PUCKER FACTOR 10

PUCKER FACTOR 10

Memoir of a U.S. Army Helicopter Pilot in Vietnam

BY JAMES JOYCE

McFarland & Company, Inc., Publishers
Jefferson, North Carolina, and London

LIBRARY OF CONGRESS CATALOGUING-IN-PUBLICATION DATA

Joyce, James, 1942–
    Pucker factor 10 : memoir of a U.S. Army helicopter pilot in
Vietnam / by James Joyce.
        p.   cm.
    Includes index.

    ISBN 0-7864-1557-6 (softcover : 50# alkaline paper) ∞

    1. Vietnamese Conflict, 1961–1975—Aerial operations, American.
    2. Vietnamese Conflict, 1961–1975—Personal narratives, American.
    3. Military helicopters—Vietnam.   4. Joyce, James, 1942–   I. Title.
    DS558.8.J69   2003
    959.704'348'092—dc21   2003006888

British Library cataloguing data are available

On the cover: James Joyce in country; background ©2003 Photospin

Manufactured in the United States of America

McFarland & Company, Inc., Publishers
    Box 611, Jefferson, North Carolina 28640
        www.mcfarlandpub.com

This book is dedicated to my wife, Barbara,
and so am I

Contents

Preface   1

Frequently Used Terms   3

1. Who Wants to Go to Flight School?   5

2. Fly This, Fly Anything   11

3. Lost Over Cleveland   20

4. Army Flight School   26

5. Boredom, Terror and Joy   34

6. Showing Off   40

7. Transition School   48

8. Welcome to Vietnam   54

9. Learning the Ropes   62

10. Missions   68

11. Settling Into the Cav   80

12. A KKK Officer   88

13. Rats   93

14. They Booed Bob Hope   99

15. To the Field   106

16. Wildlife   114

17. Ancillary Missions   119

18. There Is No Time   126
19. Infusion and Disneyland   135
20. Saigon   142
21. Welcome to the Ninth   146
22. The Major's Story   155
23. The Ox Cart   160
24. The Screaming   165
25. A Medal and a Promotion   172
26. Our Allies and the Last Mission   179
27. Welcome Home   185
28. I Get a Job   189
29. The Last Flight   192

Epilogue 1: Flying   197
Epilogue 2: War   198
Military History of James Joyce   201
Index   203

Preface

IN THE SUMMER OF 2001, relatives and friends from across the country gathered at our home for a family reunion. One evening during that weekend my nephews from California, men in their 30s, joined me on the porch and began asking me questions about Vietnam. At first I thought they were just being polite to "Uncle Jim" (they are very nice young men) but it soon became apparent to me that their interest was genuine. Moments after I'd finish telling a story they'd prod me for another. One of them reminded me they'd had no experience with war, or military life, and wanted to know what it was like. Another said, "I wish I had a tape recorder."

Fortified by their enthusiastic questioning, I continued telling stories until I got to one I could not finish. It was a story I had told before, but my audience then had not been bright, eager faces—faces that suddenly reminded me of others, faces that could have belonged to the men I had flown into battle in a helicopter so many years before. As my words slowed down I saw, in my mind's eye, those faces again and remembered how, when I returned to the battlefield to take them out, they had changed from bright and eager to ashen and, sometimes, lifeless—their spirits gone, their bodies broken. My eyes welled up and my throat constricted; had I attempted to utter another word, I would have begun sobbing. Instead, I stood up, walked into the house, and poured myself a double.

For many days after the reunion I remained puzzled and surprised at my strong emotional reaction to the story I couldn't finish. This had never happened before. On the front porch that evening in North Carolina, my nephews had unleashed an emotion that instantly dissolved 35 years and took me back to South Vietnam. That moment was the catalyst for this book. A few weeks later I began to write.

1

Most of the book is set in Vietnam, but there are also stories of us brand new second lieutenants learning to fly airplanes and helicopters before going to the war. It was a time of glory for us. As the aircraft we flew defied gravity, we defied fear. We had wings on our chests and a swagger in our gaits. We were aviators, pilots, fly boys. We were hot stuff and we knew it; we were invincible—at least at the beginning—and we loved life (boy did we love life), yet we challenged it each time we pushed the throttles forward. We were beautiful paradoxes, and to this day, "I was a pilot" is a statement I am proud to make.

There are numerous stories in the book about combat from a helicopter pilot's perspective, including what it feels like on final approach to a hot LZ, but I also include stories about people I met, lived with, and flew with. There was the ramrod straight major who cried one night, the anal-retentive quartermaster sergeant who finally broke a rule, the captain who kept a python as a pet, and the West Pointer who hated West Point. There was also the best pilot I ever knew who safely landed a helicopter after his tail rotor had been shot off—something which cannot be done.

The stories are as accurate in essence and detail as I can recall, but I have taken the necessary liberty to change the names of some people and places so that no one still living will be embarrassed and so that the memories of those who died are not tarnished. An asterisk (*) appears with the first use of any name that is a pseudonym (and only real persons' names are in the index).

James T. Joyce, 05226918
Commissioned Officer, United States Army
Active duty: January 5, 1965–January 5, 1968

Frequently Used Terms

Fixed wing aircraft   An airplane.

Rotary wing aircraft   A helicopter.

IFR   Instrument Flight Rules. Navigating by using the instruments on the control panel, charts and landing pattern approach plates. No need to look out the window to get where you're going.

VFR   Visual Flight Rules. Navigating primarily by use of maps while observing the ground. May be augmented by radio signals.

LZ   Landing zone. An area where helicopters will be landing—always unimproved and often hastily decided upon. LZs were rice paddies, beaches, holes in the jungle canopy, fields, mountain tops, and so on.

Huey Slick   UH-1 helicopter used to carry troops and supplies. No weapons are attached to the sides of the aircraft, therefore the sides are "slick."

Huey Gunship   UH-1 helicopter with machine guns, mini-guns, rocket pods, grenade launchers or a combination of same permanently attached to its sides or, in the case of the grenade launchers, its nose.

Door Gunners   The two enlisted crew members who rode in the back of Hueys, one on each side, in both slicks and gunships. M60 machine guns were post-mounted in the back of Hueys. When the door gunners were in their seats their legs straddled these weapons. They rode facing sideways, their backs against the transmission cowling. The left side door gunner was also the crew chief, in charge of the ship's maintenance.

Door gunners were killed at a slightly higher rate than pilots. Their seats did not have armored protection devices.

CHAPTER 1

Who Wants to Go to Flight School?

IF YOU WANTED TO BE A PILOT in the first half of the twentieth century, you had an advantage if you grew up around cornfields. During those years little airplanes were a part of the rural landscape, so the fledgling pilot was accustomed to seeing them and being around them. Because of this familiarity, the mystique and intimidation factors were greatly reduced for young men who grew up on farms, the first time they crawled into an airplane as beginning student pilots.

I did not grow up in pilot country. I grew up in Chicago.

Pilot country was where machinery lived. It's where tractors, trailers, hay wagons, manure spreaders, cultivators, combines and crop dusters were used, in harmony, to grow food. The people who operated these machines understood them, nurtured them and, when necessary, doctored them. There was camaraderie between man and machinery in pilot country. The only large machinery I saw on a regular basis was the garbage truck as it hissed, banged and screeched its way down our alley.

Pilot country was axle grease, elbow grease and grease up to the elbows country—the first ever airplane pilots were bicycle mechanics. It was where oily rags, socket wrenches, spark plugs, carburetors, gasoline cans and tobacco juice were most at home. In the South add Moon Pies and R.C. Cola, and pour a cellophane packet of Toms Peanuts into the bottle before drinking.

In pilot country you'd find little airports with a single grass runway and a windsock. The farmers, ranchers and small town folk gathered there to gossip, talk about the weather and the going price of crops, and generally

5

shoot the breeze. If they felt like it they could walk out of the little building, untie their airplane and take it up for a spin. These little airports also offered flight training.

In pilot country the people lived with their heifers, hogs, Holsteins and Rhode Island Reds. They also lived with their Pipers and Cessnas. It was not uncommon for a farmer or rancher to have his own airplane parked on his own land. This was a component of our rural culture, and many of these pilots never bothered to get a license from the FAA. An airplane was merely one more piece of machinery, used to visit friends and "neighbors" two counties away or, out West, to check on a summering herd of cattle up in the national forest. They'd never be landing at LAX or any other real airport, so who needed a license?

I knew a man in Mississippi—we'll call him "Slim"—who flew his brother's twin engine Beech 18 all over the South. On the trips when he'd be landing in Atlanta or Charlotte or some other large airport, he not only borrowed the Beech, he also borrowed his brother's license, just in case somebody asked to see it. Slim never got his own pilot's license (I don't think he could read), but he was one of the most skilled pilots I ever knew. Slim had "bird sense," which is the ultimate compliment you can give a pilot.

So for young people growing up in rural areas, learning to fly an airplane was not a big deal. A little white airplane parked alongside a cornfield looked natural. But a little airplane parked on a city street, in front of a row of two-flats, would look ridiculous—and that's where I came from.

On the south side of Chicago, owning an airplane or being able to fly one would make no sense at all, so the thought of becoming a pilot never crossed anyone's mind. Our intended occupations were direct reflections of our mostly Irish-Catholic, blue-collar neighborhood of bungalows and apartment buildings spaced not more than ten feet apart. No airplane necessary to visit the neighbors. Twelve baby steps or two giant steps would do it. Red Rover come over.

Our neighborhood was anchored, dominated and defined by our parish church, St. Sabina, located at 78th and Throop streets. All of us kids attended St. Sabina Grammar School and were taught by the Sinsinawa Dominican Nuns. One-day the church's Monsignor visited our eighth grade class. To host such a prestigious figure was quite the honor for the Sister and, of course, for us children.

I recall the Monsignor walking around the room asking us boys what we were going to become when we grew up. Of course we all knew what he wanted to hear, and the brown noses didn't disappoint when they answered, "Priest," the ultimate career choice for that time and place. The rest of us came up with predictable, normal jobs: policeman, fireman, carpenter, bricklayer, truck driver and, of course, baseball player for the Chicago White Sox. The Monsignor then asked the girls what they wanted to become. Those who didn't say "nun" said "nurse." There was not a future pilot in the class.

Some nuns, by the way, were not always nice to their students. One time in the third grade, as I walked past my teacher, she spun me around and pinched my face between her thumbs and forefingers. Then she bent down and yanked me toward her by the cheeks and screamed into my terrified face that I'd told her a lie earlier that day. I hadn't. Before she let me go, she shook me by the cheeks. I shall never forget the pain, which made tears fall from my eyes, and the embarrassment as my classmates saw me crying. Half of them were girls.

After grammar school we boys went on to Leo High School at 79th and Sangamon. Leo was a Catholic School taught by Irish Christian Brothers. These brothers were not full-blown priests, but they dressed like priests, wearing cassocks and Roman collars. They took religious vows and were sort of like male nuns. They were not always nice either. Many seemed to have dedicated themselves to physically punishing boys. One time, one of the brothers, a roly-poly yet muscular guy, about 30 years old and 5 feet, 4 inches tall, came up behind me during a test and hit me with his open hand on the back of my head. The blow was so hard that my face bounced off of the top of my desk. I recall thinking, "Why did he hit me and how come it doesn't hurt?" Then a few seconds later it did start to hurt, and the brother was yelling that he saw me look at the paper of the kid next to me, accusing me of cheating. He, too, was wrong. It took awhile before I quit seeing stars.

Upon graduation from Leo High School, I made a momentous decision. I decided that I had had all the formal education I could stand. I therefore decided to go into the trades and become an electrician like my dad. In those days the electricians had a "closed union," which meant the only way you could become an electrician was to be an electrician's son. I had it made. Being an electrician was one of the most prestigious jobs in the neighborhood. So I sat down with my dad and told him what I wanted to do. He heard me out and then shook his head, saying he would consider sponsoring me into the union, but we would discuss it again in four years—"After you've finished college."

Because nobody in his right mind would argue with my dad, it was now time for me to decide on a college. My parents told me I could go to any college I wanted to attend, as long as it was Catholic; even colleges in other cities were fine with them. They felt that living away from home while attending school was all part of the educational experience. This was sophisticated thinking on their part and it was, I realized later, smart. I was a bit of a hellion. No doubt they could use some relief.

I first contemplated going to Notre Dame in South Bend, Indiana. This would have made my father very proud—"The Fighting Irish" and all that stuff—but my big brother, Bob, seven years older than me, was a dedicated scholar and educator and was, at that time, on the faculty at Notre Dame. Forget it. Then I thought of Marquette in Milwaukee, but that wasn't far enough away from home. St. Joseph's College in Rennselear, Indiana, attracted lots of guys from Chicago, but Rennselear was in the middle of nowhere (speaking of cornfields).

At that time my sister, Mary, six years older than me, was dating an undertaker from the neighborhood named Dan Curley. I really liked Dan and hoped he'd become my brother-in-law. He was a graduate of a small college near Cleveland, Ohio, called John Carroll University. It was a Jesuit school with a strong academic rating and was a six-hour drive from Chicago. I couldn't have cared less about the academic rating, but I liked the distance; it was Catholic, to satisfy my parents; and here's the best part: Dan told me that in the state of Ohio you could legally drink 3.2 beer at the age of 18. Now we're talking *college*.

I made an appointment to see a Jesuit priest from John Carroll who had come to Chicago to recruit students. He was a delightfully cantankerous old man with a wonderful sense of humor. He told me all about the school but also gave me the impression he didn't really care if I attended John Carroll or not. This priest had perfected the negative sell. The only question I asked him during the interview concerned the baseball program. I thought I might like to try to play at the college level. He admitted he didn't know too much about it, but had heard someone say it was one of the best in the state of Ohio. That clinched it; I was off to John Carroll.

Two months later, when I arrived on campus to begin my college career, I quickly learned two things: (1) The undertaker had told me the truth. You could legally drink 3.2 beer in Ohio at age 18. (2) The Jesuit had told me a fib. John Carroll did not have a baseball program and never did. I told you he had a wonderful sense of humor.

There was a small detail that the priest left out of his pitch. John Carroll University had a mandatory Reserve Officers Training Corps (ROTC) program for all freshmen and sophomores. This meant that every Friday we had to wear an Army uniform to attend military science classes. Upon hearing this I was quite upset, more than I had been about the father's baseball fib, but I soon realized it couldn't be too bad because everybody had to do it. I wouldn't be the only one on campus looking like a dork.

ROTC training for junior and senior years was on a voluntary basis. If you continued with the program the Army actually paid you $27 per month, which was a lot of 3.2 beer. Upon graduation you were committed to serve on active duty for two years. However, you would be serving as an officer, having received your second lieutenant gold bars upon graduation.

This was in the 1960s (I graduated in '64), and at that time the United States had a national draft. All able bodied men were subject to service on active duty in one of the branches of the Armed Forces. So my choice to continue with ROTC was not much of a choice. Regardless of my decision, I would be on active military duty for two years. Would I do this as a commissioned officer or as a private—later to be known as a "grunt?" I continued on with the ROTC program at John Carroll. So did most of my friends.

One day during our junior year at John Carroll, I was sitting in military science class and a visiting Army captain was introduced to us by our regular teacher. He'd come from Fort Rucker, Alabama, to tell us about Army Aviation. At this time I didn't know the Army had airplanes—I thought that's what they did in the Air Force—so I was mildly interested in what the captain had to say. I also knew that his words would not be meant for me because kids from big city, blue-collar neighborhoods did not become pilots. My flying an airplane would be as foreign a thing to do as, say, my Irish father sitting down to eat a plate of spaghetti. It wouldn't happen.

But I listened as the captain explained that if we signed up today for flight training, when we got to officer's basic training camp we would be given a special physical exam. This would take place during the summer between our junior and senior years. If we passed this physical we would actually begin to fly airplanes while in our senior year at John Carroll, and could get a private pilot's license with no cost to us. Interesting.

He then explained that if we did all right flying during college we would go to the Army's flight school when we got on active duty. The flight school was almost a year long, however, so our commitment to the Army would be extended from two years to three. "This is only fair," he said. "Forget it," I said to myself.

He went on to tell us that pilots got flight pay, which was substantially higher than everybody else's pay. He also said that living conditions were better for pilots than for those whose jobs kept them on the ground. I was listening again. He then made several humorous remarks about how much easier it was to pick up women when they saw the silver wings on our chest. He told us there was something about "fly boys" that attracted them. Keep talking, Captain.

He went on to explain that being an Army aviator could be an entrée into flying as a commercial airline pilot after our tour of active duty was over. He said that most commercial pilots flying today had been initially trained as military pilots during World War II. About the time we were again civilians these men would be coming up on retirement age and new pilots would be in demand. This made sense.

Having no idea what I would be doing with my civilian life, I was now listening intently to every one of the captain's words. He concluded his talk by reiterating that the only qualifications necessary to apply for flight training were to be in good physical health and to have 20-20 uncorrected vision. He did not say that guys from blue-collar neighborhoods need not apply.

I rapidly weighed the negative—three years' active duty instead of two—against the many positives: better living conditions, a possible career opportunity after the military, a free pilot's license, more money and more women. So when he asked the question, "Who wants to go to flight school?" my hand went up in the air.

Of all the life changing, course-changing decisions I have ever made, this one probably was the most far reaching. Had I not raised my hand I would have spent two very pleasant years with the Army in Europe, been discharged, and returned to Chicago to lead the life of a normal human being. I was, I truly believe, programmed to be a normal human being.

In 1963 Vietnam was a minuscule blip on the radar screen of the general public's consciousness. There's no way I could have known, sitting in a classroom on that beautiful campus in Ohio, that by raising my hand I would be going to war in that country and that I would see things, hear things, and do things that most people cannot imagine. That hand in the air would lead me to war. It would take my soul, my spirit, or whatever you want to call it and ... torque it.

My hand in the air also determined who I would marry, where I would live and what my occupations would be (and they would be many). That hand in the air gave first names to two of my four sons. That hand in the air is why I now eat grits. There was no way to know that at the time, of course. All I knew then was that I was going to be a pilot and being a pilot was hot stuff. I was excited by the prospect, and I could hardly wait to tell everyone I knew, especially back in the neighborhood.

CHAPTER 2

Fly This, Fly Anything

OUR OFFICER'S BASIC TRAINING COURSE was held the following summer at Indian Town Gap Military Reservation near Hershey, Pennsylvania. (The whole town smelled like chocolate.) The six-week course was modeled after the standard boot camp which all military inductees are subjected to. It has been said about boot camp that if you can stay awake for the six weeks you will complete the course. There is truth to that statement. Every day you get up before dawn, and you don't get to sleep until after midnight. You learn to march in formation in regular time, quick time, and double time. You march for mile after mile with full pack on your back. You do calisthenics until you can do no more—and then you do some more.

You learn about weapons, "small arms," and you carry them up and down the hills and through the woods. There are pistols, rifles, machine guns, grenade launchers, rocket launchers, flamethrowers, and bazookas. During the six weeks you will fire them all and you'll learn to take them apart, clean them and put them back together. Shooting them is fun. Taking them apart, cleaning them and putting them back together is not. It is tedious and meticulous work. I hated it.

In boot camp you are subjected to harassment. Sergeants are constantly in your face screaming obscenities at you. "Joyce, ain't that a girl's name? You must be a pussy, Joyce. Give me 10." (Pushups.) You are subjected to frequent inspections. "Joyce, there's a fucking rope under your bunk [a piece of thread]. Your weekend pass is cancelled!" And to the guy standing at attention next to me, "There's a goddamned log by your foot locker! [A quarter-inch of bristle from a broom.] Your pass is cancelled, too!"

In boot camp you get demerits, you are assigned to K.P. duties and you lose privileges. You spit-shine boots until the toes become mirrors. You

The author (left) and First Lieutenant Dick Koenig of Wisconsin. Dick had two tours in Vietnam, one on the ground and one flying gunships. (But he's afraid of snakes.)

polish brass until it glows in the dark. You also clean toilets until they sparkle. Boot camp sucks.

The main thing I still remember from my six weeks at Indian Town Gap was that the Pennsylvania mountains were full of copperhead snakes and that they smelled like cucumbers. One of the tack sergeants cautioned us that if we were walking through the woods and smelled cucumbers we must be alert—a copperhead was near by.

One day my buddy from John Carroll, Dick Koenig, and I were walking down a dirt road. This was during the "war games" part of the training. We saw an "enemy" tank come around the bend in front of us, so Dick and I dove under a clump of bushes. We lay there motionless for a few seconds and then I whispered, "Dick, I think I smell cucumbers."

"Me too!" he yelled, and we dove back out onto the road. We stood up and looked back to make sure the snake wasn't chasing us. Then we put our hands in the air and surrendered to the tank. (Dick Koenig was also a future aviator. He survived Vietnam and eventually became publisher of *Flying* magazine.)

One morning, toward the end of the course, I was called out of formation and told to report to the camp hospital to take my physical exam for flight school. This was a nice break in the regimen as I spent the morning being checked over. I was declared healthy, physically, but then I was told to go to the psychiatrist's office for more tests. I did not know about this aspect of getting into flight school, and I must admit it made me nervous. I'd never seen a psychiatrist before. Maybe he'd tell me I was crazy.

I found his office and knocked lightly on the door. "Come in," said a pleasant voice. The psychiatrist, a major, was a tall, slender man with sandy colored hair and bright green eyes that twinkled. He gave me a big smile and shook my hand. "Have a seat," he said, pointing to the chair across from his desk. He told me this interview wouldn't take long and asked me where my home was. We exchanged pleasantries for a few minutes. I learned he was a reserve officer from Detroit and only spent two weeks a year on active duty. His real job was teaching psychiatry to medical students at Wayne State University. I liked him.

He asked me about 15 questions which he read from a paper on his desk. They were multiple choice and yes-or-no questions. He assured me there were no right or wrong answers and I should simply tell him the first thing that popped into my mind. He made little tick marks next to the answers I chose. When we finished these questions he looked up and said he wanted me to tell him, in my own words, why I wanted to be a pilot. Without hesitating I told him that I liked the idea of better living conditions, getting a job with the airlines after leaving the Army and the chance to make extra money because of the flight pay. "I was also told we'd get more women," I said.

He laughed and said that was a good answer. Then he got serious and asked about my feelings regarding the fact that flying was dangerous. He reminded me that flight pay is also called "hazardous duty" pay. "What do you say about that?" he asked. I knew this was a loaded question and probably the most important one of the interview. I thought for a moment and then said that this really wouldn't concern a person like me. He put a puzzled look on his face and asked, "Why not?" I gave him a smile and said, "Because only the good die young." This got a big laugh out of him, and he said that was the best answer he'd heard lately. He made some notes in the file and said he was recommending that I be accepted for flight training. He was still chuckling and shaking his head. "You know what, Jim?" he said. "You pilots are crazy."

"Excuse me, sir?" I replied.

"You're crazy. But it's not bad crazy, it's good crazy. Trust me: There's a difference." He stood up, shook my hand, and wished me good luck. I practically skipped out of his office. I decided that some day I'd look up the difference between good crazy and bad crazy, but for now it didn't matter. It had just become official that I'd be learning to fly an airplane.

When we returned to John Carroll to begin our senior year we were informed that the ROTC department had a contract with a civilian flight school near the small town of Cuyahoga Falls, Ohio, about 25 miles from the campus. We future Army aviators were told to use our spare time to enroll in the school and begin taking flying lessons. It was mandatory that we complete the ground school portion of the training (the textbook part), and we must acquire enough hours flying time to have soloed, i.e., flown the airplane alone. If we chose, we could accumulate forty hours of flying time and then test for an FAA private pilot's license. All of this training was compliments of the U. S. Army. Near the end of our senior year an active duty Army pilot would come to Cuyahoga Falls and give each student a "check ride." He would evaluate us based on the number of hours we had logged (flown).

Our civilian IP's (instructor pilots) at the Cuyahoga airport were young men in their early twenties. Their goal in life was to get as much flying time as possible and one day to hire on as commercial pilots with the airlines. At this time the airlines were not hiring because those World War II veterans were not quite old enough to retire. So our IP's racked up all the time they could, getting ready for the big day when the airlines would begin to interview.

But the training our IP's received was civilian, not military, and they were not college graduates. These were two big strikes against them and greatly diminished their chances of ever getting hired by the airlines, but their desire and denial kept them going. They were also aware that us ROTC students would some day be their competition for that ultimate pilot golden ring—riding up front with United, Eastern, Pan Am, American, etc. This kind of pissed them off.

They called us, derisively, "college boys," which was meant to piss us off, but it didn't. Among ourselves we laughed about it. Our IP's lived and breathed flying. We had way too many other things to think about. The expression "Get a life" wasn't invented yet, but that's what we'd have said about them, behind their backs, if it had been.

The airplanes assigned to us college boys to learn to fly were Piper J-3 Cubs. They were single engine airplanes painted bright yellow. They had only two seats, which were in tandem—one behind the other. Both seats had identical controls and instrument panels. The "skin" of the airplane was fabric rather than metal. You could punch your fist through it if you wanted to.

I'll never forget walking up to the J-3 Cub with my IP for the first time. I'd never been close to a single engine plane before. It was positively tiny! As he walked me around it, jabbering away about the pre-flight inspection he was performing, I was becoming catatonic. Not only was this thing tiny, but it was all beat up. It had cracks that went through the fabric; the I.P. pointed to one of them, saying they'd been watching it to be sure it didn't get any bigger. The little plane had rust on the wing struts, it had more than a few rivets missing, and the two main tires were bald. The tail wheel looked like it was borrowed from a roller skate. I couldn't believe I had signed on to go riding around in this thing, up in the air. If it had been an automobile they'd have junked it years ago.

Before I could come to my senses and forget this flying nonsense I was ushered into the back seat by the still jabbering IP. He showed me how to put on the seat belt harness and the headset, and then he shut the flimsy little door against me. I felt doomed. He then climbed into the front seat and called out the window for "Joe." Joe walked over and stood in front, a bit to the side of the plane. "Brakes on!" yelled the IP. "Brakes on!" yelled Joe back at him. "Switches on!" yelled the IP. "Switches on!" yelled Joe. Then Joe reached up and grabbed the propeller blade which, I now noticed, was made of wood.

"Clear!" yelled the IP and "Clear!" yelled Joe. Then Joe yanked down hard on the propeller as he backed away. The propeller started spinning, the engine sputtered a few times, then it belched, backfired, and stopped. The IP and Joe went through the same routine again, and again the engine sputtered, belched, backfired, and stopped. But the third time the engine caught and stayed caught. I couldn't believe what I was seeing.

With the engine running, the little plane was now furiously vibrating and every few seconds it would shudder all over. The noise was so loud we could only speak to each other through the headsets and even then we had to yell. The IP took his feet off the brakes and we began moving across the grass, heading for the asphalt taxiway. To the vibrations and the shudder we then added a shimmy. It felt like the thing was going to shake itself apart. We bumped up onto the asphalt and the IP said that we had to clear ourselves for take-offs and landings. He explained that this airplane didn't have a radio so we couldn't talk to the control tower. He said that if I saw a plane on "final" I was not to move on to the "active" until it had landed and "cleared" it. "You know what I'm saying?" he hollered into my headset. "Yes," I said, not having a clue.

It was at this time I decided that I really had no choice but to go for a ride, one time, in this airplane. But when we landed, if we landed, I vowed I would never, ever get in a small plane again. I had learned that the military could not make you be a pilot, not even on active duty. If you wanted to quit, you could quit. I didn't need the extra money. I couldn't really picture myself flying big jets for Delta Air Lines and, so far, I was having no problem getting women, even without the benefit of the "flyboy" wings. I would endure this one ride. But this was it.

The IP took a hard right turn, a few moments later took another one, and we came to a stop on a wide stretch of concrete, which I assumed was the runway. He told me to put my right hand lightly on the stick, my feet lightly on the pedals, and to follow along with him during the take-off—but not to fight him. "Are you ready?" he yelled into my headset. "Sure," I yelled back, as my stomach jumped up into my throat.

If I thought it was loud before, I didn't know from loud as he pushed the throttle all the way forward. We were now engulfed by roar as the plane started down the runway. I noticed the stick went forward in my hand and the rudder pedals oscillated back and forth. Within a few seconds the tail section of the plane (me) came off the ground. We were picking up speed at an alarming rate and just as I was about to yell, "Stop!" the two bald wheels came off the runway. The plane took a final shudder, then all was smooth as we gently ascended. I watched the end of the runway pass below us. "Airplanes don't like it on the ground!" yelled the IP. "They are made to be in the air!"

My stomach slowly left my throat and resettled into its proper place. I began breathing again and my heart quit pounding as more and more of northern Ohio stretched below us. I wouldn't say I was thrilled to be where I was, but I did have to admit it was now more exciting than terrifying. It was also beautiful.

The IP flew around the town of Cuyahoga Falls, pointing out certain landmarks which he said would get me oriented in this area. There was a water tower, a football stadium attached to the high school, a small lake, and a four-lane highway. After the take-off, I had "gotten off" the controls, but he then told me to get back on them. He said that the whole deal in flying a plane was the relationship between the stick and the rudder pedals. He told me to follow him through some maneuvers.

I tried to get the feel of what he was doing. When he moved the stick to the right, he pushed down on the right rudder pedal, and vice versa. When the stick went forward in my hand the nose went down, and when he pulled back on it the nose came up. We flew along like this for fifteen minutes or so. "OK, Joyce, you got it," he said. I could feel he was no longer on the rudder pedals, and he put his hands over his head to show me he was off the stick. He pointed out a twisting river below us and asked if I saw it. I told him I did and he said I should follow it and try to stay directly above it.

I followed the river as best I could and I thought I was doing a good job. I was also beginning to enjoy myself. Knowing that I was actually piloting the plane and that it pretty much did what I told it to do was neat. I couldn't imagine being able to take off or land it but at least I knew I could fly it. I was already doing that.

The IP, in fact, said I was doing a good job but to put a little more rudder into my turns; otherwise, I'd make myself sick. He told me to look for the little ball in front of me on the instrument panel, the "turn and bank" indicator, and to keep the ball between the white lines. That would show me that my turns were coordinated. So I added a bit more pressure to the pedals when I turned, and the ball pretty much stayed put. I noticed it did make a big difference. "Coordinated turns, coordinated turns, that's what we want, Joyce," he said and again told me I was doing fine.

After another ten minutes or so he told me to return to the airport; we'd had enough for the first day. His encouraging praise made me feel great, but now I looked around and realized I had no idea where we were. I flew in a wide circle searching the horizon but saw nothing that looked familiar.

"Give up, Joyce?" he asked.

"Yes," I said.

"Look directly below you. You're right on the top of it!" he said, laughing. He then got back on the controls but told me to stay on them with him through the landing. He put the little plane on its side, and we swooped down and out past the runway. We turned back around and in moments we were heading directly toward it. The landing he made could not have been smoother. I could barely feel it when the wheels touched down. He taxied back to our parking spot and turned off the engine. We unbuckled ourselves, took off the headsets, and crawled out of the plane. He told me to follow him inside the flight service building so we could schedule my next lesson. He reiterated that I did very well for the first time in an airplane. He told me he'd have me soloing in no time.

"OK," I said, and sure enough, the IP was correct. During my ninth lesson, after we'd done forty-five minutes of "touch and go's" (continually landing and taking off), he taxied the plane off of the runway, opened his door and got out. "All yours, Joyce!" he said and closed the door. He held up three fingers and waved in a circle over his head. This meant, I guessed, to take off, fly around the pattern and land—three times. I did not know he was going to do this. I almost wet my pants. Although I had gained much confidence in my ability to fly, land, and take off in the little airplane, I did not believe I was ready to do it alone. But the IP was walking away from the plane, heading back to the flight service station, so as I sat there idling, I could do only one of two things. I could do what he told me to do—take off—or I could follow behind him like a little yellow duck. I took off.

The key to learning to fly is, paradoxically, being in control of the plane on the ground, that is, while you are rolling across it on take-off and when you are touching down on it when landing. Steering an airplane while it is in the air, and making it go higher or lower, is very easy to learn, and the margins for error are as vast as the sky. It's the ground you must be wary of because it causes the most problems. The ground can kill you.

Airplanes are equipped with one of two types of landing gear, either tricycle or conventional. The tricycle gear causes the aircraft to "sit up," that is, the fuselage (body) of the aircraft is parallel to the ground. The large wheels are gathered under the wings near the plane's center of gravity. There's a small wheel under the nose. All of today's commercial airliners and most of today's smaller planes have tricycle landing gear.

With the other type of landing gear, conventional, there are two large wheels under the wings and one small wheel under the empennage (tail section). When a conventional gear airplane is sitting on the ground, the front of the plane is much higher than the back. Conventional gear airplanes are also known as "tail draggers." The J-3 Cub is a tail dragger. To solo this tiny plane the pilot has to sit in the back seat, due to weight distribution, and this poses a challenge when taxiing, landing, and taking off. When looking straight ahead from the back seat, the pilot cannot see the ground in front of him. The plane's nose is in the way. All he can see through the windshield is the sky. Therefore while taxiing he must steer back and forth, back and forth, looking through the side windows to see where he is going until he gets lined up at the end of the runway. Most people watching a J-3 being taxied would probably assume the pilot was drunk.

After lining up the Cub for take-off, which means looking through the side windows to be sure the plane is in the middle of the runway, the pilot pushes the throttle forward. For a few seconds the pilot is blind to the front, but then the tail rises up, which drops the nose, and the pilot can now see the runway through the windshield to complete the take-off.

When landing the J-3 Cub, the proper technique is for the tail wheel to touch the runway a millisecond before the main wheels touch. So before landing the pilot must raise the nose of the plane, which blocks his forward vision. He now must gauge his distance above the ground, and his location on the runway, by again using the side windows as he floats on down. After touching down he will again be blind to the front. After coming to a stop the back-and-forth taxiing begins again.

So learning to take off, land and taxi the tail-dragging J-3 Cub is more difficult than learning to handle other airplanes because of this "Solo from the back seat" feature. Because I'd never been in or around small planes I did not realize this and thought it was normal. Later, in Army flight school, it gave me a big advantage over my fellow students in the early stages of our training. When my IP told me, "Joyce, if you can fly this little piece of crap, you can fly anything," I didn't know he was telling the truth. I thought he was bragging.

CHAPTER 3

Lost Over Cleveland

EVERY PILOT I KNOW HAS at least one harrowing learning-to-fly story—the kind that obviously turned out fine (he was telling it) but could have ended in disaster. I have such a story.

One phase of pilot training is learning to fly "cross country." This does not mean flying from New York to Los Angeles. It means flying from one airport to another which is, say, 50 miles away. In order to find it you must navigate by looking at a map and matching up the symbols on the map with what you observe on the ground.

Easily identifiable objects on the ground, which are symbolized on the map, are highways, railroads, ballparks, racetracks, water towers, lakes, rivers, etc. This sounds simple enough, and it is, once you get the hang of it. But let's say the air is real bumpy and this makes you a little nervous and the map slides off your lap onto the cramped cockpit floor, and when you reach down to retrieve it you put too much pressure on one of the rudder pedals, which changes your heading, and when you put the map back up on your lap it's turned the wrong way and nothing is matching up on the ground, and then you realize your mistake and get the map oriented properly, but by this time you've flown fifteen seconds (or was it two minutes) with your head in the cockpit before you are again squared away. Now then, which river is that? It is not hard for a new pilot to get very disoriented, very quickly.

The day I took my first solo cross-country, another student from John Carroll, Tom Higgins*, was also scheduled to take his. The instructor gave us both the same route of flight but put 15 minutes between our take-off times so we couldn't cheat by flying together. Our route of flight took us west over the southern edge of Metropolitan Cleveland to a small airport near the town of North Olmsted, Ohio. From there we were to fly south-east to Brunswick, Ohio, and then northeast back to Cuyahoga Falls. At North Olmsted and Brunswick we were to land and check in at the flight service station to prove we'd been there. Simple enough. But on the first leg of the trip I got confused and then totally disoriented. There were too many things on the ground to match up with the symbols on the map, and I was beginning to get nervous. I seriously thought about turning around, but realized that this wouldn't help because I didn't know where I was.

Just as my hands began to sweat I noticed out the right window of the plane a huge body of water, which took up the entire horizon. I figured it had to be Lake Erie, so I flew toward it. The flight time to the shoreline was about ten minutes, and I used this time to calculate the correct heading from the Cleveland Indians baseball stadium to North Olmsted. I was sure I could find the stadium when I flew along the shore of the lake to downtown. And my theory was correct. I flew right over second base on a heading of 235 degrees. I then noticed, however, that my new route of flight would take me over the top of Cleveland Hopkins International Airport. Little planes without radios, like my J-3 Cub, aren't supposed to do that. But I figured I was in a crisis, and if this maneuver ended my career as a pilot, so what? At least I'd be alive.

So I did fly over Cleveland Hopkins, but luckily my route of flight was perpendicular to the active runway so I didn't pose a safety problem for the commercial airliners or myself. As an extra precaution, I had climbed to 6,000 feet—we were supposed to fly at 3,000 feet—and the planes were landing and taking off underneath me. It was kind of fun to watch, and it was most comforting knowing exactly where I was.

Shortly after leaving Cleveland Hopkins behind I spotted the little grass airstrip at North Olmsted and made a nice landing. I taxied, back and forth, back and forth, to the flight service station building and parked next to Higgins's J-3 Cub. He was standing next to it, smiling at me. "Joyce," he asked when I got out of my plane, "where the hell were you?" He said I was late and everybody was worried. I told him that I had gotten disoriented for a while but that it turned out to be a good experience. Flying over to Lake Erie to get my bearings was a confidence builder. I was lost but now I was found and I did it all by myself. I then asked Tom if he knew if the flight service station got word of an unauthorized single engine plane flying through Cleveland Hopkins airspace.

"You didn't!" he said. I told him I had to because it was on my new route of flight from the Indians Stadium. It was the only way I was sure I'd get to the appointed place. "Joyce, you're crazy," he said, with more than a little admiration.

I suggested that he take off and I'd get a Coke and check in. Then we'd see each other again at Brunswick. "See you there," he said and climbed into the cockpit. "Hope you can find it! Ha, Ha."

Later, when I got to Brunswick, Higgins had yet to arrive. Now I was the one who was worried.

But in a few minutes I looked up and saw him on final approach. After making a three-bounce landing he taxied over and parked next to me. His face had a panicky look to it. "Higgins, where the hell were you?" I asked. He told me he'd gotten lost. He said he couldn't make sense out of the map and the stuff on the ground. Finally he saw a small town with a water tower and buzzed it to get the name off of it and that's how he got squared away. " I'm lucky I got here," he said, his confidence obviously shaken. So we had two near mishaps but no harm done and now had one leg left of the cross-country flight taking us home to Cuyahoga Falls. This one should be easy as it was mostly farmland and the things to see on the ground wouldn't be bunched together on the map. But Higgins was still shaken, and he told me he had an idea. He wanted us to fly together. He said I should take off first, then fly slowly until he caught up with me. He said he'd come up on my right and to be watching for him.

I said I did not have a problem with his plan except for one thing: If I got lost we'd both be lost. He said that wouldn't happen because he was from Akron and he knew this area. If he saw I going the wrong way he'd wobble his wings and then I should follow him.

Higgins' plan did not make sense. If he knew the area why follow me? Also, he should be the first one back to Cuyahoga Falls because he took off first. But I didn't want to argue with him because he was still shook up. I figured he was using me as a second opinion. Also, I now had a great deal more confidence in my ability to navigate. When I landed first at Cuyahoga Falls we'd make up some story to tell the instructor. Higgins got stomach cramps—that would work. He agreed.

So I took off from Brunswick, and after about twenty minutes I looked to my right and sure enough there was Higgins in his little yellow J-3 Cub. We waved at each other just like real pilots—the only things missing were scarves and Snoopy hats. We flew side by side for another ten minutes or so, but then I looked over and saw Higgins wobbling his wings. Oh shit.

I looked at him, shook my head, mouthed the word "no" and held my map up to the window to assure him I was confident I knew where we were. This didn't faze him. He was shaking his head "no" and pointing to the ground and continuing to wobble his wings. We flew along this way for another minute or so and then, oh my God, Higgins took a hard 90-degree right turn and flew away!

My heart rate immediately picked up. I quickly crosschecked my map with the stuff on the ground and told myself that I was right on course and Higgins was wrong. I firmly believed this until I remembered him telling me that he was from this area of Ohio. Damn it! But I kept on flying my course, and the highways and rivers and little towns on the ground seemed to be matching up perfectly with the map on my lap. Higgins was by now completely lost or I was hallucinating.

About this time the afternoon thermals started doing their thing. The air became extremely rough, and I began bouncing around in the sky as the words "I'm from this area of Ohio" kept going through my head. The word "angst" took on real meaning. Soon it was very rough flying, the turbulence by far the roughest I'd been in, and I began wondering just how much rough air this "little piece of crap" could take. I stared hard at the struts that connected the wings to the landing gear, and it only took a few seconds to realize that at any moment these wings were going to break off. I imagined them clapping together over my head. My heart started to race and I broke out in sweat. I was about to have a panic attack.

One of our instructors told us that it was not uncommon to be overcome by fear when learning to fly and the best way to get out of it was to "stall" the airplane on purpose. I clearly remembered him saying that a couple of power-off stalls and our confidence would come right back. So I decided to do it. Why not? The wings would be gone soon anyway. I pulled the throttle back, lifted the nose by holding the stick to my stomach and waited for the stall. In moments it came: The plane quit flying and went into a dive. I reintroduced throttle, flew out of the dive, and regained control. I felt better, especially when I realized the stall put even more stress on the wing struts than the rough air. I did this one more time and calmness was restored, and the stuff on the ground was still matching up perfectly with the stuff on the map and, I'll be darned, look at that. Right in front of me was downtown Cuyahoga Falls. The airport was three minutes away and I had successfully completed my first solo cross-country. Now then, where the hell was Higgins?

"Hey, Joyce, where the hell is Higgins?" asked the flight instructor, Mr. Thompson*, as I climbed out of the Cub. He asked why he didn't land first and asked me if I had seen him at Brunswick. Realizing that this was a time to be perfectly candid, I told him what happened. Higgins had to be hopelessly lost. "Oh, shit!" he said and ran to the flight service station.

I tied down my airplane and sheepishly went into the building. Thompson and two other flight instructors were radioing and making frantic telephone calls to all of the airports in northeastern Ohio. They asked me to show them on a map exactly where Higgins left me, and because of the shock I'd felt when he turned away, I remembered precisely. One of them said that if Higgins stayed on that heading he'd run out of gas about fifty miles south of Massillon. I'd never thought about the possibility of him running out of gas. Another one added that it would still be daylight, and that Higgins was a good pilot and could probably land in a field without killing himself.

About an hour went by as I fretted and they made phone calls. Then we heard it, the low, uneven groan of a light plane. We all ran outside and looked up to see a little yellow airplane entering the downwind leg of the landing pattern. Higgins had found his way home.

Mr. Thompson was, of course, pissed off at what Higgins and I had done, but his anger was nothing in comparison with his relief at not losing a student. We were students who were obviously not quite prepared to go it alone cross-country in a radioless airplane. Had Higgins crashed, Thompson would have been the person responsible. So at the debriefing he just said that we shouldn't have flown together. Then he asked Higgins the question of the day. "Where'd you go?"

Higgins explained that after he left me he soon realized he was completely disoriented. He began looking for towns with water towers, the procedure that served him well on the second leg of our journey, but had no luck. So, in desperation, he decided to simply land the plane and ask someone where he was. He found a recently mowed field and buzzed it a couple of times to see if there were boulders or other obstacles to a safe landing. There weren't, so he landed. He walked to the farm house and the somewhat surprised farmer brought him in, calmed him down, and together they plotted his new course heading to Cuyahoga Falls. The farmer was a private pilot. He told Higgins to fly a heading of 040 degrees until he got right over the top of Akron. "Akron, you can't miss," he told him. Higgins didn't tell him he lived there. He then said that from the center of the city Higgins should take a heading of 020 degrees and fly for about 15 minutes. That would be Cuyahoga Falls. "So that's what I did," Higgins said with more than a hint of pride at his resourcefulness. "And here I am."

"Thank Jesus," said Thompson and walked out of the building.

I decided after that day that I had had enough ROTC flying, so when it came time for my check ride with the Army pilot I was to be graded at the 20-hour level. And the check ride, I thought, went very well. I flew from the front seat, the Army captain behind me. I managed a perfect take-off, recovered nicely from stalls—both power on and power off—and got out of a spin with no problem. I held my exact altitude in turns, both tight and wide, and when it was over I made a very respectable, smooth landing, missing the numbers on the end of the runway by only a few feet. After I taxied over to the tie down area and cut off the engine the check pilot said I had done very well, and he would like to give me an "A" but he couldn't because I had committed a very serious error. As he said this he reached up and handed me my seat belt. I had taken the entire check ride without wearing it. That was more than a serious error; that was a mortal sin. My flying days were over—or so I thought.

"So I'm going to have to give you a B," he said, "If you promise you'll never forget to wear it again."

"Yes, sir, I promise," I said.

"Welcome to U.S. Army Aviation, Mr. Joyce. You'll make a fine pilot."

And Higgins? Yes, he made it also, and spent a year in Vietnam flying as an aerial artillery observer.

CHAPTER 4

Army Flight School

THE U. S. ARMY AVIATION SCHOOL is located at Fort Rucker, Alabama, in the southeastern corner of the state. The small towns around Fort Rucker are Daleville, Ozark and Enterprise. Daleville and Ozark do not have a claim to fame, but Enterprise does. In the town square is a monument to the boll weevil, the insect that long ago wiped out the cotton crop. "The only town in America with a monument to a bug," boasts the Enterprise Chamber of Commerce. When cotton could no longer be grown because of boll weevil infestation, the farmers learned to grow peanuts instead and, eventually, made a lot more money on the peanuts than they ever did on the cotton.

Daleville, Ozark, and Enterprise were "dry" towns, so to find civilization from Fort Rucker we had to travel 20 miles to the small city of Dothan with a population of 40,000. Here we could get a good meal at a restaurant and also enjoy a cocktail or two. Dothan called itself the "Peanut Capital of the World." Forgiving the residents that, it was a fairly sophisticated little city, given its location in the United States.

Although the area immediately around Fort Rucker did not lend itself to fun, it was an ideal place to learn to fly. The flat land provided good "forced landing" areas. It was sparsely populated and the weather was mild. There was only one drawback. We were cautioned that if we were flying over a wooded area and saw a line of smoke coming up through the trees, we should stay clear of it. "Chances are it's moonshiners and they will shoot at you," we were told.

I had never been in the South before but had heard stories of what it was like. They're still fighting the Civil War down there; they hate Catholics; they hate Yankees; and they treat the "coloreds" like dirt. These stories turned

26

out to be mostly, but not totally, false. Segregation was still the way of life. A few months prior to my driving from Fort Eustis, Virginia, to Fort Rucker, the famous civil rights march took place in Selma, Alabama. The Deep South was in turmoil and my Yankee, Catholic self was somewhat apprehensive stopping for gas and food while driving across the Carolinas, Georgia, and into Alabama. But there were no problems, and no one could have guessed that less than three years later I'd be marrying a local girl from the "Peanut Capital of the World."

Our flight class at Fort Rucker consisted of thirty-eight officers. Most of us were lieutenants but there were a few captains. Rank, however, was not an issue during our nine months of training. We were simply fellow students trying our best to earn our wings.

Army Flight School was nine months long, and there were two distinct and equally important aspects to it. There was the actual flying part and there was the academic part. You had to pass both to graduate. In the classroom our curriculum included aircraft maintenance, navigation for both IFR and VFR, meteorology, tactics, survival, Military Code of Conduct, and radio communication. The first thing we learned in communications was to never, ever say "Over and out." That's like saying, "Speak to me. Shut up," we were told. "Only actors and assholes say 'Over and out.'" I never said it again.

The flying part of our training consisted of a total of 220 hours at the controls of an airplane. During our nine months we would fly two different planes: the 0–1 Birddog, and the brand new (to the Army) Beech Baron. We were the first class to get the Baron, which replaced the slow moving Beaver, and were the envy of all predecessors. The Baron was used to teach us instrument flying (IFR). But we not only had to learn to fly on instruments, we also had to learn to fly the airplane, which was significantly different from the tail-dragging Birddog and Beaver. It was a twin (two engines) with tricycle, retractable landing gear, and it flew almost three times faster than the Beaver.

The retractable landing gear part could be learned in seconds. After the take-off, raise a plastic toggle switch on the control panel and the gear will fold up into the belly of the plane. Before landing don't forget to put it back down. (Very important.)

But learning to fly with two engines instead of one did have its challenges, especially when one of the two engines quit running. This creates instant excitement. Let's say the number two engine, that's the one on the right (starboard) side of the plane, quits. Immediately the airplane will violently "yaw" to the right because the left engine is producing all the power. In a sense the left engine wants to "fly around" the dead, right engine.

Further adding to the wish to yaw is the fact that the still spinning propeller of the dead engine acts like a solid disc, creating tremendous "drag" from the right side. The air going past the propellers keeps them rapidly turning.

The first thing they taught us to do when we lost an engine in the Baron was ... light a cigarette. I'm not kidding. When an engine quits, the rudder pedal on its side will go to the floor and the other pedal wants to come all the way up. It takes much leg pressure to push it down to keep the plane flying straight. The reason you light the cigarette is so that you don't do anything foolish, such as shutting down the wrong engine. Although the dead engine will be on the side of the dead rudder pedal, something in your mind tells you just the opposite.

So you take a few drags of the cigarette and watch the engine temperature gauges. While one of your legs is beginning to ache from forcing the one rudder pedal down, you keep your eyes on the gauges, and when you are certain that one of them is showing cool down you gently, very gently, pull back the throttle. Then you turn off the fuel to the dead engine. Next you "feather" the dead engine's propeller, which means changing its angle (pitch) so it passes through the air like a knife rather than a fan. It will then stop turning, greatly reducing the drag. Now adjust your trim tabs (I won't bore you with that) and continue the flight. The Baron will fly on one engine just as well as on two, albeit slower.

During flight school we had to learn the above procedure for dealing with a suddenly dead engine not only while cruising at altitude but also just before landing and just after take-off. The IPs didn't actually turn off the one engine, they merely pulled its throttle back, which simulated the effect. But they were certain to keep their hand on the other throttle to keep the panicked student from pulling it back by mistake.

Lastly, regarding a twin, although the engine rpm gauges will tell you both engines are operating at the identical speed, they are not. You'll have a "waaa, waaa, waaa" unbalanced sound. You get this "waaa, waaa" out with minute throttle adjustments. Your ears will tell you when its perfect.

Most of our 220 hours would be spent in the Birddog, however, where we would acquire all-purpose aviation skills. It had tandem seating, but it was larger and more powerful than the J-3 Cub and was soloed, I'm happy to say, from the front seat. It also had a radio. The 0-1 ("0" for observation) was used extensively in Vietnam for, obviously, observation. The pilot would fly around looking for enemy soldiers, and when he spotted them he would call in artillery fire to destroy them. Flying Birddogs would be the eventual duties of most of the students in our class.

My previous college ROTC experience flying the J-3 Cub really paid off as Army flight school began. The first goal of all pilot training was to get the student to solo, and there was great competition in our class to see who would solo first. Thanks to that "little piece of crap" I learned in, I got this prize. The other students in my class had been taught in Cessna 150s and 172s with their sissy tricycle landing gear (baby carriages). The guys had to learn to take-off and land all over again, but not me. (Now who's bragging?)

Our flight instructors were civilians on contract with the Army. A few of them were nice guys and a few of them were screamers. Most were matter-of-fact teachers who did their jobs. These IP jobs were not good paying ones and some of these teachers were embittered because they were not flying big jets with the commercial airlines. All who were now in their forties and fifties had been military pilots during World War II. They could fly airplanes with more competence than most people can walk. One of them, Mr. Bud Lord, could, if the wind was right, take off in a Birddog, fly an inverted circle, and land on the exact same spot he'd taken off from seconds before. To do that took unbelievable talent and nerve.

Most of these instructors had blown it by passing up airline careers after the war. Many had started their own private flight schools, flight service stations, charter services, or their own little airlines. All had eventually failed at these enterprises and were now stuck teaching us youngsters to fly. There was no future in this for them and no glory, either.

My first instructor pilot was a screamer. His name was Pete Warren*. Screaming and belittling students was the way they taught pilots in World War II, and Mr. Warren never outgrew this method. The other students were terrified of him, but I was not. Irritable though he was, my past experiences with other professional screamers (the nuns and brothers) protected me from letting his wrath get to me on a personal level.

One time Mr. Warren and I were flying a dual cross-country, me in the front seat, him in the back. We'd flown for quite awhile without him yelling at me, so I turned around to see what was up and saw he was fast asleep. About that time we reached a checkpoint over the ground, which called for a course change. So I got my little ruler out and was measuring the distance from this checkpoint to the next. I was measuring with one hand on the ruler and one on the map and the plane veered a little off course. I quickly corrected this, which jostled the airplane. This woke Warren up. "Joyce, what the hell are you doing!" he yelled. I told him I was measuring the distance to the next checkpoint.

His tone of voice changed to normal and he told me I didn't have to use a ruler, I could use an easier reference. He asked me if I saw his thumb, which he held up next to my face.

"Yes, sir."

He said that on any aviation map in the United States the width of his thumb was exactly 5 miles long. He asked if I understood what he was saying—his thumb was an easy, reliable reference. With it he could calculate short distances in a second. I thanked him and said I understood. He then asked what I thought he used for longer distances.

"I don't know, sir."

"I use my dick, Joyce. How long do you think my dick is?"

"I have no idea, sir."

"My dick is twenty miles long. Exactly. Now quit rocking the airplane, I'm trying to get some sleep. I had a rough night last night. And Joyce?"

"Yes, sir."

"Don't tell anybody I went to sleep, OK? I'd get fired."

"No problem, Mr. Warren."

Of the thirty-eight guys who started our class, seven of them washed out, three for academic failures and four for not grasping the instrument phase of training. Learning to fly on instruments was like learning geometry—either the light came on and you "got it" or you didn't. Four guys never got it.

Of the 31 of us who graduated, most wound up as pilots with the major airlines, so what the captain told us at John Carroll turned out to be true. Army Flight School was indeed a viable path to a career as a commercial pilot. Most of the students who did not go with the airlines were career military. One of them, Rudolph Ostovich, from Milwaukee, became a major general (two stars), and 23 years after we graduated Rudy would be the commanding general of Fort Rucker, Alabama.

About half of the guys in our class were married and lived with their wives and children in small, normal looking houses on the base. We single guys were housed in BOQs (Bachelor Officer's Quarters) which were similar to motels. Each room had a bed, desk, chair, and an easy chair. There was a good-sized closet and a full bathroom. They were nice.

I quickly became good friends with First Lieutenant Palmer Haines from Texas and Second Lieutenant Joe Mulheran from Minnesota. Joe took ROTC at North Dakota State. Palmer was a West Point graduate and the son of a lieutenant general (three stars). Palmer, when anyone asked him where he went to college, would reply, "I didn't go to college; I spent four years in prison." One time he got plastered on a beach in Florida, took off his college ring and threw it as far as he could across the sand. It took me an hour to find it. (I gave it back to him the next day.) Palmer did not enjoy his time at West Point.

Palmer, Joe and I became the three musketeer bachelors. Flight school, like real school, was Monday through Friday and we spent almost every weekend together on the road looking for fun. Our quests took us to Atlanta, Mobile, and New Orleans, but the favorite spot, and the closest, was Panama City Beach in Florida. It was less than two hours away. Panama City claims to have the most beautiful beaches in the world, and it does. The sand is pure white and so fine it squeaks when you walk on it.

One weekend we got into an auto accident in Panama City. A lady, drunk, pulled her big Lincoln in front of Joe's Volkswagen. I got pieces of glass in my left hand, which I used to protect my head as it broke the windshield. The medics at Tyndall Air Force Base spent hours using tweezers to remove glass shards from my hand but said they probably didn't get them all. Those remaining, they said, should work themselves out over time. A couple of years later I would be grateful for those glass shards. As it turned out, the medics' inability to get them all may well have saved my life.

We were warned in flight school that many non-flying officers would resent us, and be jealous, because we were pilots. There was a sexiness to being a pilot. There was also the extra pay and better living conditions, especially when compared to the combat branches of infantry, armor and artillery. We were told that from time to time we would be confronted by our fellow officers who were non-pilots. They would claim we were somehow dogging it by not experiencing the joys of Army hardships. When we were accused, our instructors suggested, we should tell them that there were only two tests required to become a pilot. One was physical and the other was mental. Ask them which one they couldn't pass.

Overall, the nine months of flight school was a good time. It was more like going to college than "Being in the Army"—although the pressure to do well, meaning not wash out, was sometimes intense. I recall once having the thought that none of our presidents were pilots and they did well in life. So what if I didn't make it? Somehow that thought didn't help. Washing out of flight school would have been extremely embarrassing.

Palmer, Joe and I sometimes visited each other's homes. One time Palmer invited Joe and me to visit his "home" which was then at Fort Hood, Texas, where his dad was the commanding general. Palmer got there a day before us. Joe and I flew military standby, eventually getting to the general's residence at 7:30 A.M. I must admit I was intimidated. Generals in the Army are akin to God. I had only seen one before, and that was from a distance. General Haines was famous for having moved the First Armored Division from Texas to South Florida in record time during the Cuban missile crisis. Palmer had a picture of his dad and President Kennedy walking together, heads down, in subdued conversation. The picture was on the cover of *Life* magazine.

First Lieutenant Palmer Haines (Texas) with proud parents Sally and Ralph on graduation day at Ft. Rucker. If the cameraman had been taller you'd see his Dad's four stars.

So Joe and I, two pipsqueak ROTC second lieutenants, were a little nervous when we rang the doorbell of Commanding General Ralph E. Haines, Jr. at Fort Hood, Texas. To our surprise a smiling General Haines himself opened the door and welcomed us inside. He shook our hands, said that Mrs. Haines and Palmer would be joining us shortly for breakfast, and ushered us into the dining room. He was a large man, but those three stars on his shoulders and the blaze of ribbons on his chest made him a giant. I would have been too intimidated to talk except for one thing. The general wasn't wearing pants.

At that time Palmer bounced into the room, followed by his mom, and soon we were sitting down to breakfast. The general sat at the head of the table, decorations galore on top, boxer shorts below. He held us spellbound with his knowledge of Vietnam. "No doubt you gentlemen will be serving there." He'd become especially well versed on the newly discovered tunnel system that the enemy was using to confound us. He then told us stories of his experiences in World War II and Korea. The general was a great storyteller and a gracious host, and before long I forgot he was sitting there in his underpants.

When the breakfast was over General Haines stood up, and instantly one of his aides, a lieutenant colonel, appeared at the door of the room, like a valet, with a pair of pants over his forearm. The general took the pants, stepped into them, zipped up, buckled up and was gone. I looked at Palmer. When his dad was out of earshot, Palmer explained that his dad never put his pants on until he walked out the door. "It keeps them from getting creased." He laughed. "Dad is old Army."

Later that day the general ordered up a Huey helicopter to give us an aerial tour of Fort Hood, and we took turns sitting in the right seat being "co-pilots." He sat in the back and pointed out the sights. General Haines wasn't really being a general now; he was simply being Palmer's dad, being nice to Palmer's friends. I'll never forget it. Shortly after this he received his fourth star and moved to the Pentagon as the Army Vice Chief of Staff. When our class graduated from flight school, General Haines came down to Fort Rucker from Washington to give the commencement address. He began his speech with the words, "Tempus fugit," then paused, looked out over the audience of brand new aviators, smiled and said, "And, now, so do you."

CHAPTER 5

Boredom, Terror and Joy

A DEFINITION OF FLYING IS, "Hours and hours of boredom interspersed by moments of sheer terror." In my experiences this definition is accurate. During the nine months of Army flight school I had two instances which scared the hell out of me.

The first one took place on our first night time solo cross-country and, yes, I got lost, but this time I had a legitimate excuse. The flight plan did not call for any landings. We were merely to fly from Fort Rucker southeast to the town of Marianna, Florida, then due west to Crestview, Florida, and then northeast back to Fort Rucker. We had a nice, clear night and there should have been nothing to it. But halfway between Marianna and Crestview, over the town of De Funiak Springs, I began to smell something burning in the cockpit. Then there was a "pop" sound and a large puff of smoke came out of the instrument panel. I was engulfed in smoke, started choking, and couldn't see.

As my heart began pounding I groped for the window latch, twisted it, and pushed the window open. In a second the smoke was gone. However, the lights on the instrument panel were no longer working and most of the instruments themselves were now dead. I touched the panel and it was hot. The only instrument I had that I could rely on was the magnetic compass, and magnetic compasses are erratic at best. I was able to regain some composure by telling myself that I was not far from home base and had a nearly full tank of gas. The night was clear and nothing else seemed to be burning.

I radioed the airfield at Rucker and told them my predicament. The air traffic controller told me to hold while he got a flight instructor to talk to me. Within moments an IP came on the radio. I told him what happened and, after some discussion with other IPs, it was agreed that I should abort the cross-country mission and return to Rucker immediately. He told me to fly back over De Funiak Springs and from there take a heading of 025 degrees. He asked if I was sure there was no more fire. I told him I didn't think so. He assured me that I would be fine. I felt there could have been more conviction in his voice.

I turned around and flew back to De Funiak Springs and then took the heading north by northeast, using the magnetic compass, which wobbled back and forth. I tried to track my flight path with my map and the landmarks on the ground, but because the interior lights in the cockpit were burned out, the only light I had was from matches. Trying to get a quick look at the map, fly the plane, and keep from burning my fingers became impossible. Also, in this part of north Florida and southern Alabama there was very little to see. It was mostly woodlands, farms, and a few tiny towns. Ninety-nine percent of the ground below me was pitch black.

There was really nothing I could do now but try to maintain the 025-degree heading and hope there wasn't significant cross wind, which would require a course adjustment. I would have no way of knowing this. In all the excitement I neglected to check my time over De Funiak Springs, so I had no idea when I should be coming up on Rucker. I just kept flying over the blackness. Soon I lost all sense of time as I desperately looked for lights on the horizon in front of me. There were none. Panic began to set in again as I realized I was really lost. Missing the Fort Rucker area would be easy to do, and then there would be nothing but blackness for God only knew how far. For all I knew I had already flown past it.

I decided the smartest—actually, the only—thing I could do was to keep flying north in the hopes of finding an airport. If I didn't find one I would eventually run out of gas. At that point I would jump out of the plane. Although in the Birddog we wore parachutes, we had never used them. We'd had instructions, of course. The instructions were to be sure we were clear of the aircraft and then pull hard on the ripcord. When we got near the ground we were to keep our feet together and bend our knees, not trying to land standing up—we couldn't anyway, we'd be going too fast. When our feet touched the ground we were to roll onto it and get out of the chute. That was our parachute training—all verbal. The Army had too much money invested in pilots to allow them to get hurt by actually jumping out of airplanes. In the Airborne School at Fort Benning many students do get hurt. Besides, the chances of us pilots actually needing the parachutes were remote.

I decided to start climbing. I wanted my parachute to have all the time in the world to get fully open. I called Rucker on the radio to tell the IP my plan. He asked me where I was and I told him I had no idea. I told him I was climbing and when I ran out of gas I was going to jump. Then I added, "Oh shit, I just flew into clouds."

"Get out of the clouds, get out of the clouds!" he yelled at me. He sounded almost as panicked as I was. Fortunately, it was a flat layer of stratus. I dropped the nose and, within a few seconds, I was under them again. The IP now told me that I had been flying for 37 minutes since I'd left De Funiak Springs and that I had to be somewhere near Fort Rucker. Then, like an apparition, I saw lights on the horizon. I told him I saw a bunch of lights in front of me and I'd call him when I got closer. In a few minutes I was nearing a good-sized city. Had he not told me 37 minutes I would have guessed Montgomery or even Birmingham. Then I saw this city had a perfect circle around it, which was a four-lane highway. Only one city like that around here, or anywhere. It was Dothan.

I called Rucker and told this to the very relieved IP, who told me to take a heading of 280 degrees. I'd be at the airport in nine minutes. I was already cleared to land, straight in, on runway two-seven. I confirmed the instructions, and in nine minutes I made a perfect landing. (You know a perfect landing when the tires go "erk-erk"). On either side of me were fire trucks racing along with lights flashing and sirens wailing. It was embarrassing.

What I remembered most about that night was how terrified I had become. As events unfolded I recall thinking that I didn't realize that it was possible for me to become that afraid, which made me even more afraid. "Hours and hours of boredom interspersed by 37 minutes of sheer terror," described that cross-country.

While I was having my difficulties that night, one of the other guys in our class, Jim Sumler, experienced engine failure. As he glided down through the darkness he pulled the release lever in his door, which jettisoned it from the plane. He unlocked his seatbelt and was preparing to bail out into the night when he realized that he had merely run out of gas in one tank. He flipped the switch to the other tank and the engine came to life. He flew safely back to Rucker, one door short. They never found it.

Mike Jones admitted, later, that the night of the cross country he had set up a final approach to Main Street in Ozark, Alabama—mistaking it for the runway at Rucker. He'd aborted his landing just in time. His excuse was that the main runway at Rucker was on the exact same heading as downtown Ozark's Main Street. (I've lost track of Jim. Mike went with United Airlines after his Vietnam tour.)

Another heart pounding experience happened to me much later in our training during the IFR phase in the Beech Baron. The Baron is a four place (seat) aircraft. The seating arrangement during flight school was one student in the left seat, who was flying the plane, and the instructor pilot in the right seat, who was teaching him. In one of the back seats was another student whose job it was to watch out for other aircraft, while the flying student and the IP were concentrating on the instrument panel.

The first student pilot would fly to his destination wearing a hood device. This device prohibited him from seeing outside of the windows of the aircraft. This was called "flying under the hood," and it simulated flying in clouds. The only thing visible to the student was the instrument panel. When flying on instruments that's all you needed to see until just before touching down. When the first student pilot got to his destination, he would be debriefed by the IP over coffee in the pilots' lounge. Then student pilot number two would take the controls and fly under the hood back to Fort Rucker. Student number one would ride in the back seat.

VORs (VHF Omni Directional Ranges) are the white conical structures you see in fields near airports all over the country. The signals they emit allow pilots to navigate without ever looking at the ground. The pilot dials in the frequency of a VOR, and a needle on the instrument panel points to its direction, which is expressed in one of the 360 degrees of a circle. The pilot heads the plane in that direction, "flying the needle." He knows when he passes over the VOR because the needle flips 180 degrees. He tunes in the next VOR on his route of flight. VORs are still used today, but much more sophisticated navigational equipment is available via satellites.

Once I was flying under the hood as we were approaching the Dothan VOR en route back to Fort Rucker. All of a sudden the student in the back seat screamed, "Plane on our right!" I popped my hood off and looked out the right window. There was another airplane at our exact altitude. He could not have been two hundred feet away and was within a millisecond of slamming into our side. The IP grabbed the yoke and yanked it back, and the other plane went under us. We could not have missed each other by more than an inch. I am not exaggerating. My heart was pounding, the student in the back seat was chalk white, and the IP had beads of sweat all over his face. He kept the controls and flew the plane back to Rucker and landed it. None of us said a word until we had exited the plane and were walking to the main building. Finally the other student said, "Holy shit. I thought we were dead."

"Me, too," I said.

"Me, too," said the IP.

I don't know how we missed colliding.

I've never heard this definition of flying, but it is true: "Flying is hours and hours of boredom interspersed by moments of pure joy." During flight school and beyond I experienced many moments of pure joy in an aircraft.

One of the things IPs did in the Birddogs was turn off the engine. This was simple to do. The IPs rode in the back seat. There was a "mag switch" in the ceiling behind the student pilot's head. The IP would merely reach up and switch off the magnetos and the engine would go dead, always a total surprise to the student. We would then have to immediately drop the nose and enter a glide to maintain airspeed, which prevents a stall, and find a place to make what was called a "forced landing."

The IPs would never turn the engine off near an airport so we would have to rapidly pick out a suitable field—long enough, flat enough, and with no obstructions on it. Then we'd have to determine wind direction on the ground and set up an approach. (Airplanes always land and take off into the wind.) Our approach could not be too high, and it certainly could not be too low. We then had to land the plane, without power—a so-called "dead stick" landing—and do so without crashing. If we were hopelessly screwing up, the IP would simply switch the mags back on. After the engine roared to life, the IP would proceed to chew us out.

To make a successful dead stick landing into a farmer's field we'd never seen before was pure joy, and the joy was increased if the landing was silky smooth onto the grass. Over the course of our training we budding Army pilots became experts at instantly spotting forced landing areas and getting into them safely. One day this training would save my life.

Other moments of pure joy were frequently provided during the instrument phase of training. We got so good "under the hood" that we could take off without looking outside of the airplane. Then, using only charts and our instruments, we would fly hundreds of miles to our destination airport and then set up an approach to the active runway, which would be assigned by the tower. We would hit the glide slope with precise airspeed and altitude and then descend, descend, descend until the IP said, "OK, take off your hood," and there, directly in front of us, would be the numbers of the runway. It was like a miracle.

One time during instrument training we flew the Baron from Fort Rucker to Memphis International Airport. It was the first time we'd flown into an airport of this size. We were flying with the "big boys"—commercial airliners and large cargo aircraft. The other student had flown to Memphis, so it was my turn to fly back to Rucker. We left the tarmac and fell in behind an Eastern Airlines 727 to taxi to the end of the active runway. It was just about dark.

The 727 got cleared to take off, and as he began rolling we were cleared onto the runway to wait our turn to go. We watched the huge (to us) Eastern jet gain speed, break ground, and then stretch its nose into the sky. We were on the same radio frequency and listened to his conversation with the Memphis control tower. A few seconds after he broke ground the tower told him to switch frequencies to be picked up by air traffic control. The pilot repeated the frequency numbers he'd been given and then said, "Roger that. Goodnight, Memphis." And the Memphis tower said, "Goodnight, Eastern." I thought it was the coolest thing I'd ever heard.

We went through the same procedure, and when we broke ground I got my new radio frequency from the tower. I repeated it and then I just had to say, "Roger that. Goodnight, Memphis." Without hesitation Memphis replied, "Goodnight, Army."

I was a pilot.

CHAPTER 6

Showing Off

DURING THE TIME OF THE Vietnam War the Army had two different flight schools. The one at Fort Rucker taught fixed wing flying. The other one, the rotary wing school, began at Fort Wolters, Texas, and finished up at Fort Rucker. The fixed wing school was for commissioned officers only and the helicopter school was for commissioned and warrant officers. (I'll explain what a warrant officer is later.) Both schools were nine months long.

With one month left to go before our graduation from fixed wing school, we students received notices requesting volunteers to "transition" from fixed wing into rotary wing after graduation. The notice explained that this would entail an additional six weeks of schooling to learn to fly helicopters. This added six weeks of training would be held at Fort Rucker, where we would learn to fly the little H-13—that's a two seater with a clear plastic bubble around the pilots. Then we would go to Fort Benning, Georgia, for three additional weeks of training in the HU-1, the "Huey" that was rapidly becoming famous. In the most matter-of-fact wording the notice explained that more helicopter pilots were needed in Vietnam because helicopters were playing an expanded role there. The war was now being fought throughout the country. The notice did not say that chopper pilots were being killed at a far greater rate than fixed wing pilots, but of course we knew that. Anyone who watched the six o'clock news knew that.

The Army's rotary wing school could not keep up with the demand for helicopter pilots and needed augmentation from the fixed wing school. It also needed more commissioned officers in helicopter cockpits to fill command responsibilities. Of the 31 of us who graduated from our fixed wing class, six of us took the Army up on its offer to be cross-trained. I was one of them.

I volunteered to fly helicopters in Vietnam, instead of staying in the relatively safer Birddog, for the following well thought-out reasons:

First, I figured that as long as I was going to participate in a war I might as well experience it as up-close as possible. We had learned in history classes that there are five ways of chronicling the history of mankind, and one of them was by merely following his wars, warfare and history being inextricably linked. So I reasoned that I would be a close-up witness to history. Here was a unique, once in a lifetime opportunity. This was, I realized later, a distorted take on the expression, "If you're going, go first class."

Second, I liked the idea of being qualified to fly both fixed wing and rotary wing aircraft. To have a commercial, instrument pilot's license in both fixed and rotary wing aircraft would put me in a very elite group, adding stock, I thought, to my net worth as an employable pilot in civilian life.

Third, I was single and had no current love interest. Most importantly, I didn't have any kids. It was guys like me, I reasoned, who should be flying the helicopters in Vietnam, not married guys with families.

Fourth, I was 23 years old, and I knew in my heart and felt in my soul that I was bullet proof and could not be killed no matter what I did. I was an idiot.

After our graduation from fixed wing school, I was given a two-week leave of absence before starting the transition school. I drove home to Chicago.

Chicago, to me, was two entities. There was my family—mom, dad, brother, sister and grandmother—and there was my "gang" of fifteen guys I hung out with on the street corner of 79th and Racine. Our friendships had begun at St. Sabina's Grammar School and in some instances even before that. "Gang" was a misnomer—we were actually just a tight knit group of friends—but we referred to ourselves as "the guys in the gang." All of us lived in the same neighborhood. We could walk to each other's houses, and all of us were the same age and the same grade in school.

I could hardly wait to see them again, and I drove straight through from Alabama to Chicago. I was proud of my accomplishment, now being an Army pilot, but I was not naïve enough to think the guys in the gang would openly compliment me. In fact it would barely be mentioned. Behind my back they would say, "Did you hear Jimmy is going to fly helicopters in Vietnam?" This would be a newsworthy topic for the guys in the gang, and a slight touch of wonder would be attached to it. But to me, directly, there would be nothing. "Atta boy" and "congratulations" simply were not cool things to say and were doled out with studied reluctance by the guys in the gang. "Nice hit," "good catch," "good throw," "nice shot," were where most compliments began and ended.

There was a word we guys in the gang used—I've never known why. It was "pimp." If we said a person was a pimp we meant he: A) was not from our street corner; B) was different; C) was wimpy or nerdy; D) liked cars (we were sports nuts); or E) showed emotion. (Note: Girls could not be pimps.)

To pimp somebody was to tease them. To give a compliment was not cool, it was pimpy. Now that I think about it, flying an airplane would have been considered pimpy also, if the war hadn't been attached to it. To this day if I hit a particularly bad golf shot I will call myself a pimp. People look at me funny.

I loved the guys in the gang. We were a surrogate family and in many ways more siblings than friends. Impressing the guys in the gang was often more important than impressing family. But this was as hard to accomplish as impressing a brother who's only a year older than you. If he were impressed he'd never show it.

Nevertheless, I did make an effort to impress the guys by showing them that I could fly an airplane. After getting home, one of the first things I did was go to Midway Airport to get myself checked out in a Cessna 172. This is a tricycle gear, four-place aircraft—a pilot and three passengers. This airplane would serve my purpose perfectly. I got an IP to check me out, and we spent less than an hour together doing take-offs and landings, a few tight turns and a couple of power-off stalls. Piece of cake.

That night I walked into Chris Quinn's Tavern near the corner of 79th and Racine. Now that we were over 21 years of age, this was our hangout. We'd graduated from DeLites, the ice cream parlor and restaurant on the corner itself, which had been our hangout since early high school. Most of the guys in the gang were at Chris's, and after I was duly welcomed home with 15¢ glasses of drought beer, paid for by the guys, I told them what I'd done at Midway. I announced that if anybody wanted to see Chicago from the air, I'd be glad to take them for a ride. Naturally, and naively, I expected everybody to be excited about this prospect, but of the potential 15 passengers, only four had nerve enough to take me up on the offer. In retrospect I can now understand their reluctance. These guys had known me for most of my life and, though I wasn't the wildest guy in the gang, I wasn't the most stable, either. Would I have gone with me? Let me think about it.

The next day I met three of the guys who wanted to go for a ride in an airplane. There was Mike Watson and Tom McNally, who would become engineers, and Tom McDonough, who was in law school at Notre Dame. We got into my car and drove over to Midway, stopping on the way at a liquor store on Cicero Avenue for a couple of six-packs. It was not illegal to drink and fly, only to drink and drive.

To their credit, no one chickened out at the last minute when they realized just how small a single engine plane was. Watson and McDonough sat in the back seats—they'd be the bartenders—and McNally sat up front with me. The air that day was smooth as glass and the visibility was unlimited. We took off to the west, and as I reached 5,000 feet I turned south, heading toward 79th Street. When we got over 79th I turned due east and flew over the neighborhood. The guys were excited to be able to pick out DeLites, Chris Quinn's, St. Sabina's Church, Leo High School, and even their individual houses. I continued down 79th to its easternmost end at Rainbow Beach. I then headed north along the shore of Lake Michigan. Below us now was the Museum of Science and Industry and the University of Chicago complex. In front of us was the beautiful Chicago Loop.

I couldn't fly all the way to the Loop because it was on an approach path to O'Hare, so at 35th street I took a left, and we flew right over the top of Comiskey Park. By now the guys were very impressed and the beer cans were popping. I heard, "Look, there's Maxwell Street. Hey, there's the Prudential Building. Right below us is the new Dan Ryan Expressway." And so on. A good time was being had by all and I, being responsible, limited myself to two beers.

We followed 35th Street all the way out to the western suburbs, and then I called Midway tower to get landing instructions. The tower told me to get behind a DC-9 and come on in. This, too, impressed the guys. I made a perfect, no-bounce landing just moments after the DC-9 pulled off the runway, and taxied over to the flight service station and shut off the engine. I now had three witnesses, all important gang members, who could attest to the fact that Jimmy Joyce really was a pilot and a good one, too. And my witnesses were very happy—all the beer was gone, McDonough having knocked down the last one on final approach.

As we walked away from the airplane the bottom of the paper bag with the empties in it broke through: "*tink, tink, tink, tink, tink*" as the beer cans scattered all over the tarmac. We gathered them up and were directed to a garbage can by the man who rented me the plane. He thought this was very funny, especially when one of the guys walked over to the chain link fence and threw up. I won't say which one—he might sue me.

The next day I took my last volunteer for a ride. This was my best friend in the gang. His name was (is) James Thomas Joyce. Same as mine. Joyce is a common Irish name. There was another Joyce in the gang, Jeremiah, who would become a state senator. None of us were related to each other, nor were we related to the famous James Joyce, the Irish author. At this time the other Jimmy had just begun his career as a fireman. Today he is the commissioner of the Chicago Fire Department.

Like the day before, we picked up a six-pack on the way to Midway, climbed into the little Cessna and took off. But unlike the day before, the air was bumpy, really bumpy, and this takes a lot of the fun out of flying. The stiff-winged airplane rocked, rolled, lurched, dropped, and rose, and I noticed by the time we got to Lake Michigan Jim was looking kind of gray. I also noticed he wasn't drinking his beer. I decided to cut the trip short—I was sure he wouldn't mind—and when I got over Comiskey Park I called the tower for landing instructions. Jim had now gone from gray to pure white.

I was cleared for a straight-in approach to runway three-zero. I told Jim that we were heading in, and he nodded his head. Before we got to the airport the tower called and asked me if I'd "go around"; there was a Lear Jet closing fast behind me. It was a courtesy that little planes yield to the bigger, faster ones. I told the tower "No problem" and aborted the approach. I made a rather severe left turn to get out of the Lear's way and to re-enter the approach pattern behind him, and that's when Jim threw up.

I've always felt bad about this unpleasant experience for my best buddy on his first ride in a small plane. Within minutes of being on the ground, though, he was fully revived. Bumpy air sucks, especially real bumpy like that day. Over the years I've heard pilots say they didn't care if the air was bumpy or not. They're lying.

A few days later I took my dad for a ride in the 172. He'd never been in a small plane either, and he'd been on only one commercial flight. I gave him the same tour, and he loved it. As we approached the western suburbs, however, I noticed something at our altitude—directly in front of us. " Dad, look at that!" I yelled, pointing. "I wonder what it is?" I then realized we were closing very fast on the thing, and I laid the plane on its right side and pushed the nose down to avoid it. As we went under it I looked up out of my side window to see a kid's helium balloon, complete with streamer, pass above us. "Damn!" I yelled, then felt immediately embarrassed. "Damn" was a bad word—never said in my father's presence. But this time he ignored it.

Dad really enjoyed the flight, and on the way home from the airport he and I decided it would be great fun to rent the plane again, this time for a few days, and fly up to St. Cloud, Minnesota, to visit my brother Bob and his wife Mary. By the time we got home we were full of enthusiasm for this adventure and could hardly wait to tell Mom and Granny about it. They heard the plan and Granny was the first to say how much she'd love to go. Granny was 88 years old at this time and had become famous for having her hat on her head and her purse in her lap, ready to go anywhere, at anytime, with anybody. She was a great one for going.

But Mom was reluctant. She could find reasons to say "no" to any proposal. It was just her nature. However, a stronger point of her nature was not to be left out, so with a flurry of "tsk, tsk, tsks," and a bunch of questions pertaining to my ability to find St. Cloud, Minnesota, from the air she agreed to the deal.

Two days later we took off. Dad sat up front with me and I gave him the map. He would be the official navigator, which he loved. Mom and Granny took up the back seats.

One of the things we were never concerned about in flight school was being "over gross." This means having too much weight on board for the particular airplane we were flying. Although we'd learned about it in ground school it was never a practical consideration in a Birddog or a Baron. Four people in a Cessna 172 was not a problem either—but four people and all their luggage was a whole new ball game. When I pushed the throttle forward I thought I noticed that the plane didn't respond as it had before. It was slower picking up speed. Then I thought I noticed that I was eating up a lot of runway before gaining enough airspeed to pull back on the yoke and lift off. Then I noticed, for sure, that the fence at the end of the runway was almost upon us. We were going way too fast to stop, so I eased back on the yoke. We did clear the fence and we did clear the buildings beyond it but just barely! A few more miles per hour slower and we would have stalled and Mr. Show Off would have killed his mother, his father, his grandmother, and himself. Not checking on the gross weight was the height of carelessness; even as I write these words today, my palms are getting moist.

Of course I never indicated to my folks how dangerous the take-off was. We slowly, very slowly, gained altitude, and I didn't dare raise my take-off flaps until I was over 1,000 feet in the air. I didn't turn one degree in either direction or raise the nose one degree. I "held it" until I was sure we were high enough and going fast enough to be safe. God, it was scary.

Eventually we reached our cruising altitude of 7500 feet. It was a beautiful day with deep blue sky, puffy white clouds and barely a bump. Dad was having a good time finding things on the map that he saw on the ground. I was navigating from VOR to VOR, so I didn't need the map. As we passed over Rockford, Illinois, on the Wisconsin border, I thought I heard a strange sound coming from behind me. I turned around and sure enough Granny was throwing up into a plastic bag—not a lot, just a little. I asked if she wanted me to land or turn back and she said, " No, of course not. I'll be fine."

A little while later I heard a similar strange sound and looked back to see Mom throwing up into her plastic bag—not a lot, just a little. She, too, said she'd be fine and told me to keep going. And then a few minutes later Granny threw up again, and that's the way it went all the way to St. Cloud, Minnesota. Every fifteen minutes or so either Mom or Granny threw up. A pattern had definitely developed. My flying made people sick.

While in St. Cloud my sister-in-law, to everyone's surprise, said she'd like to take a ride in the plane. Mary had never been in an airplane, so I made sure she had a plastic bag, just in case, and we took off. I flew her over the beautiful campus of St. John's University, where Bob now taught, and over St. Benedict's College, where she taught, and all around the St. Cloud area. The air was slightly bumpy and I was waiting for her to be sick, but it didn't happen. She thoroughly enjoyed herself, she really did, and I maintain it is only a coincidence that to this day Mary has yet to set foot on another airplane.

So the pattern of my passengers getting sick was broken, and for that I was pleased. Two days later Mom and Granny boarded the train to return to Chicago, and Dad and I flew the Cessna back to Midway.

A few days before my leave was over I got a letter from U.S. Army Headquarters in the Pentagon. It contained my official orders. After the helicopter transition school at Rucker and the Huey school at Benning, I was to report to the 227th Assault Helicopter Battalion, First Air Cavalry Division, An Khe, South Vietnam. Travel orders would follow shortly.

So this made it official. Although I'd known since the beginning of flight school that I would no doubt be going to Vietnam, these official orders did give me and my family a bit of a jolt. Speculating about it was one thing; having official orders in hand was something else.

My family didn't know the difference between the First Air Cavalry Division and the 101st Airborne Division, but I did. The Cavalry was well known as a very aggressive division. In other words, it was taking an exceptional number of casualties. My wish to see the war up close and personal had just been granted. I was going to the First Cavalry.

But my family did know that flying a helicopter in Vietnam was dangerous. The evening news kept the country appraised of how "the helicopter war" was going. A pall was cast over the household with the arrival of my orders. Would we ever see each other again was on our minds, but it went unspoken.

On the night before I left to return to Ft. Rucker there was a party in my honor held in the basement of the Carrolls' house. Mr. and Mrs. Carroll were like second parents to me. Their son, Tom, was one of the gang;

he would also serve in Vietnam. Their daughter, Pat, was the closest of friends. All of the guys were at the party along with their girlfriends. It was a great bash with tons of food and gallons of booze. It was Irish. Some of the guys had prepared skits, complete with costumes, depicting escapades from our somewhat wild, always hilarious past.

Toward the end of the evening one of my closest gang buddies, Bob Cavanaugh, came up to me and looked me in the eyes. His eyes, I noticed, were welling up. He said he wanted me to promise I'd remember what he was about to tell me. I promised.

"Remember," he said, "that no matter how bad it gets, you'll get through it because you will say to yourself that when whatever is happening is over—and it will be—you're gonna get to sit down, relax, and have a beer."

Then he gave me a kiss on the cheek and walked away.

I have never forgotten this advice. I thought of it many times not only during Vietnam, where it was invaluable, but throughout my somewhat unorthodox life. But the advice was paled by the genuine show of emotion from Bobby. I was surprised, moved, and grateful. It was such a pimpy thing for him to do.

CHAPTER 7

Transition School

WHEN I RETURNED FOR HELICOPTER training I remained in my same BOQ room at Fort Rucker, but most of my buddies were off to Vietnam. Only one good friend remained: Mike Jones, the one who almost landed in downtown Ozark. Mike was recently married and spent every spare second with his new wife. He was no fun at all. Mike and I had bonded one night toward the end of fixed wing school. It was during the survival part of training. Our instructors emphasized that the single most important aspect of survival was: "Do not lose the will to live!" It was even more important than finding food—most healthy people can live for thirty days on water alone, we were told.

The exercise was called "escape and evasion." We were to pretend we'd escaped from a Viet Cong P.O.W. camp and had to make our way back to a friendly position, all the while evading the enemy. We were assigned to two-man teams for a night of living hell. Mike was my teammate. He was about 6 feet 2 inches tall and had muscles on top of muscles, gained while growing up on his family's dairy farm in Indiana. Fortunately, Mike had a gentle, laid back personality.

We were given a compass, a flashlight and a map. We were taken by jeep to a clearing in the woods and dropped off. The sergeant showed us on the map where we were and then showed us where we had to go. "Good luck, gentlemen," he said, and off he drove. It was about 8:30 at night and almost dark. We began walking through the woods.

And we continued walking through the woods, up and down ravines, and through swamps and brambles and cockle berries and thistles and burrs and every other thing that grows in the woods. We were constantly slapped by branches, sucked into mud, stumbling over unseen things. Our faces and hands were scraped, our uniforms were torn, and our knees were bruised and bleeding. Whenever we got to a road we had to crouch down beside it before daring to cross. The "enemy" controlled the roads. The exercise was timed, and if we didn't get to our destination within this time limit we would have to repeat it. To accomplish this it was necessary to walk all night without stopping except for brief rests. Of course, it was also necessary to not get lost. So Mike and I trudged and slipped and skidded and stumbled, all the while checking our map and evading the enemy. It was terrible.

Right at daybreak Mike and I were staggering, exhausted, along the side of a creek. I was a few feet in front of him when all of a sudden he grabbed me by the shoulders and threw me sideways to the ground. Astonished, I looked up at him and asked, "What the hell was that for?"

"Look, Jim," he said, pointing to the ground. I glanced over my shoulder and there, directly in our path, was a huge snake. Mike said it was a cottonmouth. I was about to step on it. I began sliding backwards as fast as possible as the snake woke up. Mike said the bite from one that big could kill a man, so we'd better give him plenty of room.

"God, Mike, thanks."

"You're welcome, City Boy," he smiled.

Shortly after Mike and I arrived at the rendezvous site my buddy Palmer Haines stumbled in, looking even more haggard than Mike and me. He went down to the ground, rolled over on his back, and said, "I have lost the will to live."

It was during this survival phase of training that we were taught how to capture, kill, clean, skin, cook and eat snakes. They are in almost all corners of the world and are very nutritious, we were told—and they do, honestly, taste like chicken. We learned to do the same with rabbits, squirrels, opossums and raccoons. We were also fed bugs. Our instructor, a sergeant, said bugs were all protein and the most plentiful and nutritious food we could find. All bugs are good for you, we learned, and to prove they were edible our instructor gave us dead bugs to eat. Our class was given large grasshoppers. I figured they couldn't taste too bad, once you got past the thought of what was in your mouth. So I took a bite out of one—it was too big to swallow whole—and the juice squirted onto my tongue. The taste was exactly like how I assume fresh shit must taste. It was horrible. Most of us gagged, some guys puked, none of us could get them down. This made the sergeants laugh. "When you're hungry enough, you'll eat them," they said. I don't think so.

When the helicopter school began I found the transition from fixed wing to rotary wing to be relatively smooth. The instruments on the control panels in both type aircraft were essentially the same. Also the flight rules governing helicopters, for both IFR and VFR flight, were the same as fixed wing. Helicopters also used the same approach charts and navigational maps. In a helicopter Mr. Warren's penis would still be twenty miles long.

One big difference between an airplane and a helicopter is the flight controls. An airplane is flown holding a stick or yoke in the hand, which moves the ailerons up and down on the wings and controls the horizontal elevator on the tail. A helicopter also has a stick, but it is called a cyclic, and it controls the pitch of the main rotor head, which can be tilted in any direction. An airplane has rudder pedals, which control the vertical rudder on its tail. A helicopter also has rudder pedals, but they are called anti-torque pedals and control the pitch of the tail rotor blades. Note: If a helicopter was hovering and didn't have a tail rotor, its body would spin around in the opposite direction of the main rotor blades above it. (For every action there is an equal and opposite reaction.)

The helicopter has an additional control not found on an airplane. This is a pole-like device called a collective. It is located below and next to the pilot's seat on the left side. This pole is held in the left hand, and it controls the pitch of the main rotor blades, which are connected to the head. Both aircraft have throttles controlling engine speed. In a fixed wing the throttles are located on the instrument panel or in front of it. On a helicopter the throttle is on the collective and is twisted like the throttle on a motorcycle. There is one other major difference between an airplane and a helicopter, and that is the helicopter's amazing ability to "auto rotate" if its engine quits running. An airplane will indeed glide to the ground if its engine quits, but it will need a long, smooth, runway-like surface to safely land upon. The faster the landing speed of the individual aircraft, the longer this flat surface must be. Not so for the helicopter. It can safely land in any space that can accommodate its size.

When the engine quits running in a helicopter the pilot rapidly pushes the collective all the way down. This takes the pitch (angle) out of the main rotor blades. They become "flat"—horizontal to the ground. As the aircraft falls toward the ground the air rushing up through the blades keeps them spinning at the same revolutions per minute (RPM) as though in normal, level flight with the engine running. So you have potential force up above you—the rapidly spinning rotor blades. Just prior to reaching the ground, about ten feet above it, the pilot pulls up (yanks) the collective, putting all available pitch into the blades. This is called "pulling pitch." The helicopter then comes to an almost complete stop in its descent and then slowly and gently settles onto the ground. A helicopter can be landed as accurately and gently in auto rotation as it can be with full power.

But you only get one chance.

If you pull pitch when you are too high in the air, you will lose your rotor's RPMs too soon before touching the ground. You will then come down hard and crash. On the other hand, if you wait too long to pull pitch you have already crashed. It's sort of tricky. Timing is absolutely everything in an auto rotation.

Auto rotation is practiced over and over when learning to fly helicopters. It is the prime life-saving maneuver, and it is an enormous amount of fun to do. To accomplish a perfect auto rotation, landing like a feather and right on the mark, is another pure joy of flying. So if you lose your only engine while flying, hope you are in a helicopter rather than an airplane. Your odds of a safe landing are infinitely greater.

Most people think that it is more difficult to fly a helicopter than an airplane. This is a myth. The myth survives because when a student pilot takes his or her first lesson in a small, single engine airplane, at the end of the hour of instruction the student can imagine that some day, way—way off in the future maybe, but someday—he will learn to fly the aircraft all by himself.

When student pilots have their first hour of instruction in a small, single engine helicopter, they know that if they live to be one hundred they will never learn to fly it. They also believe this after their second lesson and into the third. The problem is the hover. You cannot fly a helicopter until you learn to bring it up to a hover, a few feet above the ground, and hold it there—not drifting, not going up and not going down. This, at first, is impossible to do. Someone once said that hovering a helicopter is like trying to stand on a bowling ball.

But the truth is that both the fixed wing student pilot and the rotary wing student will both solo after about 12 hours of flying with an instructor pilot. So which is harder? Which is "harder" to drive, a stick shift car or an automatic? You may be busier driving a stick (or flying a helicopter) but it's not " harder" than driving an automatic (flying a plane). It becomes second nature.

In my experience the main difference between flying an airplane and a helicopter is that the helicopter is ten times more fun. I'll never forget the thrill and the seemingly unbelievable reality that a runway is not necessary. From where you are sitting you can merely take off. Or you're hovering along and come up to a fence. No sweat: Go over or around. Water? You can walk on it. Not really, but you can hover over it. The versatility of "taxiing" a helicopter versus an airplane is, well, there's no comparison. At a hover a helicopter can go forward or backward or sideways. All 360 degrees are yours. During the Gulf War, I saw an interview on TV with a U.S. Air

Force helicopter pilot. He was asked if he wouldn't rather be flying jet fighters. "Gosh, no," he said, "Flying a helicopter is like flying a magic carpet. It's the most fun in all aviation." Yes.

Most of the students in my helicopter transition class were captains and majors. All of them were career officers planning to spend at least 20 years on active duty and become eligible for retirement. They had all been flying fixed wing aircraft for many years. Some had flown in the Korean War. All were married.

I was still a second lieutenant, had no intention of spending one day on active duty beyond my three-year obligation, was single and fresh out of flight school. This made me very junior to my classmates in all ways, and I couldn't help feeling somewhat out of place. Although none of them pulled rank on me, ("Joyce, go to the PX and get us some beer") they pretty much ignored me. Other than being in the same school we had little in common.

After a few days, however, one of the senior captains befriended me. His name was Bob Daniels*, and he was from a small town in Idaho. Bob was one of the nicest guys I'd ever met. He was also one of the ugliest. The battle he'd had with acne years before left scars, bulges and crevices in his face the likes of which I'd never seen. It was hard not to stare at him.

Bob was what the Army called a "geographical bachelor." This was a married man whose wife was not accompanying him on his current assignment. He was therefore living in the BOQ room next to me, instead of married housing. For Bob, this arrangement was about to change, however. He was recently married to Robin*, a Eurasian girl he'd met while stationed at Schofield Barracks in Hawaii. She was due to join him soon. Bob confided to me one night at the Officer's Club that he still couldn't believe how lucky he was that Robin married him. He told me he was out of his mind in love with her and said she was really beautiful. "I know I'm ugly, Jim, but she doesn't care. She really loves me." He had tears in his eyes.

Bob and I became buddies, and when Robin arrived she became my girl buddy. And he was correct: She was gorgeous. If a "10" is as high as it goes, she was a "10." It was hard not to stare at Robin, also.

Bob and Robin had me over to their quarters often. It was a real house with a yard and driveway. They'd have me over for dinner and cookouts or just to watch TV. I loved being with them, and it was obvious they really loved each other—light touches, winks, smiles, and impromptu kisses. This was how married people should be, I determined.

Best of all, Bob also had orders for the 227th Battalion in the First Cav, so this would not be a temporary friendship as so many of them are in the military. He and I would see the war together. His orders had him leaving for Vietnam two days before me. Nice.

It was also during this time that I met Mary Morris from Dothan. She was tall, beautiful, bright and Southern! Her drawl could be cut with a two by four. You know General Motors? Everybody calls it "GM?" That's how Mary pronounced my name. I was a goner. Although together for less than two months before I left for Vietnam, the word "marriage" had actually been spoken between us. We were made for each other.

CHAPTER 8

Welcome to Vietnam

ASIDE FROM THE OBVIOUS CONCERNS regarding our reason for traveling, the trip to Vietnam was actually quite pleasant. We flew on a Northwest Orient Boeing 707 chartered by the Army. It was complete with pretty stewardesses serving excellent food and all the free drinks we wanted. The only difference between this flight and any other commercial flight was that all of the passengers wore uniforms and all had the same final destination, the city of Pleiku in the Central Highlands of South Vietnam.

It is a sixteen-hour flight from San Francisco to Pleiku. We stopped once, at Clark AFB in the Philippines, to refuel. In the Philippines we were allowed to exit the plane and go into the airbase terminal. The only thing I remember about this stop was that Mike Jones and I got into an argument about dogs. He said they, like people, had souls, and would therefore enjoy an afterlife. I told him, politely, he was full of crap. He then told me about his dog on the farm in Indiana and how much kinder and more considerate it was than most people. He made an excellent case, and though I did not back down, I think he won the argument. It's funny the stuff you remember. Eternity must have been on our minds.

Although we were exhausted and beat up from the interminable flight over the Pacific, the plane came alive with tension and excitement when the pilot announced he was beginning his initial approach into Pleiku. He told us he'd be making a high final approach and then a very steep descent at the end of it because there was fighting going on not far from the end of the runway. He told us not to be concerned about this, however, because his airplane had yet to take a bullet and he'd been flying this route for almost a year. Nobody seemed relieved. But soon we landed and taxied to a stop. We were in Vietnam.

We walked off the plane and lined up on the tarmac to retrieve our duffel bags containing all our possessions. We were then escorted to a row of portable bleachers some 50 yards from the plane. During this short walk all heads swiveled from side to side, checking out the surrounding hills for signs of mortar fire. We also couldn't help wondering about that battle the pilot mentioned. We could hear, but not pinpoint, small arms fire in the distance. What if we lost this battle and the Viet Cong came storming across the airport to slaughter us all? The sergeants who met us at the plane and who were now walking with us did not, however, look at all concerned. They were positively nonchalant. That helped.

In the past year while preparing to come to Vietnam we had heard many stories about the dangers there aside from the obvious—getting shot by the VC or the NVA. (The VC, nicknamed "Victor Charlie" or simply "Charlie," were the Viet Cong, who were indigenous South Vietnamese soldiers fighting against the American-supported political regime. The NVA were the North Vietnamese Army regulars who came south to help their VC comrades. The South Vietnamese Army, our ally, was called ARVN—the Army of the Republic of Vietnam.)

The other dangers in Vietnam included cute little Vietnamese children carrying harmless looking handbags. These were actually satchel charges that blew you up—along with the little kid if he didn't run fast enough after dropping it. There were also the punji stakes. These were bamboo poles stuck in the ground. The end pointing up was camouflaged and was whittled to razor sharpness and coated with human feces. To step on them was potentially deadly. The razor edge had no trouble penetrating the bottom of Army boots. There was another kind of punji stake, the spring-loaded edition, which was camouflaged along the side of the jungle pathways. If you activated the trip wire attached to the device, your body was instantly penetrated by a half dozen or so bamboo stakes. There was no surviving this.

But the most dangerous aspect of Vietnam was mortar shells. Only one place in the country was immune to mortar attack. (We'll discuss that place later). So there was virtually no safe haven, no front line behind which you could relax. You could be killed by mortar fire anytime, anywhere in the country. This, I believe, was the worst part of this war and made it unique among all of our wars. A complete respite from danger was not possible in Vietnam, even in the most fortified military base.

The NCO (non-commissioned officer—sergeant) who escorted us to the bleachers politely asked that we take a seat and "listen up." He said we were about to learn about the second greatest danger in Vietnam—something we hadn't heard about back in the States. He said that what he was about to tell us would determine as much as anything whether we would return home or not. Next to the sergeant was a large flip chart on a wooden easel. He had a pointer in his hand.

Our eyes left the nearby hillside where we had been searching for tell-tale puffs of white smoke and now gazed at the sergeant. I, being a college educated officer, was sure we were about to get a lecture concerning all of the deadly poisonous snakes that crawled all over this country—I'd read about them—or perhaps deadly insects or plants that we had not been told about.

The sergeant began his lecture by stating that he knew what we were thinking. We were thinking he was going to lecture us about the deadly snakes and insects in South Vietnam. "That is incorrect," he stated. He added there were lots of them here but they didn't mean shit compared to what he was about to tell us. He flipped the cover page of the chart and there in big red letters were the words "Venereal Disease!"

"Gentlemen and men," he said (gentlemen were officers and men were the rest), "This is the second greatest danger you will face during your year in Vietnam!" He then explained during the next half-hour that there were strains of VD in this country for which there was no cure. He said that even if the VD didn't kill us, we would never be allowed back to the USA because we'd be carriers. As he was talking he was flipping the pages of his chart, which showed penis after penis and scrotum after scrotum in the most horrific of swollen, oozing conditions. He had our attention. The sergeant told us that the most severe strains of VD were found in the rural areas, "carried by country girls," but nowhere would we be totally safe. His final words were that abstinence was the only assurance we wouldn't catch these diseases, but if we couldn't do that we must use rubbers—"Two is best." He would be passing them out shortly.

"One last thing," he continued: "You gentlemen and men who are going to the First Cav at An Khe are better off than most." He explained that the Army had set up a house of prostitution right next to the base. It was called "Disneyland," and the women were checked once a week by the Army doctors. He said it was the safest place in Vietnam to get laid but was still not foolproof, so rubbers must be used. He told us to line up and he'd pass them out. "And oh, yes," he smiled, "Welcome to Vietnam."

After this bewildering—make that unbelievable—introduction to Vietnam, we were assigned to barracks where we would be spending the night. Those of us going to An Khe, about 60 kilometers to the east, were to report back to the airfield at 0700 hours the next morning. But for now we were free. We were told that the city of Pleiku was secure, but we were advised that if we went into it we should go in a group and not wander beyond the center of the city ... "because you can't be certain." Although physically exhausted from the flight, Mike Jones and I decided to see Pleiku. Mike, in my mind, qualified as a group.

I remember very little about our evening in Pleiku. The combination of jet lag and culture shock must have taken effect. I do recall, however, that Mike and I found a local Vietnamese restaurant and decided to eat "on the economy." We took a pass on the traditional Vietnamese dish of fish head soup, instead ordering hamburgers and Ba M' Ba beer (pronounced "bow me bow"), the national beer of Vietnam. It was delicious, and so were the hamburgers, although later we learned that hamburgers in Vietnam did not come from beef but from water buffalo. No problem. After supper we returned to the base, found our barracks, and collapsed on top of our cots. Our first day in Vietnam was over. We had only 364 more to go. Time in country counted from when we left San Francisco.

An Army tour of duty in Vietnam was twelve months long. In this we were much more fortunate than the soldiers in other wars before us. We who served in Vietnam all had a DEROS (Date of Estimated Return from Overseas), so we knew how much time we had to serve and could count the days we had left in the war. In the other wars that America fought, the soldiers left home not knowing how long they'd be gone. Often it was many years.

At 0700 hours the following morning I boarded a twin engine Army cargo plane, called the Caribou, for the thirty-minute flight to the First Air Cavalry Division headquarters next to the town of An Khe. A Caribou was entered and exited through the rear door, and the pilot flew with this cargo door open, so we had a panoramic view of the countryside. It was jungle-covered mountain after jungle-covered mountain as far as we could see from 5000 feet. Beautiful, to be sure, but I remember thinking it was no wonder we hadn't won the war yet. Ten army divisions could hide in those mountains and never be found—and I was seeing only a small fraction of the Central Highlands. It was jarring to realize that this was the terrain I'd be flying over in a helicopter.

Soon we reached our destination and the pilot made a very steep descent into the An Khe Valley. He landed smoothly on the PSP (perforated steel panels) runway. The instant we touched down he reversed the pitch of his two large propellers and we came to an abrupt stop. (Note: Airplanes do not "reverse their engines" to slow down after landing. That's not possible. Propeller-driven planes reverse the pitch of the props. Jets mechanically divert their thrust to the sides or back around to the front.) He cut the engines and we trudged down the ramp into bright sunlight.

The most impressive sight at the headquarters of the First Air Cavalry

Division, henceforth known as the Cav, was the division's insignia, which had been painted on the side of the top of Hong Kong Mountain, which overlooked the compound, An Khe and the An Khe Valley. It was truly awesome. The Cav insignia is oblong but wider at the top than at the bottom—egg-like, if an egg were flat. The background is a very bright yellow, and on a diagonal across this background is a thick black line. Above the line is the profile of a horse's head, also in black. To the Cav members their insignia on the mountaintop was a great source of pride which stated, "This area is ours." To the villagers it was no doubt boorish, garish and an insult to their land. In any case, it made one hell of an impression when you first saw it. I don't know its dimensions, but it was huge.

As we walked from the Caribou toward a row of tents I heard someone call my name. It was John Breen, one of my JCU college buddies, standing on the tarmac grinning at me. The last time I'd seen him was over a year ago when we were briefly stationed together at Fort Eustis, Virginia. From there I'd gone to flight school and he'd been assigned to a unit in France. While there he learned that many of his JCU classmates had been sent to Vietnam, and he decided it wasn't fair that he should have a cushy, safe job in Europe. So he extended his two-year active duty obligation in order to volunteer for Vietnam, and he was now in charge of the fixed wing airfield at the Cav headquarters. Breen had a conscience at a time, the 1960s, when having a patriotic conscience had become optional. So this meant I already had two good friends here—Bob Daniels having arrived two days ago. Things were looking good.

As it turned out, John and I would see each other only once more during our tours. He'd told me at the airfield that he'd never been in a Huey and I had determined to correct that. Some months later I gave him the ride of a lifetime, a 140mph low level tour of the An Khe Valley—skids just inches above the treetops. My left side door gunner let John ride in his seat.

As John and I were catching up on news of our classmates, a jeep pulled up. The driver was looking for a Lieutenant Joyce. "That's me," I said.

"Hop in, sir, I'll take you to the 227th."

By now I was a first lieutenant, having been promoted at the end of transition school. Silver bars are more impressive than the second lieutenant's gold, and I almost felt like I deserved a jeep and driver. I climbed into the vehicle, throwing my duffel bag in the back seat. The driver said that my unit was in the field and was expected back that night. He said he'd take me to my quarters and I could get officially signed in tomorrow. We drove about five minutes and he pulled up in front of a dust-covered, hunkered-down tent. As he handed me my duffel bag he said this was where

First Lieutenant John Breen (Illinois). The airfield commander at An Khe. His conscience wouldn't let him stay in France.

I'd be living and that there was an area in the tent that wasn't taken. "Just make yourself at home, sir," he said as he got back in the jeep and sped off.

I picked up my bag and stepped up onto wooden pallets that had been nailed together to make a front porch of sorts. At that moment a captain came through the tent flap. I dropped my duffel bag and saluted him and he saluted me back. We shook hands, and I introduced myself saying I'd just arrived from the States. He said he was Captain Ray Clark and that he'd heard I was coming. He told me my bunk was the second one on the right. I asked the captain if by any chance Captain Bob Daniels was staying in the same tent. I told him we were buddies in transition school and he had orders for the 227th also. Clark hesitated and then said that Bob had been in the tent across a small ravine—he pointed to it—but he wasn't there anymore. I asked if he had been transferred to another unit.

"No, Joyce, he was killed yesterday."

My eyes got wide and my jaw dropped. "But he just got here," I said.

"Yeah, two days ago," Clark said, and told me the crash happened on Bob's second mission. It was over by the coast. Everybody was killed—Bob Daniels, his co-pilot, the door gunners and eight grunts. "My God, what happened?" I asked, "Were they shot down?"

"No," he said. "The weather was lousy and somehow they flew into the side of a mountain." He said Bob must have gotten vertigo or something but nobody knew for sure. There had been an explosion on impact. The wreckage and bodies had not yet been extracted from the mountainside. He said this happened a lot. "If Charlie doesn't get you," he added, "the weather will."

As I stood there dumbfounded, Clark continued talking. He said that after I was here awhile I'd notice that lots of guys got killed either right after they got in country or just before they went home. He said it didn't make any sense but it was true. He added that he was going home in two days so the colonel let him stay in camp instead of going to the field. "Joyce, I got stuff to do. You might as well get unpacked," he said and walked away.

This news of Bob Daniels' death did not sadden me as much as it stunned me. The way Clark told it, so matter of factly, and without a trace of emotion, made it all the more unbelievable, like it was hardly worth mentioning. Somewhere in my now dazed mind it occurred to me that had I not asked about Bob, Captain Clark would not have told me that there'd been a crash yesterday that killed four guys from our unit and eight infantrymen.

I picked up my duffel bag, pushed back the tent flap, and walked into my new home. It was dark inside, and a heavy, musty smell filled the air. There was no sound in the tent, not even a ticking clock. As my eyes adjusted to the dark I saw what must be my "space." I moved toward it, trying to make what I had just heard seem real. Bob is dead? Daniels is dead? No, he's not. This is either a dream or Captain Clark was lying.

When I got to my space I dropped the duffel bag, sat down on the cot and silently started talking to myself. Bob Daniels really is dead. This is a war, after all, what did you expect? People get killed, especially when they fly helicopters. You knew all this before you got here. Jesus Christ, what about Robin? She'll be shattered. But she'll get over it. You'll get over it. This is one friend dead. There's gonna be more. But you won't die. You weren't born to die in Vietnam. Bob was a career officer. He even talked about being killed here. You never talked about it. It's not in the cards for you. You can't die. You're too young. You're a civilian. You're a volunteer, not a regular.

This rambling of nonsense continued for I don't know how long, but then I began to feel a dullness, a numbness surround my brain. It started at the back of my head and worked its way forward, focusing all thoughts to the front, through the eyes, to the now. I continued my silent reverie. Bob Daniels crashed and died yesterday. This could happen to you. College type thoughts about philosophy, theology, and "what's it all about" no longer mean anything. Survival. You must concentrate on your survival. God. You will trust in Him ... and focus on survival. That's all you can do.

I put my face in my hands and tried to cry for my friend Bob Daniels and for his beautiful Robin. But I couldn't. All I could think about was myself.

CHAPTER 9

Learning the Ropes

I UNPACKED BY DUMPING THE contents of my duffel bag into the footlocker and then fished around in it to find a writing tablet and envelopes. I would write to Robin later when I recovered from the shock of Bob's death. For now, I wrote a letter to my parents and one to Mary, and I was half way through one to my best friend, the other Jim Joyce, when I thought I heard thunder. It was a rolling, far off rumble, but the sound was too uniform and constant to be thunder and it was getting louder by the second. I put the letter down and walked out of the tent.

I looked to the sky and saw them. It was a line of Huey helicopters, four abreast, coming in from the south. The line was so long I couldn't see the end of it. They were coming in to land at the "Golf Course," the name given to the First Cav's heliport, which was directly behind my tent. (The lieutenant colonel who oversaw the creation of the heliport said he wanted it "as clean as a golf course.") As the first wave passed over me, not more than thirty feet above my head, the earth shook and the cacophony of sounds from the rotor blades gave me goose bumps. DOOVA, DOOVA, whop, whop, POP! POP! All underscored by the high scream of the jet engines.

The backs of the Hueys were crammed with soldiers in full battle gear, each cradling a weapon. Those on the exterior sat on the helicopter's floor, legs hanging over the sides, their boots resting on the skids. Some of them waved down at me and a few actually saluted me. I felt like I should be saluting them. Their uniforms were filthy, but they all seemed to be in a good mood. Clark walked up and stood next to me to watch this endless aerial parade of descending Hueys. "There's some happy campers there, Joyce," he said.

"How come?" I asked.

He said it was because they were home from the field for a while. Living in the field, he said, was miserable; it was a lot safer here than out there. He added that I'd learn that soon enough.

That night I met the other guys who lived in the tent: First Lieutenant Glenn Hilliard* from South Carolina, First Lieutenant Wayne Lannin from California, First Lieutenant Bruce Jones* from North Carolina, First Lieutenant Walter John* from New York City, First Lieutenant Hal Trout from Missouri, and Captain Paul Silberberger from Nashville, who was the senior ranking officer in the tent. Captain Clark also lived in the tent, but Silberberger outranked him by time in grade. If there was a dispute in the tent, Silberberger would be the one to settle it. He had one more month to serve in country before his DEROS.

After supper some of us were sitting in the common area. I was full of questions about being in the Cav, and these "old timers," some with less than two months in country, were happy to answer them. About ten o'clock we began to hear "swish boom, swish boom" in the distance. Everyone in the group quit talking and tensed up, their heads cocked toward the sound. Then there were more "swish booms" and these were much closer. They all jumped up, someone yelled, "Incoming!" and they took off running through the tent flap. Figuring I should follow them, I stood up and started toward the flap when someone hit me hard from behind. I fell over the top of a lawn chair and wound up on the floor. As I landed I saw the back of Captain Silberberger as he raced through the opening. I stood up and now the "swish-booms" were very close. I heard someone yell, "Joyce, get the fuck out here! Come to the bunker!"

I ran outside to see explosions all around our area. I dashed to the bunker and was pulled inside by Jones. As the eight of us huddled in the bunker, Lannin explained to me that "swish boom" means enemy mortars are incoming. "Boom-swish" means they are friendly mortars going out. "You'll figure this out real quick," he said as the "swish booms" fell around us. I asked him how long would this last and he told me it probably wouldn't be too long. "Charlie's just welcoming us home, he said." We then heard helicopters taking off. John said they were a couple of gunships from Delta Company and with them in the air the mortar attack would be over in less than a minute. He said gunships were awesome and that he'd like to fly one. He said gunships played offense, slicks were always stuck on defense. His prediction about the mortar attack was correct: It ended a few moments later.

When we got back to the tent Captain Silberberger apologized for knocking me down. He had been asleep on his cot in the back of the tent

The place to be during "swish-boom" time.

and said he'd acted totally on reflex. He said he barely remembered doing it. "It was like I was running in my sleep, Joyce," he said, and I believed him. But even if he'd done it on purpose I really couldn't blame him. Why let some stupid FNG (Fucking New Guy) get you killed in your tent after you'd been through eleven months of the war? I told the captain not to worry about it and that next time I'd know enough to run. "Thanks, Joyce," he said, and we shook hands.

All of the personal areas in our tent were the same size, about six feet wide and eight feet long. The walkway down the middle of the tent was three feet wide. Some guys had built crude shelves to hold books, pictures, and some clothing. These also doubled as partitions separating their area from the one next to it, making things a bit more private. The floor of the tent was rough, unpainted wood. A single fluorescent light hung from the horizontal pole that ran lengthwise across the top of the tent. The only way in and out was through the flap at the front. The canvas sides could be rolled up to allow air to come through.

Each individual area had a wood-framed canvas cot. On top of the cot was a rubber inflatable air mattress. Above the cot was a metal frame which held up mosquito netting. At the back of each area was an all-purpose foot-locker. All of these items were supplied by the Army. I brought my light-weight flight jacket to Vietnam, and this, when rolled up, made an adequate pillow. (This jacket is the only souvenir I kept from the war). Everybody had a lawn chair which was privately owned. The next day I bought myself a lawn chair. It was the single improvement I made to my living conditions. There was no way I was going to build shelves or bookcases. This, to me, would have signified permanence. I wanted to maintain a sense of transience.

There were many tents like ours arranged haphazardly around the 227th area. Haphazard was not the Army way, but in this case it was necessary. Tents must be erected on flat ground. Our area had ravines with creeks running through them. Flat ground took precedence over uniformity. The pilots' tents were placed closest to the Golf Course. We could get from our cots to the helicopters and be in the air in about four minutes, if necessary.

One of the nicest features of our base camp—a true luxury, I would learn—was the officers' latrine. It was an all-wooden structure with screens framed into the walls, and it had a screen door. Only the roof was made of canvas. There were six holes cut into a large piece of plywood. The plywood had been sanded to a smooth finish and sat up high on a platform so that your feet rested on a step as though you were on a throne. On the opposite wall was a urinal made of a long drainpipe cut in half and hung on an angle so urine ran off rapidly. What more could you ask for?

You could ask for some sort of partitioning between the holes to give some privacy. That would have been a nice touch. However, we'd all been through basic training where toilets in the barracks were lined up without partitions, so we had experience sitting down with bare knees rubbing against the bare knees of the guy next to us. On the plus side, the lack of partitions did encourage conversation. At An Khe we also had a shower. It was a 55-gallon drum set on top of a wooden frame. Take your shower in late afternoon or evening—the water would be warm. In the morning the enlisted men refilled it for us. We officers had it knocked.

So all things considered, life at the base camp was fairly civilized and pleasant. Other than the frequent mortar attacks and the danger of our missions, we couldn't complain. We had the O'Club tent, the mess hall tent,

Vietnamese barbers would come "out of nowhere" and set up shop.

the chapel tent, the first rate latrine, the adequate shower, our own private area with cot and lawn chair, and even a front porch. These amenities made for very tolerable living conditions. The only really bad thing about An Khe was the rats. The rats get a chapter of their own.

Close to the opening of our tent was the above-ground bunker constructed of sandbags. It was three bags wide on all four sides and two bags high on the roof held up by PSP panels. The opening was narrow, so once inside you were 99 percent safe during a mortar attack.

In the 229th Battalion area (the 229th was our sister battalion) was the PX (Post Exchange). The PX was the place to get your lawn chair. Here we could also buy toiletries, snacks, pop, beer, liquor, socks, underwear, and other assorted items. Underwear didn't sell well, however; nobody in Vietnam wore it. Underwear promoted crotch rot in that humid country.

Our personal laundry—shirts, pants, t-shirts, and socks—was picked up and delivered to our tents. It was a service provided by the local Vietnamese women, who were called "mama-sans." Middle aged women, and

For a few extra piasters the mama-sans would also do boots.

older, were mama-sans. They would come and go silently on their rubber "flip-flops" which did not flip-flop when they walked. Unlike Westerners they walked with a shuffle, not a stride. Every one of them chewed betel nuts, which turned their teeth brown and stained the side of their chins. We were warned not to discuss anything about our missions or other duties when the mama-sans were around. There was no way of knowing if they understood English, nor was there any way of knowing if they were VC or VC sympathizers. We paid the mama-sans with piastres, the Vietnamese currency. The laundry service was dirt-cheap.

CHAPTER 10

Missions

THE MORNING AFTER MY ARRIVAL I officially reported in to battalion head-quarters. After completing the paperwork I was told by a sergeant to wait until the C.O. (commanding officer) had time to meet with me. He said "the Old Man" was currently tied up in a meeting with his company commanders. They were debriefing the crews of the most recent missions. The 227th Assault Helicopter Battalion was comprised of four companies. Three of them, Alpha, Bravo and Charlie, flew Huey slicks. Delta Company flew the Huey gunships.

Eventually the meeting ended and Lieutenant Colonel Thomas Franklin* had time to meet with his newest pilot. He was a friendly man and made me feel welcome. Although he was a career officer, his mannerisms and affect were casual. He told me to take a seat and offered to get me a cup of coffee. I declined the offer but remembered it. Lieutenant colonel battalion commanders didn't usually fix coffee for junior officers. Most of the career officers I had dealt with in the past seemed to me to be fairly tight, overly serious, with an underdeveloped sense of humor. Franklin reminded me of a college sociology teacher. He was somewhat disheveled, somewhat pre-occupied and did not appear to take himself too seriously.

Colonel Franklin explained to me that in the 227th we cared about one thing and one thing only: getting the job done. He said there were no formations, no PT (physical training), and no saluting each other in the battalion area. He said he'd get tennis elbow walking to the shit house and back if he had to return the salute of everybody he passed. He said there were no inspections, and he didn't care if our boots were clean or dirty, and that went for our belt buckles and personal areas, too. "That stuff's for back in the States. This is a war zone," he said. He told me that I was being assigned

68

to Bravo Company, so I had two things to think about: keep myself and my crew alive, and keep those soldiers I'd be carrying alive, as best I could. I liked Colonel Franklin.

He picked up my file from his desktop and rapidly flipped through the pages. He noticed that I had gone to fixed wing school and then made a transition to helicopters. He asked if I felt comfortable flying the Huey. I was surprised by the question, and I felt a sense of relief but also concern. Although tempted to lie, I thought better of it, and I think he noticed this. "No, Sir, I don't," I said hoping this honest answer would not get me reassigned to a fixed wing unit. Even though Bob Daniels' death was a mind numbing reality, I did not want to change my plan to see the war, up close, in a helicopter.

Although I had graduated near the top of my class in transition school in the H-13, there was a big difference between that little aircraft and a Huey, that difference being power. The H-13 has a small reciprocating engine, requiring constant throttle adjustments, and it carries only two people—a pilot and his passenger. The Huey has a jet engine and carries twelve or more people. It is also, of course, a much larger aircraft. Technically it is easier to fly a Huey, because throttle adjustments are not required no matter what contortions you put the aircraft through, but I was not comfortable with this extra power and size. I didn't have enough experience with it.

Colonel Franklin listened patiently as I explained to him what happened with our class during the Huey transition school. This school was supposed to provide 30 hours of flight time in a Huey, mostly with an IP. But during our class at Fort Benning the Army decided to demonstrate to President Johnson how Hueys were being used in combat assault missions in Vietnam, taking soldiers in and out of battle. Our class was chosen to fly from Fort Benning, Georgia, to Fort Campbell, Kentucky, where the demonstration was scheduled for the president. Much of our allotted 30 hours of instruction was spent flying cross-country with our IPs, from Benning to Campbell and back. There is practically nothing to be learned flying cross-country in a helicopter or an airplane. Take-offs and landings is what learning to fly is all about.

We students were not allowed to fly the actual demonstration, either. Because it had to be perfect, to impress the president, the IPs did all that flying. So, no, I was not comfortable in the Huey because I did not know its capabilities in various landing and take-off conditions, and this could be critical.

Colonel Franklin was now looking at me with a pained expression. "Damn," I thought, "I've just talked myself out of Hueys and back into Birddogs." But when I finished he asked if I had been in the same Huey transition school as Captain Bob Daniels. I told him I had.

More to himself than to me he said, "I wish I'd known about that Fort Campbell business before I made him an A/C. Goddamn it." He then looked past me, at nothing, his jaws tightening. It took him some moments to come back. He said my inexperience would not be a problem. I would fly as a co-pilot for a while to get some more time. And when I was ready I would move to the left seat. (The A/C is the aircraft commander who sits in the left seat on all aircraft. The co-pilot sits in the right seat.)

I thanked the colonel and said I appreciated getting the extra time. He stood up and reached across the desk to shake my hand. "OK, Joyce, you're excused. Welcome to the 227th," he said, but he was gone again, obviously needing to be alone. I quickly walked out of his office. Had I just told Colonel Franklin why Bob Daniels flew a fully loaded Huey into the side of a mountain, killing himself and eleven other men? Probably.

My first mission was that night. One of our infantry squads patrolling beyond the First Cav's perimeter had detected a VC unit coming up the An Khe Valley. About 30 men carrying automatic weapons and mortar tubes had been spotted. It was 9:30 when we were "scrambled"—get to the helicopters and crank them up. Ten slicks and two gunships were assigned to this mission. Each slick carried eight soldiers.

I was in the right seat of the lead slick. In the left seat was Captain James Gardner*, who had overall command of the slick helicopters. It was his job that I was being trained for—aircraft commander and team leader. A team of helicopters could be as few as two or as many as 20. More than 20 was unofficially called a "gaggle." I had only met Captain Gardner briefly earlier in the day. I now noticed he was chain-smoking Camels.

We took off into the night, Gardner barking orders over the radio to the nine ships behind us. We were flying in "trail" formation—one helicopter after another. The two gunships were on our flanks. After no more than five minutes of flying, the captain told everyone over the radio, "LZ in two"—the landing zone was two minutes ahead. We began to descend. I had no idea what was going on. There were no lights to guide us; we were getting lower and lower and I could not see the ground.

Gardner lit another cigarette as the gunships opened fire. Their rockets began exploding on the ground about three hundred yards in front of us. Then I saw the tracer bullets from their machine guns splattering in the same place. Within seconds we were at the LZ. The rockets and machine guns from the gunships now raked the area on either side of it. Gardner flipped on the landing light, our door gunners started shooting their machine guns, and Gardner took the helicopter all the way to the ground,

Mini-gun and rocket pods on a Huey gunship.

not bothering with a hover. The troops jumped out, the landing light was extinguished, and off we flew back into the black sky. The choppers behind us did the same thing and reported to the captain, "Two off," "three off," "four off," and so on.

We flew back to the Golf Course, landed, and Gardner told me to shut down the engine. "Did you get all that, Joyce?" he asked, lighting Camel number four. I told him that I didn't and that I would never be able to do what he just did. He laughed and said it just took practice and I'd be doing it soon.

I asked the captain how he knew where to land. He answered that before we took off he'd looked at a map; he had the coordinates of the LZ.

"But it was dark. What good are coordinates if you can't see the ground?" I asked.

He said he didn't know exactly where to land but he knew the general area. Then when he saw where the gunships put their ordnance he had the exact location.

"OK, how did the gunships know where to shoot?"

"Our guys on the ground told them."

"What guys on the ground?" I was baffled. He explained it was the infantry unit that called in the attack. They were on the hill to the right of the LZ. They were talking to the gunship fire team leader—vectoring him in. I said I had a hell of a lot to learn, but he told me not to sweat it. After I'd done it a few times it would get easy. Cigarette number five was lit.

We hung around the helicopter for an hour or so, the captain occasionally giving me advice: On a CA (combat assault) during daylight you don't have to land to let the troops off. A low hover is OK and let them jump. They're more anxious to get off the helicopter than we are to have them off. But at night he always took it to the ground so the soldiers wouldn't twist an ankle jumping off. When they got on the ground they had to move fast, because the choppers showed Charlie exactly where they were. They didn't need a twisted ankle. "Those guys are fighting this war. We're just their drivers," he said. He advised that if I was not comfortable with my approach to an LZ, I should slow it down and get comfortable. He said crashes kill more people than bullets.

He explained that the door gunners saw more than the pilots. They had a wider field of vision and they weren't busy on the controls. He said to give them their heads as to whether to fire their weapons or not. He also said I should teach my door gunners to land the helicopter because if my co-pilot and I were shot and couldn't fly, this might save our lives. For sure it would save theirs.

I listened carefully to all Captain Gardner told me. It was good advice and I enjoyed the easy way he dispensed it. We then got word it was time to go back and pick up the troops, so we climbed into the helicopter. When the main rotor was up to full rpm we were ready to take off, and Gardner told me to take the controls. I brought it up to a hover and then pushed the nose forward, and back into the night we went. I knew he wanted to see if I could find the location of the LZ myself. I couldn't, but I got closer to it than I expected. A flare went up about a quarter mile ahead of us, but off to the left of our course. He told me to fly to the flare and said he'd stay on the controls with me for the landing.

So I, and Captain Gardner, flew into the LZ and landed, and eight soldiers scrambled aboard. On the flight back to base we learned that ten enemy had been killed—eight of them by the initial gunship attacks. Three mortar tubes had been taken along with various other weapons. The rest of the Viet Cong had been routed but would, of course, be back.

I found the Golf Course (a no brainer with all the lights coming from the Cav compound), hovered over to our parking spot, and gently put the aircraft on its skids. "You'll be fine, Joyce," Gardner said, lighting the first Camel from pack number two as the rotor blades came to a stop. He said that all I needed was time to get used to all this and suggested we go to the O'Club and get a beer.

"Aren't we still on call until morning?" I asked.

"Yeah, so?" he said. "They've got a radio in the club." He then smiled and said we were only going to have a beer or two, not going to get drunk.

Over the next few days I flew perhaps five missions, none of them classified as combat assault. They were routine resupply missions taking hot food, mail, ammunition, and personnel to various infantry units within a 20-mile radius of An Khe. I was in the right seat, flying with experienced guys, and most of the time I had the controls. Each day I gained more confidence, but I was still not comfortable with what a Huey could do under certain conditions.

One morning, just after daybreak, our chopper and another—our "wing man" (choppers never flew alone in the Cav)—were loaded up with food prepared in the mess tent and put into metal marmite cans to keep it hot. We also had some mail and, in our ship, a courier and ammunition. We were to resupply an infantry platoon about 15 miles from camp. The mission was expected to be routine and safe, no enemy activity reported along the route. We found the infantry with no problem and landed. The courier jumped out and the ground troops came up to unload the food, ammunition, and mail. We weren't on the ground two minutes and then took off to return to base. I had the controls.

In front of us and slightly to the right was a lone palm tree. To our left was a grove of palm trees where the infantry was bivouacked. As I hovered forward to gain air speed I decided to stay as far away from the troops as possible because the down wash from our rotor blades would wreak havoc with their tents and other gear. In this attempt to be nice, however, I miscalculated how close we were to the single palm, and one of our main rotor blades clipped the trunk of the tree. The Huey helicopter instantly went berserk.

"I've got it!" screamed the A/C as he jumped on the controls, desperately trying to get the helicopter under control. But he didn't have it because it couldn't be had. When the main rotor blade struck the tree, all of the control linkages in the ship were broken. Because we were gaining speed and climbing when we hit the tree, the rotor blades were deeply pitched in order to take us up. But the last thing we wanted now was to go up. To continue to do so would mean that at some height above the ground the rotors would slow down and the helicopter would drop like a rock. The A/C screamed again, "Joyce, get on the collective with me! Help me push it down!" I did this, but it wouldn't budge, and we were now careening toward the palm grove on our left where the troops were.

Fortunately, the left skid came up under heavy palm leaves on the top of the trees. I remember that this pitched our nose downward and away from the troops. Now we were heading for the ground, but the aircraft started rolling to the left. We would have gone upside down, but we slammed into a rice paddy before this happened. We were now on the ground, on our side, and all forward motion had stopped. But...

The rotors were still turning, and one broke free and was about to come through the windshield cutting us in half. But it hit the dike that formed the rice paddy and bounced over the top of us. Now all motion ceased, helicopter-wise, and it was time to get the hell out of there before the thing blew up. We had a full tank of gas.

In Vietnam the Huey's doors to the cockpit had been modified to give the pilots extra protection against small arms fire. An armored panel had been installed which slid back and forth next to the pilots, protecting their sides. It was difficult for the pilots, while sitting in their seats, to slide these panels, so normal procedure was for the door gunners to do this for them. Just before take-off they would slide the panels forward. When we landed they'd come up to the doors and slide them back. The pilots also wore an armor-plated vest and a flak jacket and it was impossible for them, with all that bulk, to get themselves between the panel and the small opening behind the doorframe.

Well, actually, not impossible. In the case of this "landing" both the A/C and I squeezed through this tiny opening in approximately 1/10th of a second. The only injury suffered in the crash was to the left side door gunner, who broke his thumb. In this we were extremely fortunate, but a $279,000 Huey D model helicopter (1966 prices) was completely destroyed ... and it was my fault.

That would be the end of the story about the time I crashed a helicopter in Vietnam, except for one thing: The hover, the take-off, the striking of the palm tree, and the crash that followed were all on film.

The infantry platoon we resupplied was commanded by Lieutenant Joseph Anderson, who was one of the few African American graduates from West Point up to that time. A French filmmaker, Pierre Schoendorffer, had gotten the idea, and permission from the Army, to join Anderson and his platoon and document their day-to-day activities. This turned out to be Pierre's lucky day. When we took off he decided to roll his camera to show how the U.S. soldiers, in the middle of nowhere, had gotten their mail and a warm meal, cooked for them at the base camp's mess tent. This documentary became famous and eventually won Hollywood's Academy Award (1968) in the category of Best Documentary. It was called *The Anderson Platoon*. My crash, naturally, was the highlight of the film.

I have seen *The Anderson Platoon* (it is still available for rent at video stores), and the crash is pretty much as I remember it, with some exceptions.

Let's go to the Golf Course and see what the new guy, Joyce, did to a Huey "D" model.

The film shows it took only about four seconds from the time we hit the tree until we crashed in the rice paddy. I thought we'd futilely fought that whirling dervish of a broken aircraft for at least ten seconds. The film also revealed that we did not roll on our side but slid up against a dike on the A/C's side. That's why we both had to exit through the door on the right. The rotor blades did not leave the ship; they just kept bouncing off the dike. There were no leaves hit to point us toward the ground. (I have no idea why I remember that there were.) We also bounced once before settling in. I don't remember that, either. What I know for sure, after watching the film, is that there are four guys who are very fortunate.

One of the sights I was spared at the time, but saw dramatically highlighted in the film, was the carrying away of the remains of the busted up Huey. A Chinook helicopter was dispatched to the crash site. The different pieces of the Huey were strapped together, and a sling came down from the belly of the huge aircraft. It picked up the hunk of junk and slowly flew away. This was sickening for me to watch.

Our crew flew back to base in our wingman's helicopter. It took no time at all for the word to go through Bravo Company that the new guy, Joyce, had flown into a solitary palm tree, totaling a "D" model. I had to face much teasing by the other pilots in the unit, and their teasing was tinged with knowing smirks as they asked me to tell them, again, exactly how I had done it. The guys in my tent were especially curious. Wink, wink.

Of the eight of us in the tent I was the only one who had gone to fixed wing flight school. The rest were graduates of the helicopter flight program. As it was unheard of to make a transition from helicopter to fixed wing, they were stuck as chopper pilots only. So those of us fortunate to have both ratings were envied, and the envy was justifiable. Most pilots who did not plan to make a career of the Army wanted to fly with the airlines. It was well known that the airlines did not put as much value on helicopter time as fixed wing time. Wrong thinking by the airlines, but that's the way it was.

The knowing smirks of my fellow pilots were understandable. Even if I hadn't had the excuse of the lost instruction time flying to Fort Campbell, we transition pilots were not as good as those who'd spent nine solid months in choppers. How could we be? Just look at what Lieutenant Joyce did. He flew an empty Huey into a lone palm tree. "How the hell did you do that?" They couldn't help asking. I was mortified.

Unfortunately for the A/C who crashed with me, the accident initially went on his record, too. He was in charge; he allowed me to screw up. I felt terrible for him. But Lieutenant Anderson came to our rescue. An inquiry was held to determine exactly what happened. In other words, who was going to pay for this Huey? But the lieutenant testified that shortly after we began hovering forward, a gust of wind came up and pushed us into the palm tree. I, of course, had felt no gust of wind, but what the hell did I know? And this did explain how the A/C could let me fly into a tree. So we owe one to Anderson. His explanation of the crash got us officially exonerated. Unofficially, in our own minds, we'd always know we screwed up, big time.

The day after the crash Captain Silberberger, the one who knocked me down the night of the mortar attack, came to me and said the Old Man wanted him to take a couple of days to "fly around with Joyce." Silberberger told me to meet him at the Golf Course at 0900 and gave me the tail number of the ship we'd be flying. After pre-flighting, the captain told me to take the left seat. He said that Franklin told him to spend as much time with me as needed to see if he thought I'd ever qualify to be an A/C. If he didn't think I'd make the grade, Franklin was going to transfer me to a fixed wing assignment. Silberberger had been an IP in Hueys before coming to Vietnam and told me he was a pretty good judge of a pilot's ability. He said it was up to me, and added that he wasn't supposed to tell me this, but the Old Man also wanted him to determine if I flew into that tree on purpose.

Since the crash the day before I felt that my confidence as a helicopter pilot could not get any lower. I really thought that I had been progressing and recalled the total shock I felt as the helicopter went nuts after we "nicked" the tree. During the wild ride to the ground I had actually had the thought, "How could this thing be doing this to me?" It was like having a pleasant conversation with a new friend when, without warning, he punches you in the nose. Then Silberberger saying Franklin thought I did it on purpose took the last of my self-esteem and laid it flat.

But in a few seconds I recovered enough to get pissed off. "Captain, I may not be able to fly a Huey worth a shit, but I'm not a suicide. Does the Old Man think I tried to kill myself and three other guys?"

He replied that he didn't know what the colonel thought. He told me to crank up the helicopter and he and I would work together. He told me to take the controls and fly up to the top of Hong Kong Mountain. He said it was over to our right with the First Cav patch painted on top. "I know where Hong Kong Mountain is, goddamn it," I said, under my breath but loud enough for him to hear. He let it pass.

One of the major differences between flying airplanes and helicopters is a phenomenon called "ground effect," which only applies to helicopters. When a helicopter is hovering a few feet above the ground it is, in a sense, sitting on a cushion of air created by the down draft from the main rotors. The air coming down (under a Huey, it is 100 mph) hits the ground and bounces back up and to the sides. This creates the ground effect "cushion." Ground effect can be lost by hovering too high, in which case the air loses its compaction, or by hovering too fast in any direction, which causes the helicopter to "slide off of" the cushion.

The take-off procedure we learned in the little H-13 was to come up to a three-foot hover, establish ground effect and then slowly start forward and increase speed until the helicopter slid off of ground effect but now moving fast enough to fly. The rotors above the aircraft create a "wing" that functions like the wings on an airplane. It was now forward motion (air speed) which kept the aircraft in the air. When the helicopter left ground effect and began to fly, utilizing air speed, this was known as "transition." So I slowly raised the collective, bringing the Huey up to a solid three-foot hover, then slowly started forward. As we slid off of ground effect the helicopter dropped a few inches, reached transition speed and began to fly.

The mountain's sides were steep, so I flew around it as we climbed. I made sure I maintained plenty of air speed, as there would be no ground effect available on the mountain's side. I circled the mountain four times before reaching the top and flying over the First Cav patch. Silberberger had said nothing from the time I took off. As I circled the patch for the second time I asked him what he wanted me to do next. He told me to go back and land at our space on the Golf Course.

A mountain top LZ has just been "prepped." Now it's our turn to participate in the battle by taking in the troops.

I called the tower, told them I was over Hong Kong Mountain, and requested landing instructions. The controller simply told me I was clear to land. So I entered the downwind leg on a 45° angle, then made a 90° turn onto base and another 90° turn on to final. A textbook approach. I came to a hover directly over our space and slowly and gently put the helicopter on its skids. Perfect.

I looked over at the captain, knowing he would tell me that was a good approach and landing. He didn't. He said I'd been cleared to land and didn't need to go into a pattern. I should have flown directly to our space. "Oh," I said.

He then asked what I'd have done differently if he had told me to get up to the top of the mountain as fast as possible. What if there were troops up there in deep shit and needed to get off? I told him I would have flown faster circles around the mountain. He asked why I wouldn't just fly straight up to the top. I told him that would be like a very high hover and we wouldn't have any ground effect. Silberberger looked at me and shook his head. He said I was flying an empty Huey with only us and two door gunners aboard. We were as light as we could be, just like yesterday when the ammo boxes and marmite cans were unloaded. "I've got it," he said, "and I think I just figured out your problem."

He took the controls and the helicopter shot into the air like a rocket. In less than 15 seconds we were looking down at the horse's head, the black line and the yellow background of the First Cav patch. My chin was on my chest protector.

"Now you take it, Jim, and slowly hover around the sides of the mountain. There will be no ground effect. You don't need it."

For the rest of that day and the next, Captain Silberberger and I spent 15 hours of flight time together. He had me doing things with the Huey that I had no idea I, or the Huey, could do. He kept adding weight, by using full ammo boxes, until we could barely get the aircraft to a hover. In those two days of intensive instruction Captain Paul Silberberger made me a Huey pilot. I will forever be appreciative of his patience, his skill as an IP and his calm demeanor. I remain in awe of his superb flying and teaching skills.

I am pleased to report that Paul made it to his DEROS and left Vietnam a relieved, happy man. A career officer, his next assignment was Germany, where he would be shuttling VIPs around Europe. His wife and child would be joining him. It was a plush assignment, and after a year flying combat assaults in Vietnam he deserved this. I was very happy for him.

I am saddened to report that after his one-year tour in Germany, Paul Silberberger was reassigned to Vietnam, and was killed in a Huey the third month of his return.

CHAPTER 11

Settling Into the Cav

CAPTAIN SILBERBERGER "SIGNED OFF" on me and convinced Lieutenant Colonel Franklin that I was not inept as a helicopter pilot—merely under-trained in the capabilities of the Huey. He assured the colonel that he had corrected my lack of training. Captain Silberberger also assured Colonel Franklin that I would make a good A/C and that I was not suicidal. I flew another half dozen or so missions, but now from the left seat, being "checked out" as an A/C by more experienced co-pilots. Two of these missions were combat assaults into hot (under enemy fire) LZs.

I must have done fine, because one week after my crash Colonel Franklin called me into his office and told me I was now a team leader. A team leader is an A/C who is in charge of the helicopter he is flying and at least one more. And the teasing had stopped. Shortly after my crash the Cav had had two more. One was pilot error when a captain with eight months in country caught the tip of a skid under a tree branch coming out of an LZ at night. The helicopter crashed, seriously injuring three soldiers. This was the captain's fourth crash. Kirk* was his name—Crash Kirk behind his back. The second crash killed pilot and co-pilot but everybody else survived. This one was weather related. Captain Clark had been correct when he said weather, especially in the mountains, killed more pilots than the Viet Cong.

The First Cav loved a fight. It was always looking for one, and fights were easy to find in Vietnam because the Viet Cong were everywhere. The Cav, with four brigades, 16 battalions, and 64 infantry companies, usually had something going on, but if things got too slow for them they would rely on those little H-13 helicopters to get things heated back up.

In the Cav the H-13s took on the role of reconnaissance. A pair of

80

A typical Vietnamese farm-house (hooch).

them—they never flew alone—would be dispatched to an area where enemy activity was suspected. They would fly along at tree top level, or just above the ground, hoping someone would take a shot at them. I say "fly along," but it was more like buzzing than flying. They would swoop, spin, and go sideways and backwards working a tree line, a valley, or a row of dikes or ditches. They'd hover up next to a hooch (farmhouse) and peek in the windows or the door. They'd fly down the streets of little hamlets just a few feet off the ground—stop, start, pop over the buildings to the next street. They truly did act more like bees than aircraft.

The H-13s had a pilot flying left seat and a door gunner in the right seat. Between the two of them the helicopter was full. The two little choppers in the team would take turns covering each other, as best they could, while trying to draw enemy fire. Darting here and there across the countryside, their mission was to surprise the enemy by all of a sudden "appearing." Then the VC would shoot at them out of surprise and fear.

When they did draw fire they would return it—the door gunners blaz-

ing away with their handheld automatic rifles and the pilots shooting shot-
guns, M-16s, pistols, or whatever they had. Flying an H-13 demanded more
attention from the pilot than flying a Huey because of the constant throttle adjustments. But these pilots were able to fly the helicopter, shoot their
weapons, talk to each other on their radios, talk to the command post, and
be super-vigilant to any activity on the ground—all at the same time and
often while being shot at. They were, in my opinion and anyone else's who
saw them in action, the most proficient aviators in the war.

If the enemy who shot at them was a few isolated VC, the H-13s would
engage them without help from anyone else. If they encountered a unit of
any size they would detach themselves to a safe distance and radio the enemy
coordinates to base. Huey gunships would then be dispatched and be vec-
tored to the target by the H-13s. When the gunships got their bearings the
H-13s would go home, their mission accomplished. If the gunships determined the enemy was sizeable, more than they could handle alone, then
slicks would be called in carrying troops to be deposited on the ground.
The Cav had a fight.

Sometimes the H-13s got real lucky and buzzed up on a serious-sized
VC or NVA unit. When this happened we were in for a spectacular show.
First to be called would be Air Force B-52s. They flew so high (50,000 feet)
they could barely be seen from the ground, but their bombs were spookily
accurate. Bombs of 500 pounds, 1000 pounds and even more would be
dropped on the enemy's location to soften it up. If the area was jungle covered with three different tree canopies, even more bombs would be dropped,
in effect creating an LZ. I couldn't believe my eyes the first time I saw that
these bombs actually made the air "move." Of course there were explosions
and fire, with dust, dirt, smoke and debris flying through the air, but that's
not what I mean. I mean the air itself moved and you could see it—wave
after wave of clear air concussions. It was at once thrilling and daunting to
see this show of raw power and destructive force.

When the B-52s were done, either Air Force or Navy fighter planes
showed up. They'd start diving toward the area from about 2,000 feet, flying
at 500 mph. They had more bombs to drop and also covered the area with
rockets, napalm and twenty-millimeter canon fire. They worked in pairs,
and their accuracy was equally effective. When the fighters left, Huey gun
ships attacked the area with rockets, grenades and machine guns. After
watching this demonstration of incredible destruction it was impossible to
believe that enemy soldiers could still be alive in the target area. But there
always were, lots of them, waiting for the slicks to come in with their cargo
of soldiers.

During the aerial attacks we slicks would be circling nearby until we

First Cav Hueys in formation over the Central Highlands.

got word to go in. There might be 20 of us or 100, depending. When the word came, we would fly in a formation suitable to get as many helicopters as possible into the LZ at the same time. Sometimes 20 or more choppers could fit into an LZ. Sometimes we had to go in one at a time. The LZ size and enemy activity determined this.

As we got near an LZ, our door gunners would begin firing their mounted M-60 machine guns, and on our flanks would be the gunships. It was incredibly noisy, exciting and often terrifying, especially if we began hearing that ships in front of us were being hit and shot down. Every combat assault mission was given a "pucker factor" grade. The pucker factor referred to how tight the pilots' sphincter muscles became during the mission. Ten was the highest.

Just as Captain Gardner had said, slicks did not land (touch their skids to the ground) when they got to the LZ, except at night. A low hover was all that was required for the troops to jump off the ships. They were indeed as anxious to get on the ground as we were to have them leave us. A Huey

When the infantry exited the slicks, they hit the ground running.

helicopter on approach, at hover and on climb out was a very vulnerable and easy target. So, too, were the soldiers riding in back. Sometimes I envied the Viet Cong. We were hard to miss.

Fortunately a Huey could be shot in almost any place without its ability to fly being affected. Main rotor blades could look like Swiss cheese—as could the fuselage, doors, windows, and even windshields—and it would still fly. But it could not continue to function if hit in the engine, the control cables, the tail rotor gearbox, or the hydraulic system. Then it must be landed immediately, if possible.

On one of my first daytime combat assaults we had been briefed, as had our soldier passengers, that we should expect to find the LZ "hot." A combined force of American and South Vietnamese Army troops were engaged in fierce fighting with an NVA unit. Our side was outnumbered and losing the battle. They had taken heavy casualties. Our mission was to reinforce the friendly troops. Fifty Huey slicks were involved in the mission along with five gunship teams. My helicopter was about twenty back from the lead ship.

The LZ could accommodate ten ships at a time. However, in the first wave two helicopters were disabled by enemy fire and had to be abandoned in the LZ. Now it could take only eight at a time. We heard all of this on our radios and rearranged our in-flight formation. We also heard yelling, swearing, and orders being barked by the commander on the ground—and lots of gunfire. We were going to fly into a real mess.

When we were a few minutes from the LZ, I turned around in my seat to look at the faces of the American soldiers about to go into battle. I did this as part of my plan, hatched months ago, to see the war up close from a helicopter. Although I guess I knew better, what I expected to see were grim, masculine faces with determined, steely eyes and firmly set jaws. The image of GI Joe. But that was not what I saw. I saw pimples and peach fuzz and eyes full of fear. Some of the soldiers were big guys and some were slight, but they all had one thing in common—they were young, really young. I'll never forget that image. The typical American infantryman was a kid.

When it was our turn to land, these kids didn't even wait for us to come to a hover. As soon as we were low enough to the ground, yet still moving forward, they jumped off of the ship, hit the ground, and opened fire with their weapons as they raced to the nearest cover. Within seconds we were out of there climbing up to safety. The kids remained on the ground to fight and, often, to die.

One of my favorite diversions from the war was to go to the battalion officer's club at night and play craps. I'd never played craps before getting to Vietnam, but I learned the game and became quite good at it. So good that I rarely lost at craps, the main exception being when an older pilot, Joe Ryan*, would come over and stand next to me while I was rolling the dice. It had to be coincidence, but it really did seem like whenever Ryan was near me I'd crap out. Eventually it got to where I would ask him to please go stand back at the bar while the dice were mine. And I'd given him the nickname Joe Btfsplk, after the diminutive Li'l Abner comic strip character who walked around with a rain cloud over his head. He was known as the world's worst jinx. Joe Ryan, too, was short and slight of stature, and he was my jinx.

It became a standard joke at the club, and whenever I got really hot the other guys would call Joe over and buy him a drink while he stood next to me. Sure enough, I would crap out. I am not superstitious, and I loved the ongoing teasing and camaraderie, even though it did seem like Joe was costing me money. Then it got to the point where Ryan would bribe me. "Give me $5, Joyce, and I'll go back to the bar." Good fun.

Joe Ryan was a Chinook pilot. The Chinook, nicknamed "Shithook" by us Huey pilots, is the very large brown boxcar-like aircraft with two main rotor heads placed atop either end of it. It's a powerful helicopter designed to carry many troops or heavy equipment. It was also used to sling-carry the huge rubber bladders of fuel and potable water out to the field and, as you know, to sling-load crashed Hueys.

Joe was a warrant officer. Warrant officers are highly trained specialists in one specific field. They are not commissioned officers (second lieutenants),

An ACH-47 Chinook outfitted as a gunship. They were nicknamed "Guns-a-Go-Go." The Army has had better ideas.

nor are they non-commissioned officers (sergeants). They are in between these ranks but enjoy commissioned status in that they have officer's club privileges and are saluted when met by non-commissioned officers. They, in turn, must salute commissioned officers, second lieutenants and up. Warrants have five grades of rank, chief warrant officer V being the highest.

The overwhelming majority of helicopter pilots in Vietnam were warrant officers—flying helicopters being their unique specialty. In theory they were to be pilots only, with no command responsibility—in other words, not team leaders. Practically speaking, this was not how it was, because there were not enough commissioned officers to fill these slots, and warrant officers were often more capable and experienced in leadership, while in the air, than were the commissioned officers. Personally, if I were going to fly into difficult conditions, I would most likely choose a warrant officer to fly with me. The warrants were almost always better pilots than us commissioned types.

During this time the Cav received four Chinooks that had been retro-fitted to be gunships. These were experimental aircraft, with .50 caliber machine guns mounted in the doors and out the back. These were fired by door gunners. Two 20mm cannons and rocket pods were mounted on each side of the aircraft and a grenade launcher was attached to the nose. These weapons were fired by the pilots.

One night Joe Ryan was flying one of these new, improvised gunships. He was in the middle of an attack shooting the cannons when there was a failure in one of the stops that limited the travel of the barrel. Joe had no way of knowing this and continued shooting. The barrel soon pointed straight up, cutting the rotor blades in half on the front end of the ship. Joe Ryan, my chief warrant officer buddy from the O'Club, his fellow pilot, and six door gunners perished.

CHAPTER 12

A KKK Officer

AT THE AN KHE BASE WE HAD a chapel tent, and on Sunday mornings we Catholics would attend mass. The chaplain was a young captain and a nice guy. The penances he would mete out after confession were extraordinarily lenient, no matter, it seemed, the grievousness of the sins. (We penitents sometimes compared notes.) Standard penance was only one "Our Father" and three "Hail Marys" along with a promise not to do it again. This must have been a Vietnam perk. If you walked slowly you could knock off the prayers before reaching the back of the tent. The "not do it again" part could, of course, take a lifetime.

One Sunday morning the chaplain was about to begin the offertory of the mass when a spec 4 (like a corporal) came running into the tent. "Sorry, Father, but we're about to be attacked! All pilots to the flight line!" As we bolted from the church he called out, "Come back after the mission. I'll save communion for you!"

We ran to the Golf Course, cranked up the Hueys, and took off—the soldiers were already on board when we got to the helicopters. En route to the LZ, which was only a three-minute flight, we could see the gunships working the area—two teams, four ships. The gun leader was very excited. "We got about 20 of them mother fuckers! They were setting up mortars!" he radioed to us slicks. He then told us there were many more of them down there and they had at least one "50." The gun leader advised us to go in and out of the LZ "hot" (fast). He further advised that the "50" would be on our left and he'd cover us. A "50" is a .50 caliber machine gun, an extremely deadly weapon.

So we flew in and out hot, leaving our troops behind, and returned to the Golf Course. It was procedure to wait at the helicopters until we got word to either go back to the LZ and pick up the troops or return to our living area, because the troops would not be ready to come back for a while. That was the case on this Sunday morning, and we were released.

We Catholics returned to the chapel to receive our communion. The mass was now over, but true to his word, the priest was waiting for us with his chalice of unleavened wafers. We lined up and took our turn standing in front of him as he placed a host on our tongues with the ancient Latin words "Corpus Christi"—the body of Christ.

I found a corner of the tent and knelt down to begin saying my standard prayers, the "thank yous" and the "pleases," when an unwelcomed and irreverent thought crossed my mind: "I wonder how many of those mother fuckers we just killed were Roman Catholics?" There were many Vietnamese Catholics because of the years of French influence. It's unbelievable what you'll think about sometimes when you're supposed to be praying.

One Sunday after mass I returned to our tent and one of the other pilots, First Lieutenant David Durbin*, came into my area. Dave was from Alabama and had graduated from a small state college with a degree in engineering. I liked him. He was soft-spoken, obviously bright, and friendly, and he had an easy smile. He had been very helpful and encouraging to me when I was the newest guy in the company. He was also one of the few who had not teased me about my accident. He said he wanted to ask me a couple of questions but they were kind of personal and would that be OK. "Sure," I said. "What do you want to know?"

He looked around the tent to be certain no one else was there and then asked if we could take lawn chairs and go outside. He said he didn't want anybody to hear us. "No problem," I said, my curiosity growing, and suggested we sit under the palm tree. It was a huge, leafy palm about 100 feet from the tent, providing plenty of shade. When we got settled Dave started talking. He was nervous.

He told me that he liked me and didn't want to upset me but there was something he wanted to understand. He said he couldn't help but notice that I was a Catholic and that he'd never known a Catholic before. He'd seen a few of them in college but never talked to them. David told me he came from a rural area of Alabama—"Some people would call it backwoods"—and there were no Catholics there. But he'd been taught about Catholics by his preacher, who told him that Catholics weren't really Americans because we had sworn allegiance to a foreign power, the Pope in Rome. The preacher had also told him that Catholics were evil and should never be trusted. David said he knew I was not evil and untrustworthy but he wanted me to tell him about the Pope.

My first impulse was to laugh, but Dave was being so sincere and concerned about my feelings that I repressed the urge. I told him that the Pope was the spiritual leader of Catholics, but he had nothing to do with our politics or citizenship. There were Catholics in almost every country in the world, I explained, and we sure didn't think alike about politics. I then told him my recent realization that I was probably involved in killing Catholics here in Vietnam. I reminded him that President Kennedy, who got us into this war, was a Catholic and not once did he consult with the Pope on any of his political decisions.

I explained to Dave that about 25 percent of all American citizens were Catholic—"That's one out of every four," I said, for emphasis—and that there were about one billion of us worldwide. He was obviously surprised. He asked me what Catholics believed in, and I told him we believed in Jesus Christ and his message. "You mean Catholics are Christians?" This really surprised him. There was a long pause; then Dave looked me in the eyes and said, "Jim, can I trust you to keep a secret?"

I told him he could.

"Back home I am a member of the Ku Klux Klan."

If he had told me he was a double agent for the Red Chinese I could not have been more surprised. He was staring at my face, waiting for my reaction. It came out of my mouth immediately. "No shit?" I said. Asking him to please not to take offense, I confessed that I thought all Klan members were uneducated morons. He was obviously a college graduate and not a moron. I asked him to tell me about the Klan. " Do you wear the white sheet and the hood with the holes in it?" I asked. He told me that he did wear the sheet on special occasions.

He then said that if the Army knew he was KKK he'd lose his commission and probably get a dishonorable discharge. I promised him I wouldn't tell anyone and asked him to tell me what it was like to be a Klan member. I was fascinated. He said he didn't know why he even told me but "I had to tell someone, you know what I mean?" He had lied on his ROTC application about not being a member of a subversive organization. Now he was stuck with the lie. I reassured him that his secret was safe with me and that I really did want to know about the Klan from somebody who really knew. "Please educate me."

Although no one was near us, he lowered his voice. He said the Klan believed the white race should remain pure. It didn't believe in socializing or intermarrying with "nigras" and other dark skinned people. (That was the first time I'd heard the word "nigra." I guessed it was intended to modify the word "nigger," thus softening the insult. Then again, maybe it intensified it. Hard to tell.)

Dave said the Klan thought Jews were out to destroy society economically, but he'd never met a Jew either. In his area back home all they had were the blacks, who outnumbered the whites three to one. He explained that the Klan's primary activities were in helping the police and sheriff's deputies in keeping law and order among both the white and black communities. He said there were nowhere near enough lawmen to cover the huge areas of rural Alabama, and the Klan filled this need. He went on to say that the Klan was as much a social organization as a political one, with wives and children involved in many functions. He said he had been a member all of his life, like his father and grandfather before him, and that the Klan did many good works for both blacks and whites by distributing food and clothing to the needy and by providing shelter when necessary. He would never mistreat a black person; he simply believed they belonged with their own kind.

"But what about the hangings?" I asked.

He answered by saying that was in the old days when a black killed a white man or raped a white woman, but even that wouldn't bring on a hanging today. He said the regular law would handle that. I reminded him that the previous year in Alabama the Klan had hung a black army lieutenant colonel just for being black. He said that wasn't Klan. That was dumb, hate-filled rednecks.

I looked skeptical, but Dave insisted he was telling the truth. The Klan was needed to keep peace where he lived. It protected all the people who lived there, including blacks. The black community welcomed its presence. He said he'd like me to visit his home after Vietnam so he could show me that what he said was true. And his sincerity was convincing. I began to think that his misguided beliefs about the Catholic Church might somehow be analogous to my beliefs about the Klan. I told him it was hard for me to believe him, but if he said it was true, then it was—at least where he lived. I reassured him his secret was safe with me. We did not speak of it again. We didn't have a chance.

The next day Dave was given a standard resupply mission flying food and ammo to a U.S. company in the field. He was the team leader of a two-ship team. Shortly after take-off his wingman radioed that he had a "red light" on the instrument panel indicating a problem with the engine. Dave told him to return to the Golf Course and he would continue the mission alone. When they neared the LZ a Viet Cong bullet blew out his hydraulics and the helicopter crashed. The impact killed the co-pilot and right door gunner. Both of Dave's legs and one arm were broken, and his ribs were crushed. The left door gunner, Dick Hamilton*, who was also the helicopter crew chief, was miraculously unhurt.

Moments after the crash, the downed helicopter came under attack from VC ground forces. Hamilton rapidly removed his machine gun from its mount and set it up behind a rice paddy dike. He fired off enough rounds to keep the enemy at bay and then stood up, got Dave's door open, and slid the plate back. He unbuckled Dave's harness and dragged him out of his seat, then carried him to safety, placing him behind the dike. Hamilton used all of his ammunition and most of the dead door gunner's to hold off the VC until the U. S. company could fight their way to them. When the battle was over the cockpit windshield was riddled with bullet holes. Dick Hamilton heroically saved the life of Lt. Dave Durbin. Dick Hamilton was a nigra.

After I returned to Fort Rucker from my tour in Vietnam, I was sitting in my BOQ room when there was a knock on my door. I opened it and standing there was a grinning Dave Durbin. He was leaning on a cane. He'd been so badly banged up in the crash that the Army sent him to the States for surgery. He said he'd heard I was back and invited me to the club for a beer.

We went to the officer's club and I waited until we were well into the second beer. I then told him that everyone in Bravo Company heard what Hamilton did after the helicopter was shot down, and I had to ask: When he got out of the Army and returned home, was he still going to be a member of the Ku Klux Kan?

A big smile crossed his face. He said he knew I'd ask that question. The answer was, he was not going back home to Alabama. He'd gotten a job in Houston.

"That's not fair, Dave," I protested. "What if you were going home?"

The smile disappeared and Dave's eyes welled up. After a long drink of his beer, he said that if Dick Hamilton hadn't risked his life by standing up and pulling him out of the helicopter, he would be dead. So the answer was, "It just wouldn't be right." He said many members of his family had also given up their membership in the Ku Klux Klan because of what Specialist Fourth Class Dick Hamilton had done.

CHAPTER 13

Rats

ONE OF THE HANDOUTS WE RECEIVED upon checking in to the 227th Battalion concerned rats. It explained that the rats at An Khe—in fact, throughout Vietnam—were more aggressive than most of the rats of the world and did not need to be cornered or provoked before biting. The handout, prepared by the medical corps, went on to say that rabies among these rats was a serious problem and if we were bitten or scratched we must report this immediately. The handout stressed the importance of tucking in our mosquito netting between the air mattress and cot to prevent the rats from climbing up inside the netting and biting us while we slept. The handout stated that we could not kill the rats because they carried germs that would then leave the dead body and become airborne. These germs could make human beings deathly ill. The only way to control the rat population was by catching them alive in metal cages and then transporting the cages to the medical corps, where they would dispose of the contents.

I read this handout with growing concern. I was terribly afraid of rats, having seen hundreds of them growing up. Our house was a standard brick bungalow, three bedrooms, one bath, living room, dining room, and kitchen—one of thousands that stretched for miles across Chicago. The fronts of the bungalows faced the city streets and the backs faced the alleys. Behind the back of the house was a tiny patch of grass (the backyard), and then a garage which touched the alley. Next to the garage was a concrete trash receptacle into which you put the garbage. On the alley side of this receptacle was a metal door which hung down over an opening. When the garbage truck came down the alley the garbage men lifted the hanging metal door, shoveled out the garbage and put it in the back of the truck. There were no plastic garbage bags in those days.

Naturally the metal tops for the receptacles and the metal doors that hung down were not always in place, or they were missing, so these concrete garbage receptacles were the perfect place for rats. We kids would hear story after story of garbage men and others being bitten by rats. The adults told us to notice that all the garbage men had their pants legs tied tight at the ankles. This kept the rats from running up inside their pants and biting them.

When I was little and would get sick I got to stay in my parents' bed during the day while I recovered. From their bed you could see out the window toward the alley. Often I would see rats playing on our side of the garbage receptacle, just out of sight of the people who walked up and down the alley. The alleys were used as much as the streets for coming and going. This gave me the creeps when I realized that when I walked down the alley I, too, was within just a few feet of playing rats. So I made sure to make a lot of noise walking down the alley—whistling, talking, or hitting a baseball bat on the concrete. Bouncing a basketball was also good. I didn't want to surprise a rat into thinking he was cornered. But now I was in Vietnam learning that cornering doesn't mean much to these rodents—they'd bite you out of meanness.

I asked the other guys in the tent about the rat problem, but they didn't seem concerned. They admitted there were a lot of rats around, especially at night, but nobody in our tent had been bitten. They also said to tuck in my mosquito net because that was what it was for—not mosquitoes. They said that when everybody was back at base camp you didn't see nearly as many rats as when the unit was in the field. The guys at headquarters who stayed behind said that was when the rats took over. So of the eight of us who lived in the tent I was the only one with rat phobia, and of course, I was the only one who was bitten.

It was a few nights before Christmas. Our unit was back at An Khe because of the Christmas Truce. The nice folks back home had sent their loved ones cookies, candies, cakes, pies, and other treats for our holiday enjoyment. The Army sprang for free beer and booze, all we wanted. On this particular night our tent was littered with sweets of every description and I was polluted with booze, of the vodka description, and when I tumbled onto my cot to go to sleep I forgot to tuck in my mosquito netting.

I was awaked in the night by a sharp pain at the tip of my ring finger, left hand. "Damn!" I remember saying to myself. "A rat is chewing on me!" I slung my hand out, and thought I heard a rat drop to the floor. I rolled over and went back to sleep.

In the morning when I awoke I immediately remembered the incident and started hoping it had been a bad dream. "Please make it a dream," I thought (make that prayed) as I lifted my arm. It was not a dream. Dried blood covered my hand and part of my forearm. I couldn't believe it. The place was strewn with open cans and boxes of every kind of sweet food you could name, and a rat decided to chew on me instead. That's a mean rat.

I vacillated for perhaps half an hour before deciding to turn myself in as a rat bite victim. We all knew the medical procedure for rabies prevention—sixteen extremely painful shots in the stomach. But we also knew that to die of rabies was about as bad as dying got. When my head was fully cleared (how much vodka did I drink?) I walked over to the medic's tent and told our flight surgeon what happened. He examined my finger and said, "Yep, that's a rat bite." He said the skin would grow back over it, however, and he didn't think there'd be a scar. "He must have just gotten started on you," he said and told me I was lucky I woke up. Yesterday he had seen a soldier who was missing most of his upper lip. He'd gotten drunk, too, but he passed out with peanut butter on his lips. The doctor said there must have been three or four rats working on him before he woke up screaming.

The doctor then outlined the procedure I'd have to go through to protect against contracting rabies. He told me I had to report, today, to the medic tent of our sister battalion, the 229th, which was "next door," about 500 yards away. That was where the rabies shots were administered between 1:00 and 2:00. He said I'd get one injection every day for fourteen days in a row. If I missed any day I'd have to start all over again. After the fourteenth injection I'd get another a week later. The last one would be a week after that. These were boosters, and I couldn't miss them either. He explained that the shots were administered in the abdomen in the four quadrants around the navel. They were given in that area because it was the largest part of the body and so it best absorbed the pain. They could be given in the arm, but the next day you wouldn't be able to move your arm. If they were given in the butt, the next day you couldn't walk. He wrote a note to my CO telling him I must be available every day between 1:00 and 2:00.

The flight surgeon said that as the days went by I would be in more and more discomfort in the abdominal area and sitting in one position would be painful. He said I could continue to fly for now but to let him know when the pain got too bad and he would ground me until it was better. "Most guys make it about a week," he said.

So at 1300 hours that day I found the 229th medic tent and reported in. There were already about 20 guys forming a line. Fortunately for me I had some fat on my stomach, which allowed the corpsman who administered the shots to pinch up the fat and stick the needle into it sideways. The needle itself was not very long, perhaps an inch or so, but it was brutally thick. Getting it stuck in was most uncomfortable, and when he plunged the medicine in, it burned like hell.

Of the sixteen shots I received, the one I remember most clearly is the Christmas Day shot (about the fourth in the series). The Bravo Company cooks outdid themselves for the Christmas meal served at noon. They cooked not only turkeys but also hams, beef, lasagna, and all the stuff that goes with them. I believed then, and still do, it was the greatest Christmas dinner I ever had. Absolutely spectacular. I don't know how they pulled it off. Unfortunately, because I ate so much and obviously wasn't planning ahead, when I got to the clinic and lay down on the table to get the shot, the corpsman couldn't get hold of any fat. My stomach was stretched to its limit. "Sorry, Lieutenant," he said and stuck the needle straight in. God. And sure enough, just like the doctor had predicted, after about seven days I was looking like a decrepit old man. To walk I had to stoop way over, and I couldn't straighten my legs without shooting pain up into my trunk. So I shuffled over to see the doc, and he grounded me.

The very next day the 227th was told to saddle up and head for the field. Apparently those H-13s had come across a brigade-sized unit of NVA working its way south down the An Lao Valley. An Khe was too far away to support the infantry, so a field camp would be established close to the fighting. I was not going, of course; I was grounded and had to keep getting the shots. I would be alone in the tent ... with the rats.

After the unit departed I made my way to the supply tent. A sergeant was sitting behind the counter reading a *Playboy*. "Help you, Lieutenant?" he said, barely looking up.

"I need another mosquito net, Sergeant," I said.

He told me I had to turn in my old one before he'd give me a new one. "Make an exception will you, Sarge?" I said. "I really need two."

Now he looked at me and I could see he thought he was about to have some fun with a lieutenant. Sometimes NCOs, especially quartermaster types, enjoyed having power over officers. The smirk appeared. "Rules are rules, sir," he said.

I asked him to please give me a break. I said I was now alone in my tent and I wanted two nets to keep the rats away from me. I told him I got bit by one last week and had to stay in camp to get rabies shots. I lifted up my shirt. My stomach was black, blue, and yellow.

"Holy shit," he said, his eyes wide. "You're gettin' them rabies shots in the belly?"

"Yes, 16 of them," I said.

"Gawd damn! OK, here's another one," he said, handing me a brand new mosquito net. "They hurt as bad as they say?"

"Worse," I said and shuffled out. I knew I'd get another net. Only the meanest of pricks wouldn't take pity on someone gettin' them rabies shots.

When darkness came I crawled onto my cot and double-tucked myself in. I had a flashlight to read by and felt fairly safe from the rats. And you should have seen the rats. The story about them taking over when the unit left for the field could not have been more accurate. They were everywhere—but I wouldn't expect you to believe me. Luckily I have a witness.

My witness was my buddy Palmer Haines. We had been corresponding by in-country mail, and he'd learned about me getting grounded. He was a Birddog pilot supporting a Marine unit to our north and was able to get an overnight pass to come visit me. The next day he arrived. I told him how bad the rats had been the night before, but he didn't believe me. "Jim, they can't be that bad," he laughed.

"Just wait," I said.

After supper Palmer and I went back to my tent. We sat in the common area on lawn chairs facing each other and were talking about everything and nothing as good friends can do. Just as it got dark outside a rat came in under the tent flap, saw us, and ran between us toward the back of the tent. "Holy shit," Palmer said. "That was a big one."

Not a minute passed and another one ran past our side. Then another one ran past our other side. Then another one ran between our feet, followed by another one. "OK, OK," he said. "What do we do?"

Palmer got into the cot next to mine, and we tucked ourselves in and talked until the wee hours as the rats scurried to and fro across the floor. The rats owned the tent and we were their prisoners. "This is unbelievable," Palmer said many times that night. (After a year in Birddogs Palmer returned to the States, transferred to the Marines, attended their flight school, and returned to Vietnam flying A-4 "Skyhawks," a jet attack aircraft. He then hired on with Delta Airlines.)

About a month after I got bit one of the warrant officers in the tent next to ours got bit. Whereas my only response to getting bit was to get the shots and double the mosquito net, the warrant took aggressive revenge. Every night he'd set out as many rattraps as he could get his hands on, and every morning each contained a rat. He would line up the traps facing their doors away from the tents toward a shallow ravine with a creek running through it. Then he would douse the rats with lighter fluid, set them on fire, and then open the trap doors. It was quite a sight to see burning fur ball after burning fur ball trying to get to the creek. They never made it.

As much as I feared and detested the rats I could only watch this one time. To me it was more cruelty than revenge, but that was me. Most of the guys thought it was the proper thing to do. Besides, it was by fire that the medics killed the rats when we delivered them. In any case the Old Man made the warrant officer stop the practice because the medics warned that if the rats didn't completely burn up those germs they carried might get airborne. End of fun with rats.

An Khe was not the only place in Vietnam with an overabundance of rats. About a month after my last shot we were bivouacked in the field near Kim San. I was sleeping on a cot and had to relieve myself in the middle of the night. When I shown my flashlight on the ground I saw, to my horror, a sea of rats running around, perhaps one every five feet on center. I knelt on the cot and pissed off the side. Nothing else to do.

CHAPTER 14

They Booed Bob Hope

TWO DAYS AFTER THE RAT BITE, but before I was grounded, the First Cav was given a special treat. Bob Hope was coming to entertain us. There had been rumors circulating to this effect for a few days but nobody took them seriously. An Khe was simply too dangerous a place for Hope and his entourage. With less than 24 hours' notice, however, it became official: Hope was indeed coming, and all troops in camp were invited to the show. Just outside our perimeter a crude stage was hastily built at the base of a gently sloping hill, which made an ideal outdoor arena.

Bob Hope had been entertaining American troops on location during Christmas-time for many years, beginning in World War II. To actually get to see him was something to tell one's grandchildren because Hope had become a legend. The words war, Christmas, and Bob Hope belonged together when America had soldiers fighting in foreign lands.

My team of two slicks was particularly fortunate with Bob's visit because we were assigned the mission of getting Bob and other entertainer dignitaries the hell out of there should Charlie decide to lob mortars into the area. We were to get into the air, climb to 1500 feet as fast as possible, and circle around until we were told when and where it was safe to land with our famous cargo. So our helicopters were parked on a small knoll just to the left of the front of the stage. Best seats in the house.

Thousands of troops blanketed the hillside. They were in a very good mood, laughing, drinking beer, and generally enjoying themselves. They felt safe for this one afternoon and were about to be entertained by one of the most famous comedians who ever lived. The next couple of hours would be pure joy. And safe they should have felt. Two gunship fire teams could be seen circling the outer reaches of the arena area, and two sets of Air Force

99

jet fighters circled high above them. The First Cav brass was making very sure that Bob Hope and company would not be harmed during their brief visit to An Khe.

The show began about 2:00, and the opening act was the singer and comedienne Martha Raye. Martha Raye was well known to us from early television days. She was bawdy (at least for 1960s TV), she was funny, she had a good singing voice, and she had a large mouth. Today I couldn't tell you the songs Martha sang or the jokes she told, but I'll never forget what she did.

When singers perform with bands, there are usually instrumental interludes when the singer stops and the band continues to play. During these interludes, the singers usually snap their fingers keeping time to the music, or they sway their hips, or dance, or look dreamily off into the distance. Martha did none of that.

During the first lull in the lyrics she looked back at the band; then she looked at the microphone in her hand. Then she looked out at the troops, put that huge smile on her face and, pretending the microphone was an electric razor, she mimicked shaving her armpit. It was unexpected and funny and the troops loved it. When the next lull in the singing came, she did it again with her other armpit, and again the troops laughed, cheered, and applauded. Then there was another pause in the lyrics and Martha looked out at the troops, winked at them, and then began shaving her pubic hair. The troops went nuts, whooping and hollering. If Charlie was watching with his binoculars from some far off hill he was probably laughing, too.

I laughed also, of course, but being essentially a prude I now began to worry about the priest, a colonel, who was the division chaplain and who was sitting in the front row, right in front of Martha and next to the general. I assumed the chaplain would be offended by this sort of lewd gesture, but when I saw his face he was laughing just like everyone else. I relaxed with the knowledge he was not going to get up and leave.

With Bob Hope was Les Brown and his Band of Renown. They'd been accompanying him since the beginning of his wartime shows. Jerry Colona was there, another Hope fixture, and of course the drop-dead beautiful Hollywood starlets who danced and sang and gave Bob ample material for guy-type jokes. Most of us had not seen American women since we got in country and those starlets were something to see—and think about. (There were American nurses on the base, but I only saw one once.)

The highlight of the Bob Hope Christmas Show was Bob Hope himself. When he finally strolled out onto the stage with his knowing smile, his ski jump nose, and his trademark golf club, it was magical. Les Brown's band began playing Hope's theme song, "Thanks for the Memories," and all of us were momentarily spellbound. Here, in one of the most remote and hostile places on earth, some 12,000 miles from home, stood Bob Hope grinning at us. If we didn't know it before, we sure knew it now—we were American servicemen overseas. We'd just become the stuff of newsreels.

Bob's monologue started just fine, and he was getting one uproarious laugh after another. Many of the jokes made reference to the starlets on the stage and to us poor, horny bastards in the audience. Hope pulled this off with sophistication and hilarity, all the while wearing his shit-eating grin. Even the chaplain was in stitches.

These jokes were followed by jokes about being in the military. One was about General Eisenhower who, in the 1950s, decided to run for president. "Some guys will do anything to get out of the Army," Hope said. The troops howled.

Then Bob segued into Vietnam jokes, but unfortunately for him, they were all centered on the city of Saigon and how dangerous it was to be there. After the third such joke the laughter noticeably died down, and after one more of these jokes there was no laughter at all. Then Bob made the disastrous mistake of telling a joke which compared the dangers in Saigon with the dangers in the First Cav, as though they were similar, and now the troops started to boo! He told one more like this and the boo became a roar. Hope was obviously confused and shaken, and he looked down into the first row for help. I was embarrassed for him. Fortunately the commanding general of the First Cav came to the rescue. He jumped up on the stage and whispered into Bob Hope's ear. No doubt he told him that as far as this audience was concerned, the city of Saigon was one of the safest places on earth. They'd do almost anything to be stationed there. A Saigon assignment was more coveted than gold by most members of the First Cav.

Unfortunately for Bob, he didn't have any other type of Vietnam jokes, but he did have the good sense to stop. He regained his composure and looked back at Les Brown, and the band started softly playing a patriotic song. Over this music Bob waxed nostalgic and then thanked us for the sacrifices we were making for our country. We could feel it was genuine. The show ended and the audience, having already forgiven Hope for his gaffe (how could he have known?) and having gotten their point across, now gave Bob, Les Brown and his Band of Renown, Martha Raye, Jerry Colona, and the starlets a very loud, very long standing ovation.

I don't know if this was the only time in his life that Bob was booed by U.S. troops, but I suspect it was. This war zone was very different than any he'd been to before. That afternoon in the An Khe Valley, Bob Hope learned this truth loud and clear.

Serving a tour of duty in Vietnam did not necessarily mean that you were in serious, imminent danger. In fact there were some assignments that had no danger to them at all. For instance, there was a combination military base involving U.S. Air Force, Navy, and Army personnel. It was on the coast at Cam Ranh Bay. This base was so large an area that if you lived and worked near the beach, where most did, you could not be reached by mortar attack. The fortification here was so strong there was no way the enemy could fight their way into it. Not even an NVA division with suicide in mind could have penetrated it. When President Johnson made his symbolic trip to South Vietnam, he confined his visit to Cam Ranh. During the Vietnam War that certain area of Cam Ranh Bay was possibly the safest place on earth.

Years later, a famous personality appeared as a pitchman in a series of TV ads selling some sort of product. The ads were geared to ex-military people and this person supposedly had credibility because he was a Vietnam vet. He was, but his tour of duty was spent at Cam Rahn Bay. He was in a lot more danger driving on a freeway in the United States than serving in the military in Vietnam. His "veteran" pitch frankly pissed me off.

There were many jobs in Vietnam that were exceptionally dangerous, however, taking the highest percentage of casualties. The "tunnel rats" are the first group to come to mind. These men, all volunteers, were perhaps the boldest, bravest soldiers in the war.

In early 1948 the Vietnamese began constructing a tunnel system in which they could hide and also store food, weapons, and ammunition. As the years progressed the tunnel complex became so sophisticated it had surgical hospitals, restaurants, and an amphitheatre. By the time we Americans came to fight, the tunnel system was 130 miles in length with innumerable offshoots. It ran unbroken from the Cambodian border all the way to Saigon. It was an ingenious network, and an engineering wonder, and in that area of the country gave our enemy a huge tactical advantage over us.

Early in the war our infantry became aware of the tunnels. They would be engaged in a firefight with the VC and then, like ghosts, the VC would disappear. An entire platoon could vanish in moments by slipping down into the tunnels and then closing trap doors behind them. These doors were highly camouflaged and were all but impossible to detect. When they were located it was the tunnel rats' job to enter them and to fight the Viet Cong in the dark or try to smoke them out. A terrifying mission, to say the least, and practically impossible because the tunnels were not straight.

The imaginative Vietnamese tunnel builders had purposely curved the tunnels. A bullet could travel only a few yards before slamming into the tunnel wall. The shrapnel from grenades, therefore, was also contained, often posing the most danger to the one tossing it. To make working in the tunnels even more harrowing, the tunnels had become home to bats, fire ants, giant crab spiders, scorpions, the extremely poisonous bamboo viper, and banded krait snakes, and of course, they were lousy with rats. The tunnels were also booby trapped to the max with dung-covered punji stakes.

All Vietnam veterans still hold tunnel rats in the highest regard. If today I turned on my TV and an ex-tunnel rat was selling something, I'd have to buy whatever it was out of respect.

Another high-risk job in Vietnam was being in the Special Forces. These super-trained soldiers generally operated independently from the large American units, concentrating their efforts on bolstering the ARVN forces. Our slicks were used to resupply the Special Forces in their "camps." These were often minuscule outposts located in some of the most out-of-the-way areas of the country. It was unnerving to fly in and out of their camps because they were so remote. Living there, to me, would be unimaginable.

Being a LRRP (lerp) is another job most people wouldn't want. Long Range Reconnaissance Patrols were squad sized—eleven men. They would walk out of a base camp after nightfall and then wander around in the dark trying to locate enemy units. When they found one they would whisper into their radios the unit's size, location and direction of movement. During daylight hours they would hide. LRRP were highly skilled infantrymen, but for a job like theirs a great deal of luck was needed. Sometimes the luck was good—an enemy unit was located, an air strike would be called (either Huey gun ships or jet fighters), and the unit would be destroyed.

But sometimes the luck was bad. Working in the dark, LRRP could come upon an enemy unit that was large and too spread out for immediate attack, so they'd have to wait until daylight to better assess what they'd found. One of our LRRP units discovered one morning, to their dismay, that they were completely surrounded by a large NVA force. The LRRP had inadvertently penetrated their perimeter in the dark. The NVA, so far, was unaware of their presence. The LRRP leader, Lieutenant Rick Stetson, did the most prudent thing he could do. He got his men into a shallow ravine and then called an air strike on his own position. Some of the men were wounded but none were killed. Rick was awarded the Bronze Star.

Artillery units were sometimes stationed in base camps. Though actively engaged in the fighting they were, by necessity, removed from it. Howitzers are not designed to shoot close-up targets. But often artillery units relocated to the field to get closer to the action. That's when their combat pay was earned. They'd be isolated from the infantry they were supporting with their long-range weapons. One of our Cav artillery units, consisting of 20 men, was overrun while I was there. There were no survivors.

Most pilots were also in high-risk jobs. Once I had a three-day, mini R&R (Rest and Recuperation) in Bangkok. In the hotel lobby I was talking to some Air Force pilots who were stationed there. Their living conditions couldn't have been better, but their daily missions took them on bombing runs over North Vietnam. "You guys fly over North Vietnam every day?" I asked. "You ought to have your heads examined." (Being a military pilot was a voluntary job.)

When they asked me what I did, and I told them I was a helicopter pilot with the First Cav, they started laughing and one of them said, "You call us crazy? If we're crazy then you're a fucking lunatic!"

In World War I they were "doughboys," in World War II and Korea they were "G.I.s," and in Vietnam they were known as "grunts." These were the infantrymen (the soldiers) who did the day-to-day, slug-it-out fighting on the ground. Of the 58,000 casualties the U.S. suffered in Vietnam, the overwhelming majority were infantrymen. The infantrymen—and this included Marines—carried their rifles, grenades, grenade launchers, rocket launchers, and machine guns through the jungles, the rice paddies, and the open plains. Not only was their job the most dangerous on a daily basis, their living conditions really sucked. They lived "outside" and what many of them saw, heard, and felt provided the stuff of legitimate, lifelong nightmares.

Some Vietnam duty, however, was actually pleasant. There was a resort city on the coast called Vung Tao. It was a place the Army used to give in-country R&Rs. Rumor had it that the Viet Cong also used it for R&R and a covert agreement had been reached that when in Vung Tao there was no fighting allowed. I spent two nights in heaven there, and I'd have given anything to be assigned to the chopper unit in Vung Tao flying VIPs back and forth to Saigon. It would have been only slightly more dangerous than flying from Virginia Beach to Richmond.

I applaud everyone who heard the call and served their nation in Vietnam. However, over the years I've been sometimes irked by vets who stated, or implied, that their time in the war zone was much more hazardous than it really was. That's not right. It is an insult to the memory of those who died in battle. (I have also heard people tell stories, with Homeric bravado, about how they "almost went to Vietnam." Good grief.)

So I have compiled a list of Vietnam War jobs and given each one a hazard rating. One is least hazardous and ten is most. The list is totally subjective and is based on my experience, not on official statistics—if such statistics exist.

A) Infantry, enlisted man = 10
B) Infantry, officer (major or below) = 10
C) Clerk typist in Saigon = 1
D) Mechanic in a base camp = 3
E) Cook in a base camp = 3
F) Cook in a field camp = 6
G) Special Forces = 10
H) LRRP = 10
I) Artillery at base camp = 3
J) Artillery at field camp = 10
K) General = 0
L) Pilot of helicopter = 10
M) Pilot of jet fighter = 10
N) Pilot of B-52 flying over South Vietnam = 1
O) Pilot of B-52 flying over North Vietnam = 10
P) Pilot of Birddog = 8
Q) Colonel = 1
R) U.S. Navy Seal = 10
S) On a U.S. Navy gunboat in the Delta = 10
T) On a U.S. Navy boat off shore = you don't count
U) Stationed in Thailand at an air base = you don't count, either
V) Stationed in Thailand flying over North Vietnam = 10
W) Army band = 1
X) Medic in the field = 10
Y) Medic in a MASH = 3
Z) Tunnel rat = off the chart

Of course there were numerous exceptions to the above list, and dozens of jobs not listed. The easiest and most accurate way to determine a veteran's true danger quotient would be to simply ask: "How many friends did you lose who had the exact same job, and rank, as you?" Then the exaggerator will either have to shut up or lie.

December of 1966 was early in the war, and it was then that Bob Hope learned that Vietnam was many different experiences for the men and women who served. There was Vietnam, Mr. Hope ... and then there was Vietnam.

CHAPTER 15

To the Field

DURING MY FIRST TWO MONTHS OR SO with the Cav, the 227th Battalion was based at An Khe, so no matter what the day's or night's missions had been I got to sleep on my own cot in my own area of our tent. At An Khe were the officer's club, the chapel, the mess tent serving three meals per day, warm showers, and the extraordinary officer's latrine. Other than the missions, which produced casualties, life was good and we had little to complain about. But this good life, unfortunately, was about to change.

Our nosey H-13 pilots caught up with a prize they'd been seeking for a long time. They buzzed up on a North Vietnamese Army unit, which was at least regiment size, and possibly as big as a division. Upon contact one of the helicopters and crew were lost. This NVA unit was discovered heading south, near the village of Kontum, some 40 miles to our north and west. We therefore could not support our ground troops from as far away as An Khe. We had to set up a base camp closer to where the combat was about to take place. The 227th Assault Helicopter Battalion was off "to the field" and from then on most of my time with the Cav would be spent in the field, living in one temporary base camp after another.

Our missions from the field would be essentially the same as those flown from An Khe except that a much higher percentage of them would be combat assault, and medevac under fire, and the percentage of hot LZs would increase dramatically. One of the main differences between the base at An Khe and a hastily erected field camp was that the field camp would not be nearly as secure. The Cav "owned" the An Khe valley—sort of. Near Kontum we owned nothing, and therefore mortar attacks would be much more frequent. The chance of being overrun became a distinct possibility.

The author filling sandbags.

Another main difference between An Khe and a field camp were the creature comforts, which took a dramatic nosedive. Although we usually had a tent over our heads and a cot to sleep on, the floor of the tent was now dirt, or, in the rainy season, mud. There were no showers, hot or cold. We bathed and shaved with cold water, which we carried from the potable water station in our steel pots (helmets). A helmet held about two quarts, not nearly enough to get the job done. We urinated into empty mortar tubes called, of course, "piss tubes." Those were driven into the ground on an angle and were moved around every couple of days for sanitary (odor) reasons.

We defecated into "honey buckets." These were metal 55-gallon drums cut in half with a crude piece of plywood placed on them. There was, naturally, a hole in the plywood. You had to be careful because the plywood was not fastened to the drum and tended to slide around. No privacy was afforded to the piss tubes or the honey buckets, and after awhile, it didn't matter. You either stood there taking a piss or you sat there taking a dump and people walked by and didn't even notice.

Like the piss tubes, the honey buckets were strategically placed around the camp. But unlike the piss tubes, the honey buckets were not moved. When they filled up, the "latrine patrol" would simply pour gasoline into them and light the contents on fire. You can imagine (actually you can't) the smell of burning shit.

One time, immediately after finishing my business, I thought I felt something touching my scrotum. I jumped up and turned around to see the largest bug I'd ever seen, a beetle I suppose. His dark blue body was in two sections, both the size of golf balls. His plan, apparently, was to use my genitals as a ladder. He was standing on his hind legs, on the pile of shit, and his pincers were frantically grabbing at the air above him. Incredible.

There were times when a field camp became large, which told us we would be there awhile, and the mess personnel from An Khe would be dispatched to set up a real mess tent with real food. But most times this was not the case and C-rations were the only food available. This sounds like a terrible hardship, but in reality it was not.

C-rations came in cardboard boxes containing plastic spoons, salt and pepper, instant coffee, sugar, creamer, gum, matches, toilet paper and cigarettes—4 smokes to a pack. Also in the boxes were the tin cans that contained the food. These tin cans could be heated so the food inside was quite edible. We would drain some fuel from the helicopter gas tanks into an empty can, with holes punched along the sides near the top. This allowed oxygen in, to keep the fire going. Then we'd light the fuel and put the can with the food in it on top. This was not as efficient as a Coleman stove, but it worked just fine and wasn't nearly the hassle.

The C-ration menu was diverse and the food tasted good. Not great, of course, but not bad at all. We had ham and eggs, ham and lima beans, spaghetti and meatballs, beans and wieners, beef and gravy with potatoes (my favorite), turkey loaf, boned chicken, chicken and noodles, and spiced beef (my second favorite). And there were canned peaches, pears, little pound cakes, and a bunch of other stuff. We did not go hungry.

Sometimes when based in a field camp we would be temporarily assigned to spend our nights in a "field-field" camp. This occurred when the fighting was intense, and our need to support the infantry was potentially immediate, so we had to live with them. Medevac missions under fire, extraction of units from LZs under fire, and resupply under fire were now the rule. It was hairy flying and the living conditions were primitive and transient—a night here, a night there. There were no tents, no cots, no piss tubes, no honey buckets. In a field-field camp the Army got out of the bathroom business—you were on your own. We slept on the ground under, or next to, the helicopters. If it was raining, or the ground was too muddy, we slept inside of them—pilots in their seats and door gunners on the metal floor in back.

Supper is almost ready.

One time my team of four slicks was assigned to an infantry platoon. For the night the platoon leader had chosen a hill with unobstructed visibility (fields of fire) in all directions. The hill was in an area where lots of enemy activity had been reported. We felt certain that we would be attacked before daybreak. It had been raining without relief for many days. We were soaked to the bone and miserable. Our mission in the morning was to take the platoon to an LZ that was yet to be determined. Our mission that night was to get the helicopters into the air as soon as possible after the first mortar landed or if a ground attack was launched. The helicopters sitting on the ground were prime targets and very vulnerable. As soon as we were in the air we were to call in the coordinates from where the attack was coming, if that could be determined. Perhaps friendly artillery some distance away could help repel it, or this information would hasten the repelling fire from the gunships when they arrived. We would then simply circle the area high overhead until it was safe to land. If medevac was then needed we would perform that mission.

All of us had been in field-field camps before, so no one needed a briefing. The rules were simple: Pilots alternate sleeping every other hour. Door gunners do not tie down the rotor blade (done to prevent wind damage) as it takes four or five seconds to untie it. If a helicopter was started while its main rotor was tied down, the drive train was instant junk and the aircraft could not be flown. Happened all the time.

With about a half hour to go before total darkness, we eight pilots gathered at the edge of the hill to eat supper. Because of the rain we ate cold and standing up. As we ate we idly watched the soldiers placing claymore mines along the side of the hill. The soldiers could remotely activate these mines. There were also flares with trip wires connecting them, and they would be our first warning should the enemy decide on a land attack.

The valley was now shrouded by a thick, gray fog with an opaque mist above it. It was an eerie, ghostly scene, and had the circumstances been different it would have been enchantingly beautiful. But this particular evening it was terribly depressing and utterly frightening. The fog and mist provided excellent cover for the enemy to get within 50 yards of us without being seen. We were all thinking, but not saying, the obvious: If the VC singled out this infantry platoon bivouacked on this hill and decided to take it they could. They would suffer casualties but they might decide it was worth it.

We wore our ponchos and the rainwater found its way down the creases into our eyes, our boots, our food and under our sleeves with each bite. No one spoke; the only sounds were the plastic spoons quietly scraping the sides and bottoms of tin cans. This was our sixth night in a row living with the infantry in a field-field camp. We were wet, we were filthy, we stank, we were exhausted, and of course we were scared. This spot, this hill protruding up from the fog-shrouded rice paddies, was that night one of the most dangerous places on earth for an American to be.

Many more minutes passed without a word. Then, in the lowest of voices and the deepest of southern accents, one of the guys said, "If, when ah git home, mah wife says to me 'Honey, let's take the chillun and go on a picnic ... ah'm gonna punch her right in the mouth."

All of us lost it. Charlie must have heard us laughing a mile away. The infantry guys looked at us like we'd gone nuts. Those were the most perfectly grouped words I think I've ever heard.

Of course, there was a mortar attack that night and we followed rote procedures getting the choppers into the air. Soon the gunships arrived and did their thing. (I envied gunship pilots.) Fortunately there were no casualties so no medevac was required. It was a token mortar attack (*we know where you are*) with only a few rounds landing on the hill.

The next day, just after dawn, I got my new orders to fly the platoon to LZ Foxtrot, where they would join up with another platoon from their company coming from a different location. I knew Foxtrot's location from memory and off we went. Twenty-five minutes of flying and we arrived. I was now in radio contact with the other slick team leader coming in with the other platoon. He was a few minutes behind us so we were the first team into the LZ. We did not know if it was hot, so as a precaution I told the door gunners to lay down fire just prior to landing. It was not hot. Good news. Then more good news. I contacted base to receive my next mission and was told my team was being replaced by fresh crews, and we were to return to An Khe for a 24-hour break. No sweeter words could be heard. Hot showers, hot food, dry clothes, and cots with air mattresses awaited us. And, of course, there was the officer's club. Life is good.

When flying cross-country in a helicopter in Vietnam there were two altitude alternatives—either above 1500 feet or down "on the deck." These altitudes minimized the chances of being hit by small arms fire. An altitude of 1500 feet is too high for most small arms fire and the target at that altitude was small. Flying on the deck, skids just inches above tree tops, is also good because the enemy can't hear you approaching and you're over them and gone in a millisecond. Flying treetops is more fun than you can imagine—and that was how we flew all the way back to An Khe.

Although the rain continued at An Khe, we had our tent, and for the first time in a week we got dry. Who would ever think that simply being dry would be a luxury? The mess hall guys fixed us steaks for supper, we got our mail, we pounded down drinks at the club and were fast asleep by 9:00 p.m. No mortar attacks, no nothing. It was great to be home.

But by noon the next day we were in the air again, this time bound for a field camp in the Ia Drang Valley south of Pleiku. The Cav was getting spread out as fighting continued to increase all across the Central Highlands.

Most of the time missions just happened, with no warning or preparation—ammo resupply, troop reinforcement or evacuation, and medevac. It was the slick's job to perform medevac missions from hot LZs because we had machine guns manned by the door gunners. The official medevac Hueys had a large red cross painted on their sides. They did not carry mounted weapons so they were totally without protection, and therefore relegated to flying wounded from MASH hospitals to more sophisticated base hospitals.

Other missions, the larger, planned combat assault missions, were usually begun with a briefing by a high-ranking officer, a major or above. We would then learn the big picture—where the friendly units were located,

The versatile Huey slick. The South China Sea is in the background.

where the unfriendlies were concentrated (more frequently a guess than a fact), and the route we would be taking to transport our troops from point A to an LZ, which would enable them to "make contact" with the enemy. Charts and maps were used and casualty guesses were made. It was nice to occasionally get these formal briefings because 90 percent of the time we had no notion of the big picture—not the big picture of the entire war effort nor even the big picture of what the Cav, or its individual units, were up to.

While with the Cav I probably attended about 20 of these formal, pre-flight briefings. After most of them were over, I would say to myself as we walked to our helicopters, "Well, I guess this is it." I determined that if the conditions we were about to fly into were as bad as we had just been told, my chances of surviving were about 50/50. Of course I knew from statistics that 50/50 remained 50/50 on each mission, but at the same time common sense told me that if I had ten 50/50 missions I was going to die. Even two 50/50's weren't good.

So I had my back-up plan (dying plan) all set. On the top of the cyclic there was a button. The right forefinger rested on it. When this button was depressed you were immediately transmitting over the radio. All the aircraft involved in the mission would hear what you had to say because they were all tuned to the same frequency. So I knew that many people would hear me say, "Tell Mary I loved her and my parents I went to heaven." I felt sure I could get those words out before slamming into the ground. I practiced saying them fast, but not too fast. I wanted my girlfriend to know how I felt about her, and because my parents' main concern was for my immortal soul, I knew they'd be relieved to learn it had been in ready-to-die shape.

The mission briefings were usually accurate. If they said we'd be encountering heavy resistance then we did. This warning was good for us. It kept us sharp, on our toes, heads up. During the flying time from point A to the LZ the radio communication between slicks and gunships always started out curt and polite. Our formations were tight and professional; our senses were at their peak. But as we got closer to the LZ, and began hearing from the ground forces that we would be under heavy fire on the way into it, then the fear crept up. It started in the gut, and when that was filled it sweated the palms, beaded the forehead, and drenched the armpits. As reports came in of helicopters down and helicopters being waved off, the formations loosened and so did tongues. It was now every chopper for itself. Somehow get into that LZ, get the troops off (never a problem) and get the fuck out of there.

Guys would start cursing and screaming advice to each other. When final approach arrived our door gunners would open up. On our flanks the gunships would be punching off rockets, chunking grenades and blazing away with their machine guns. The noise was absurd. The smell of gunpowder and sulphur was intense.

And then you were there. Your turn. Find a spot. Get to it as fast as possible. Drop to a low hover. Troops out. Nose down. Grab airspeed. Grab altitude. Clear! Now climb! Climb! Climb! Made it! Safe! Fifteen hundred feet! Out of harm's way again! Armpits and foreheads dried up. Stomach back to normal. Fifteen hundred feet. Nothing bad could happen to us now.

The feeling experienced by the crew of a Huey helicopter, after successfully completing a combat assault into a hot LZ, was exhilaration!

CHAPTER 16

Wildlife

VIETNAM IS HOME TO MANY WILDLIFE species. During my tour there I saw elephant, monkey, deer, wild boar, water buffalo, peacock, parrots, king cobra, python, and tiger.

When a patrolling infantry unit bivouacs for the night, forward perimeter guards are sometimes used as a first line of defense and warning against impending enemy attack. Holes are dug in the ground 50 meters outside the perimeter, deep enough to stand in so that only the head and shoulders are exposed. Standing guard in these holes is about as much fun as being the point man on patrol and nobody wants it, so the soldiers assigned to the duty are rotated to make it fair. Mysteriously, one of our infantry companies operating near Bong Son reported that two of their forward perimeter guards had gone missing—one last night and one the night before. There was no explanation for this. They could not have deserted because there was no place to desert to. They were simply gone.

So the next night they assigned two men to occupy the hole in the ground, and this solved the riddle. As the one soldier was looking forward, toward where the enemy might be, the other one was facing backward toward his own unit. He was the one that saw something large moving slowly toward him. He yelled, "Halt!" and raised his rifle. Through the scope he saw the stripes of a Bengal tiger as it bolted across the darkness. He was too shocked to shoot, and that was a good thing, since the tiger was between him and his unit. Apparently it had been sneaking up behind the guards and soundlessly "taking" them.

Bravo Company was assigned the mission to search for, and destroy, this tiger. That mission fell to my team of two Huey slicks. For a mission of this nature you'd think they'd assign gunships, but slicks actually made more sense. The First Cav had thirty times more slicks than guns, and our M-60 machine guns were more than enough firepower to kill a tiger. Also an empty slick is much more maneuverable than a fully loaded gunship.

We flew up to the area where the tiger had been spotted and then began our search. We flew around the mountains and down the valleys and ravines of the Bong Son area for an entire day, looking for a tiger on the ground. We all assessed our chances of seeing it at less than one million to one, but we didn't care. It was a safe mission and a nice respite from combat assault. Tigers weren't much of a threat to men in helicopters.

Then, incredibly, we did see him—no more than a kilometer away from where he'd been spotted the night before. He bounded from one tree line to another across a huge boulder. My door gunner on the left side sprayed the area the tiger had run into, and so did my wingman's left door gunner. We then circled around and let the right side door gunners do the same, just for the hell of it. I couldn't imagine we killed him or even hit him— he was really moving—but then I had never thought we'd even see him. Who knows?

When it got dark we flew back to base. We were hoping we'd get the same mission the next day, and maybe even become famous as the tiger hunting team of slicks. I'd change my call sign from "Dog Fight" to "Tiger Killer." That had a nice ring to it, I thought. But this was not to be. Things were now quieted down in the Bong Son area, and the next day we airlifted out the infantry units and took them to a more exciting location, enemy wise. Nuts.

In the aftermath of the war, continuing even to this day, we are attempting to find MIAs (missing in action). I have wondered how many of those MIAs fell prey to tigers. Although the man hunter we chased was, I think, fairly unique, tigers were prevalent in the Central Highlands and probably carried off some of our dead. In the elephant grass areas it could take days after a battle to find the dead bodies, which were often located by smell. We had to assume tigers beat us to some of them. This was not the kind of stuff we wanted to dwell on, however.

We were Bravo Company 227 and the neighborhood next door, back at the An Khe base, was Charlie. One of the guys in Charlie Company, a Captain Tom Wilson* from Tennessee, had somehow managed to catch a python, which he kept outside his tent in a large enclosure fashioned out of 2 × 4s and chicken wire.

The python's favorite food, he learned, was live rat, so getting food for the python was no problem at An Khe. Captain Wilson got permission from the medical corps to feed live rats to the snake. Because the rats were totally consumed there were no residual germs to worry about.

Wilson would release a rat into the cage, and guys would stand around the sides and watch as the snake stalked the terrified rat, grabbed it with his mouth, squeezed it with his body, and then slowly swallowed it. I'd been hearing about this from other guys in Bravo Company who'd wandered over to Charlie around feeding time. Still suffering from rat phobia, I thought it might be good for me to see this, so one day I joined a group and over to Charlie Company we went. I wish I hadn't.

This was the day that Captain Wilson learned something about his snake: It could only eat one rat per day. The way he learned this was by releasing two rats at once into the cage. I don't know why he did this, but I suppose he had a theory that if the snake ate both rats at once he'd sleep longer, cutting down on the time it took Wilson to feed him. Or perhaps he thought the snake would eat one rat today and save the other for tomorrow. In either case this would mean less work for the captain.

I stood there with about ten other guys. The python was ready for food when the captain showed up, and when the rats were released it began stalking. The rats were absolutely freaked. They saw the snake and started running, climbing, dodging, and hiding behind rocks and logs. All this to no avail. The python honed in on one of them, and with lightning speed he nailed it. A few minutes later it was swallowed and the snake curled up and went to sleep.

Now the other rat got an idea. Sensing the snake was immobilized by his meal, the rat attacked. It bit the python on the face, the sides, and the end of its tail. It was a vicious attack and each bite brought blood. The snake could barely move, and Tom Wilson panicked. "Fuckin' rat's gonna kill my snake!" he yelled. He opened the cage door, and the rat ran through it and across the compound, never to be seen again. Just one more reason to be afraid of the little bastards. They are really smart.

We were in the officer's club one night and some of the guys were getting hammered. They had just returned from a particularly nasty mission. Somebody suggested that they go get the python and let him loose in the club, just to see what would happen. So two guys got the snake, carried it into the club and put it on the floor by the bar. It went to sleep and stayed asleep for at least ten minutes. Disappointed, one of the drunker guys staggered over and reached down to pick it up. The instant he touched it the python woke up, reared back, and nailed the drunk in the leg just below the knee. "Shit!" he screamed, and everybody laughed. Captain Wilson put his snake back in the cage.

There was a radio tower on Hong Kong Mountain, and from time to time it needed to be repaired. One day our mission was to fly two technicians up to the tower, wait for them to do their repairs, and fly them back down to base. This was a cushy, non-hazardous mission—my favorite kind. On the way up the mountain my co-pilot, Charlie Harris*, asked me if I'd like to see an extraordinary sight. Charlie was a CW-3 and had been in country almost a year. He was getting "short," which meant his time in country was about up. "Sure," I said. "What is it?" He said I'd have to see it to believe it and asked if he could have the controls. "All yours," I said and lit a cigarette.

Over the intercom Charlie told the door gunner to tell the technicians that after we dropped them off we'd be gone about 15 minutes and would then return to pick them up. We landed, and the technicians jumped off the ship and grabbed their bag of tools. Charlie picked up to a high hover and slowly moved sideways until we were clear of the mountain. Below us was a solid jungle canopy all the way down to the valley floor.

Slowly he began descending down the side of the mountain until we were about one fourth of the way down. I then heard one of the door gunners say over the intercom, "Wow! Look at that!" I looked down into the trees where there was an explosion of activity, stretching in every direction. Monkeys! There were hundreds of them, maybe thousands, jumping through the treetops. An area the size of a football field was boiling with monkeys as big as baboons, but without the red hind end. Some stopped long enough to shake their hairy fists at us before jumping to the next tree. "I thought you'd enjoy this, Lieutenant," Chief Harris said as he slowly hovered back and forth across the tops of the trees. He told me he'd discovered them by accident some months ago but he hadn't told many people because he was sure it was not good for them to be bothered.

"This is one I'll never forget, Chief. Thank you," I said as he hovered back up to the mountain's top.

Setting up a field camp one day, shoveling dirt into canvas bags to stack around our tents, we heard, "It's a cobra!" coming from a guy about 100 feet away. We looked over and saw a lieutenant running backward away from his small tent. We walked over to him, entrenching tools (shovels) in hand and heard him telling the gathering crowd that he'd stepped into the tent, which he had just erected, and in the back corner a king cobra rose up. "It was huge!" he said, wide-eyed.

"Is it still in there?" somebody asked.

"Where else could it be?" the lieutenant answered, his voice high and quivering.

The sides of the tent were to the ground and the flap was shut. We all stared at the flap knowing a snake could easily crawl under it. We backed up a few more yards.

A master sergeant now appeared, and Lieutenant Ray Blyde* told him that he thought the snake was still in there. The sergeant said he knew how to find out. He picked up a stone and walked to the side of the tent. He then lobbed the stone, underhanded, so it struck the side about four feet above the ground. In something less than one tenth of a second, bam! From inside the tent the cobra struck the exact same spot the stone had hit. The side of the tent bulged out about a foot. "Holy shit!" was shouted all around.

Then the sergeant threw another stone—hit, bam! Then another one—hit, bam! "He is a big one," said the sergeant. "But we'll tire him out." He continued to throw stones at the tent, moving from the side to the back and to the other side. Soon the bams were getting lower than the hits. By this time there must have been 30 of us gathered near the tent—but not too close.

Now the company C.O., Major Ed Keefe*, showed up with a shotgun in his hand and asked, "He wore out yet, Sergeant?"

"Yes sir."

"Lieutenant Blyde," the major asked, "is this your tent?"

"Yes sir," said Blyde.

He told Blyde to walk up to the flap and grab the rope hanging down. "When I say 'pull'" said the major, "yank it back hard and keep the flap between yourself and the opening."

Blyde didn't move. He gave the major an incredulous look. But Keefe stared back at him. "Now, Lieutenant!" he said. (Keefe was a small man with a terrible temper.)

Blyde slowly walked to the tent flap and reached for the rope. He was bent way over, keeping his feet as far from the tent as possible. Keefe then walked to within five feet of the opening, raised his gun, and said, "Pull it!"

Blyde yanked the rope. The snake slithered out and Keefe blew its head off. He then told us we'd had enough entertainment for today and to return to filling the sand bags making certain they were stacked high. "Charlie's gonna mortar us tonight. You can count on it," Keefe said. He was correct, of course.

CHAPTER 17

Ancillary Missions

COMBAT ASSAULT MISSIONS WERE the most prevalent for Huey pilots in the Cav—that was the concept that created the First "Air" Cavalry Division—but we were also given other, usually less exciting and therefore less dangerous, missions. We could be aerial chauffeurs flying high-ranking officers from one place to another. We could be used as high altitude observers—flying the commanding officer of a battalion over a battle his unit was engaged in. This way he could be on the scene, direct certain elements of the battle, get a sense of the big picture, and not get himself killed in the process.

Sometimes we took a Birddog type job of spotting for artillery units. First we would locate the target area and call its coordinates to an artillery officer—often miles away. He would relay this to his troops, who would fire a round, and we would watch where the round landed. If the round was off target, we would tell him how far off and in what direction. He would then fire another round and we would tell him where that one landed. He would make an additional adjustment and shoot another round. When the artillery shells were "bracketing" the target we would tell him to split the difference and "fire for effect." Then all the guns would open up and all hell would break loose on the ground. This was great fun for us, in a wartime sort of a way, and the best part was that we were in no danger, flying at 2,000 feet in the air.

Another mission we sometimes got was airlifting P.O.W.s from where they were captured to an internment camp. The typical Viet Cong soldier was dressed in a T-shirt and shorts. He had a conical hat on his head and Ho Chi Minh sneakers on his feet. Ho Chi Minh sneakers were what we would call "flip-flops" only their flip-flops were formed from the rubber of discarded automobile tires—very durable, very cheap and very smart.

On these P.O.W. flights there was usually a Vietnamese soldier from the ARVN—the good guys who were on our side. We had heard stories that sometimes when the helicopter was high in the air, the ARVN soldier would begin interrogating the prisoners, and if they wouldn't talk, or did talk but were lying, he would start throwing them out of the helicopter, one by one, until those who remained on board were talking their heads off. I didn't know if these stories were true or not, but I suspected not. War stories told in war zones are often more outrageous than those told years later.

One day we picked up a load of P.O.W.s along with an ARVN officer. About ten minutes into the flight I felt a rocking of the helicopter and heard yelling coming from behind me. I turned around to see that the ARVN had a prisoner by the seat of his pants with his right hand, and his left hand was around the man's throat. The prisoner's arms were tied behind his back. The ARVN was screaming into his ear as he edged him closer to the open door. The prisoner, who was about to go airborne, was crying, and the others were terror struck. I hit the intercom button and told the door gunner to tell the ARVN that if he threw the prisoner out of my helicopter, I was going to go back there and throw him out. The door gunner got this message across by yelling in pidgin English and waving his arms. The ARVN threw the prisoner to the floor of the helicopter, spit on him, and then gave me a look of disgust that I will never forget. So the stories were true.

We had a mission one time near the coast in conjunction with the U. S. Navy, which had a destroyer anchored about a half mile off shore. The destroyer's guns could reach for many miles with incredible accuracy. So whenever the Navy's ships were available, and the fighting was close enough to the sea, the Cav teamed up with them.

One morning about 11:00, after a mission with the Navy, I was told to fly to the field base camp near Qui Nhon where a naval officer would be waiting for me. He was the liaison officer between the Army and the Navy, and he needed a ride back to his ship. I was happy to get this mission, because no one would be shooting at me over open water, and because I had never landed on a ship before. It was the perfect little mission, safe and different. I picked up the Navy officer, a lieutenant commander, and his assistant, a chief petty officer. The flight from base out to the destroyer took only a few minutes—about 45 seconds of it over the water. There was a raised helipad at the back of the destroyer with a windsock near it, which enabled us to set up an approach directly into the wind. Nothing to it.

But when I came to a hover over the landing pad and began to set down, all of a sudden my skids touched the pad and we were down. Then a moment later we were hovering. Then we touched again and then back to

The author and a slick. The mud on his boots will wind up on the Navy's carpet.

a hover. "What the hell?" I said to the co-pilot and pulled up to a high hover. At this time the Navy officer leaned over my shoulder and yelled in my ear that the ship was moving up and down in the swell. "Lieutenant, you're going to have to plant this helicopter!" he said. I'd never planted a helicopter before, but at least now I knew what the hell, so down we went until we were touched by the ship in the up-swell and I pushed the collective all the way down and chopped the power. I held the collective down until the spinning rotors lost their lift. "Fine job," said the Navy officer. "How about joining us for lunch? It's that time."

All services were aware that the Navy had superior cuisine, so I accepted this unique invitation with pleasure. The door gunners went off with the CPO to the enlisted mess, and my co-pilot and I followed the lieutenant commander through the spotless corridor of the ship until we got to a door marked "Officers Dining Room."

"After you, gentlemen," said the lieutenant commander and opened the door.

We walked into the room and I could hardly believe my eyes. The floor was covered with a plush blue carpet, and the windows were treated with ornate drapes. The tables had linen tablecloths on them, and on the tablecloths were real plates with the Naval insignia emblazoned in the middle of them. Next to the plates were real knives, forks, spoons and soup spoons. Next to the utensils were linen napkins folded into peaks. There were cups in saucers and stemmed water glasses with ice in them. The lieutenant commander escorted us to a table, and when we sat down I saw the most amazing thing of all. At each place setting there was a menu with three different entrée choices!

I cannot recall what I had for lunch that day with the Navy. I don't even remember if it was extraordinarily delicious. I assume it was. What I do remember is how very out of place I felt, and how embarrassed I was to the point of being ashamed. There were about 20 Naval officers in the dining room, all wearing crisp, perfectly starched and creased white uniforms. Their insignias were polished metal which gleamed, just like their belt buckles. Their shoes were black mirrors. They were clean-shaven, had fresh haircuts and smelled good. Their table manners were impeccable and their table conversation was carried out in subdued tones. My co-pilot and I felt like bums off the street who'd somehow wound up lunching at Delmonico's.

For the past many weeks we had been living in the field. Our jungle boots were caked with dried mud—no doubt some of it now dropped onto the blue carpet. Our uniforms were rumpled and filthy. Our insignias were made of cloth, my white bars more gray than white. But worst of all, we stunk, badly. I hadn't known just how badly until I smelled myself sitting in the air-conditioned dining room of the USS *Whatever*. I recall keeping my upper arms as close to my body as possible to try to contain the stink. I did the same with my legs. The lunch was an embarrassing nightmare.

I also recall that the Navy officers were not particularly friendly. Courteous and impersonally polite, but not friendly. No one asked us about our lives in the war, the missions we flew, and the living conditions. Forget the last one. The living conditions must have been obvious. Perhaps these Navy guys were embarrassed, or shocked, to see fellow officers—pilots, no less—looking like we did. "Is he really a first lieutenant?" they must have thought. "How come he smells like a pig?" Or maybe they were embarrassed and then intimidated in some convoluted, macho kind of a way. They would never be in any danger on that ship, and seeing us had to drive home the point that they had little to complain about regarding their tour in the Vietnam War. I'll never know, of course—and speaking of convoluted, I was glad to get off the ship. That immaculate, safe, culture-shocking vessel floating a mere half-mile off shore was just too much to bear.

An infantry extraction from an elephant grass LZ. They'll be happy campers back at the An Khe base. Living in the field really does suck.

Another ancillary mission we flew was called a psychological warfare mission, "Psy-war" for short. Two huge speakers were loaded in the back of my Huey slick. They were placed pointing out and down from both sides of the ship. Accompanying the speakers was an ARVN officer and a G-2 (intelligence) officer from our Army. This officer, a captain, understood the Vietnamese language. The ARVN carried a piece of paper, which turned out to be a script he would read when we got to our destination. The U. S. captain gave us a copy of it in English.

When everyone was settled in we took off and flew about 20 minutes to a small town (hamlet) nestled at the base of a mountain range. This range and the one across from it were separated by a wide valley of open fields, farmhouses, rice paddies and palm groves. The valley was the shortest route from our newest field location to the current fighting the Cav was engaged in. The problem, as the psy-war captain explained it, was that every time our helicopters would fly down this valley and past the hamlet below us, they would receive small arms fire. He said that nobody'd been hit yet, it was probably just two or three old guys who couldn't shoot straight, but one day they might get lucky. I asked why we didn't simply take them out with gunships, and he explained that the Army wanted to try something new—give the Viet Cong sympathizers a chance to change their ways. The Army thought it would be good P.R. here in the mountains. "Show the locals we don't really want to kill them, we just want them to behave," he said.

A moment or so later, sure enough, we saw a flame and a puff of smoke came from a window of one of the hooches. Over the intercom I told the psy-war captain that somebody just took a shot at us. I was not concerned as we were above that magic number of 1500 feet. The psy-war officer told me to continue flying past the hamlet for about two minutes, and then to circle back and fly over it again. We did this, and near the edge of town the Vietnamese soldier started broadcasting his message. I followed along in English: "Please do not shoot at the helicopters as they pass by. They will not harm you; we are here to assure you of that."

Poof. Another puff of smoke. We kept on flying over the town until we were well beyond it and then circled back to over fly it again. "I am serious about this," continued the ARVN. "If you keep shooting at the helicopters the Americans will destroy your village. They do not want to do that."

Poof. Poof.

We circled back. "Please listen. We are not here to harm you. Neither are the other helicopters that fly over you. Do not shoot at us or we will have no choice but to destroy your village. This is your last chance."

Poof, poof, poof. Three shots this time. The ARVN had followed his script word for word. It must have been assumed it would do no good.

Over the intercom the American captain told me to dial in the frequency of an air force Phantom fire team. The message: Spook Six says to proceed with Mission Valley Pest. He then told me to circle over the mountain range to the west, as the fighters would be coming up from the south.

In about five minutes the two Phantoms came up the valley—throttles full forward. On the first pass they raked the village with their .20mm cannons. On the second pass they dropped 750-pound bombs. Direct hits. One more pass and they laid down napalm. The hamlet was a smoldering memory.

"Well, we tried," said the psy-war guy. "Let's go home, Lieutenant."

That night I reflected on this bizarre mission and, frankly, I had a feeling of pride in being an American. Yes, the hamlet was destroyed and maybe a bunch of people were killed. Or maybe none had been silenced. They had

had plenty of time to scurry up the jungle-covered mountain before the fighters showed up. In any case, at least we warned them. Had other armies done that in the past? I didn't know, but I didn't think so. I sincerely felt that we were good guys. We turned the other cheek, three times, before we let them have it.

One day our mission was to fly into a ravine halfway up the side of a mountain. The team consisted of three Huey slicks. We were to be met by a platoon of ARVN soldiers who were accompanied by a U.S. Special Forces advisor. I was given his radio frequency and was told to contact him when we got close to his location. So far, routine—but we were also told to be sure our gas masks were in good working order, and if they weren't, to get one that was. I hadn't heard that before.

We found the ARVN unit with no problem, and after we landed, the Special Forces advisor came up to the window of my ship and told us our mission. His ARVN platoon had located a cave, which contained the bodies of 20 Vietnamese soldiers who'd been killed and tossed into it many weeks before. He told us they must be transported to a processing area so they could then be sent home to their families. He said the problem was the stench. It was unbelievable, and he hoped we were told to bring our gas masks. Without them, he said, we would never be able to accomplish this mission.

Back in the States we had been told that sometimes the heat in Vietnam was almost unbearable. I never found this to be true. Hot, yes, but not unbearable. Unbearable was Alabama in August. What they didn't tell us was how cold it could get. Once, at An Khe, we were scrambled in the middle of the night. Our mission was to fly to the top of a mountain and extract an infantry platoon. They had been walking in the rain for days, and were thoroughly soaked, and that night it got so cold on the mountain they were literally in danger of freezing to death. When they got on board their teeth were chattering and their lips were blue. I told the door gunners to shut the side doors to protect the soldiers from the wind. It's the only time I flew with the back doors closed. Vietnam was one surprise after another.

CHAPTER 18

There Is No Time

WHETHER AT AN KHE OR in the field, when not flying missions we pilots had few other duties. During the day, time on the ground was spent reading, writing letters, playing cards, playing volleyball (An Khe only) or just hanging around. Because the Cav was never in a safe area, seeing the local sights, if any, was out of the question.

Time on the ground after dark was spent drinking. I drank a lot in Vietnam, beer and vodka mostly. Beer was so cheap it was practically free, and vodka didn't cost much more. Beer was always available, even in the field camps. The Army was good about that. Mixers for the vodka were often in short supply, however, so I developed a taste for vodka and Kool Aid. Kool Aid was always there for the asking. Ice was frequently a problem, but I adjusted. The use of drugs would become a big issue in the war as the years went by, but not during my time. I did not see any drug use, not even marijuana. We just drank, and that was fine.

I couldn't tell you how many missions I flew under the influence of alcohol. Dozens for sure. I do not mean to the point of being drunk. That would have been irresponsible and stupid. I mean two or three drinks under the influence, to the point where if a Breathalyzer test had been issued, I would probably have flunked (at least by today's standards).

Paradoxically, my drinking and the drinking of many of my fellow pilots probably saved lives. On any number of occasions we would be called out at night to fly a medevac mission. Medevac missions were not planned, of course; they were always emergencies. If one or more soldiers had just been wounded, it was obvious there was fighting taking place at that location. So to medevac them to safety meant coping with a hot LZ. The booze, frankly, bolstered the nerves.

But even more dangerous than a hot LZ (Hueys can take lots of hits without being disabled) were the tight LZs. For instance, an infantry unit moving through the jungle took wounded. The soldiers then carried the wounded to an opening in the trees and declared it to be an LZ. Then they called for the helicopters. In the panic of being in a firefight and having wounded men, the infantry sometimes used the term LZ for an opening that Harry Houdini couldn't have gotten in and out of. So we slick pilots had to do the best we could. We would come to a hover over the opening in the jungle canopy and then gingerly begin to descend down into it. We would now be relying on our door gunners, more than ourselves, to determine if we would "fit." The door gunners were connected to the helicopters by a metal wire attached to their harness. This enabled them to lean way out of the chopper, without falling out, and observe the tail rotor. To clip a tail rotor on anything was much more devastating than chopping some leaves with the main rotor blades. All exterior lights were kept on, including the landing light and search light, which could be pointed all around and had the luminescence of floodlights. Their light helped us gingerly navigate through the trees. (It also made a great target.)

After we got to the jungle floor and loaded the wounded, we'd have to hover back up through the hole. This was hairy, precise flying. We pilots could not be ordered to land, even by a general, if we determined the LZ was unsafe. We were a crew of four men and often had a medic on board to tend the wounded we'd be picking up. It was strictly the aircraft commander's decision whether to risk those 5 lives. But the combination of the pleas from the ground troops and the vodka and Kool Aid usually won out, and we would slowly, slowly, slowly go in and then slowly, slowly, slowly come back out. I've wondered over the years how many men are alive today because some Huey pilot had had a few drinks.

Although based in the field, my team had not had a mission in two days. We had written all the letters we could think to write and all the books were read. Hard to believe you could get bored in a war zone, but we were coming up on it. Then we got a call.

This mission would be a routine ammunition resupply, but there was some urgency to it in that the American company we'd be flying to had been in a protracted fight the night before and was almost out of ordnance. We would also be picking up a KIA (Killed in Action). The unit was about 10 miles north of us in the Bong Son Valley. There were two Hueys in the team. We cranked them up and flew a couple hundred yards to the ammo dump

A safe LZ. An infantry "Pathfinder" shows us where to put down.

where they were waiting for us. The ground personnel quickly loaded my ship and my wingman's with metal boxes of .30 caliber rounds, grenades, and other ammunition. We were then set to go. When the engine got back up to full rpm I pulled up on the collective, but the helicopter stayed on the ground. "Shit, we're too heavy," I said to the co-pilot.

There is a technique that can sometimes be used in these instances. It is called the "running take-off." If you can get the helicopter "light" on its skids, even though you're still mostly touching the ground, and if you have a long smooth area in front of you, you can take off pretending you're an airplane. Get the skids light, inch the cyclic forward and the helicopter will start sliding across the ground. If you can do this, eventually you'll be going fast enough over the ground until the main rotor head takes on its airfoil roll. You'll reach transition and into the air you will go. Although I'd never done this in actual conditions, I was by now so confident in my prowess as a Huey pilot I decided to try it. I had a good 300 feet of smooth dirt in front of me, and the American outfit needed all the ammunition it could get. So we started forward and were gaining speed nicely, and about the time we ran out of smooth dirt we broke ground. Nothing to it.

Then I noticed a low, wide, shed-like structure directly in front of us. It had solid wooden sides and a metal roof. Shit! Because of a garbage pile on one side of it and some trees on the other, the only thing I could now do was go over it. I couldn't stop and set down—below us were large boulders—and I couldn't come to a hover because we were too heavy. Right and left wouldn't work either; we were in a ravine.

Our ascending angle of attack had us hitting the shed with the toes of the skids about one foot below the roof line, so one half of a second before we slammed into it, I popped the cyclic back. That popped the Huey higher in the air, and over the shed we went, the bottom of our skids gently scraping the tin roof. This little maneuver got us over the shed, but it cost us air speed and we momentarily quit flying. But luck was on our side: The ground dropped off just beyond the shed, giving us more air to go through. We started gaining air speed, again reached transition, and slowly staggered into the sky.

"Holy shit," I said and looked over at my co-pilot, who was ashen. I then radioed back to my wingman and told him to dump some of his ammo boxes. "You don't need a rat fuck take-off like we just had," I said.

"I'll roger that," he replied, laughing.

Because he was now lighter, my wingman caught up with me in a few minutes and we "formed up." Helicopters always flew in formation, the configuration of the formation being determined by the team leader keeping the particular mission in mind. Our formations were tight, usually not more than 20 feet of air space separating the tips of the rotor blades. In the Cav we took pride in tight, precise formations. It spelled professionalism. From time to time we would hear stories of hot shots flying formation with rotor blades actually overlapping. This caused more than one fatal accident, and the practice was outlawed by most units. I only did it once—just to say I did. Boys will be boys, and boys can be very foolish.

When we were five minutes from the LZ, I contacted the ground unit and told them our location. They started looking for us—they'd probably hear us first—and when they made visual contact they called to tell us they were "popping smoke." When flying to troops who were constantly on the move, finding them often posed a challenge. Seeing the smoke was how helicopters pinpointed their exact destination. The ground troops carried smoke canisters which contained a powder. There were five colors—blue, white, green, red, and yellow. When the top of the canister was popped, like a grenade, the powder was ignited and the smoke would billow out. The ground troops didn't tell the helicopter pilots what color smoke was going to be popped, for a very good reason. The VC could sometimes monitor our radio transmissions, and if they were in the same area and heard yellow smoke was going to be popped, they would quickly pop yellow smoke. The pilots might see the VC smoke instead of the friendlies and fly to it, and then be ambushed. This happened more than once.

In front of us, and off to the right, we saw green smoke. "I have green smoke," I transmitted. "Roger," replied the unit's radioman. "Green smoke." (The smoke served another valuable purpose as it showed the wind direction on the ground. If practical, it's best to land a helicopter into the wind. This day it was not practical.)

The radioman went on: "Thank God you're here. We're down to our last few rounds!" He told us they were in contact with the enemy and that we should come in low and fast because the VC were in the tree line just west of them. "They are shooting at us now!" he yelled. He was scared, and we were going into the middle of a fight without gunship support. Now I was scared.

Technically we did not have to go in until gunships arrived, but even if they were available they were at least ten minutes away, back at the camp we'd just come from. The radio operator saying they were in trouble took the technicality out of it anyway. We dropped to the deck about a quarter of a mile before the LZ and did what the private on the radio told us to do: went in low and fast. When we came within range of the tree line to the west I told our left side door gunners to spray it. They opened up and we flew to the green smoke, skids just a few feet above the ground. We landed as close as we could to the tree line on the right, which was where the U.S. troops were bivouacked.

"Stop firing," I said.

My door gunner told me that we had been taking fire until a few seconds ago. I told him, and the other ship's door gunner, that if they saw more fire coming at us to return it, but not to use all of their ammunition because we had to have some left for the take-off. Our infantry, too, had been laying down fire on the tree line as we approached. But that now stopped. Perhaps they had expended the last of their rounds to cover us.

Upon landing we backed off our throttles to idle, and the soldiers came running from the tree line and started unloading the ammo. The right side door gunners were helping them. The left side door gunners again opened up with another five-second burst. "They started to shoot again, sir!"

As the last of the ordnance was removed from our ships the infantry radio operator called to say his captain needed to talk to me and to please wait. In a few moments the captain got on the radio. "Dog Fight, this is Bandit 6, I've got a problem here. I've got to move my unit out of this loca-

Approaching a hot LZ at dusk. The squiggles on the photo are enemy tracers. (The pucker factor just hit "10.")

tion now." He told me he had two WIAs (wounded in action) and couldn't move fast enough carrying them. He asked if I would please wait a couple minutes so his medics could tend to them, getting them ready for transport. The left door gunner punched off another five seconds from his M-60 as Bandit 6 continued. I could hear the panic in his voice. "I know this isn't part of your mission but I need your help!"

Of course we had no choice. We would do whatever we had to do to help him. My fear level, however, was now approaching terror. We were the VCs' number one target. My two helicopters were positioned directly between them and the American company, and we were completely in the open. I had the clearest image of a bullet smashing through the left side of my helmet. I could practically see it coming. I crouched lower in my seat, giving them less head and more leg to shoot at, and said, "Roger, Bandit, but please hurry it up. We are sitting ducks."

"Thank you," he said. "You're saving our ass." Again my door gunner let out a five-second burst, and the infantry in front and to the right of us, newly rearmed, also started shooting again.

It seemed like an hour, but was no doubt only a few minutes, when we saw from our right the troops carrying one of the wounded soldiers out of the tree line. He looked to be unconscious, his head wrapped in bloody gauze. They placed him on my wingman's ship which was directly behind us. Another group now came toward our ship carrying the other WIA. His shirt was off and he had a huge bandage over his chest which was also full of blood. His eyes were open but glazed over.

Lastly, from the tree line, came the soldiers slowly and reverently carrying the body of the KIA, their faces reflecting their anguish and disbelief. He was a large kid, and the muscles on the arms of the soldiers carrying him were bulging under the strain. One of them, the biggest, had tears running down his face. His chin was quivering. When the body was placed on the helicopter floor he briefly paused and put his hand on the dead soldier's head, and then he completely broke down. One of the other soldiers put an arm around him and guided him back into the trees.

It was then I realized there had been no shooting from either side since the first wounded soldier was carried out. The only sounds had been the low, deep rumble of the slowed down rotor blades and the soft whine of the engines. Sounds of sadness.

Some of the American troops were gathered at the tree line. They were standing at attention as the bodies of the dead and wounded were being secured to the floor of the helicopters. They were paying their last respects as best they could.

I turned in my seat to watch so I would know when to throttle back up and take off. But I was no longer in a hurry. My fear, like the shooting, had mysteriously gone away.

It was then that I saw something, felt something, that has been with me ever since. In that softly idling Huey I saw, and felt, time cease to exist. It was like I'd become part of the cosmos, part of eternity—at one with the living, the dying, and the dead. I was enveloped by peace.

I do not know how long I was in this psychic state, surely no more than a minute, and even while in it I was aware that I was hallucinating. The feeling was no doubt prompted by the fact that we living, dying and dead all looked the same. We were all young men and we were dressed identically—same shirts, pants, belt buckles, helmets, and boots. I recall staring at the dead soldier's boots and hearing them say, "It could be you in these boots and it wouldn't matter. We're not going anywhere, really."

The door gunners finished strapping down the two soldiers and nodded to me that they were secure. I turned back around in my seat and brought the engine and rotor blades back up to full rpm. It was time to leave.

Before we lifted off I told the door gunners to hold their fire unless they were sure we were being shot at. Something told me we would not be. I pulled up on the collective, pushed the cyclic forward, and we smoothly ascended. When we got to 200 feet I turned back to fly over the friendly position which was the shortest route to the nearest MASH. I looked down to see the fighting had begun again—but not one shot was fired at us.

I would like to think that the Viet Cong quit shooting at us while we were on the ground when we made the transition from being a resupply helicopter to a flying ambulance and hearse. I would also like to think that's why they didn't shoot at us when we took off. I don't really think that, but I'd like to, and maybe it's true. If there were ever two helicopters that could have been shot up coming out of an LZ, it was us.

After a few minutes of flying my wingman radioed to say he thought his WIA looked like he was dying and suggested we fly at red line (top speed). My left door gunner then said over the intercom, "I think this one's dying, too, sir." So we put the helicopters on their noses, and the airspeed dials went past the red lines, but it didn't do any good. When we got to the MASH, three KIAs were removed from our ships.

Of all the missions I flew in Vietnam, this is the one I think of most often. Not because it was more dangerous than most, and not because of the closeness to death. These factors did not make this mission unique. Rather it was that brief glimpse into what I felt was another reality, that the living and the dead were sharing the same existence. The soldier's boots spoke to me that day, and sometimes I can still hear them. "We're still here," say the boots. "I know," I say back to them.

Every combat veteran has a right to a little post-traumatic, isolated psychosis, and as far as I can tell this is the only one that lingers with me. Whenever I wish, I can return to the Bong Son Valley and relive the feeling of oneness with the dead. Shrinks would call this "survivor's guilt," coupled with rationalization and denial. Religious people would say it's one more proof of a hereafter. I don't know what it is ... but I like it.

A few years ago I was given a biography of Albert Einstein. In it was a quote that I read over and over. When I first read it, it shocked me, and then it pleased me no end. Einstein said: "The distinction between past, present and future is only an illusion, however persistent." So seeing—feeling—time cease to exist may not have been as hallucinatory as I once thought. It was heartening to read that my psychosis was in good company—the company of a genius.

I have often thought how nice life on earth would be if I could hold on to the feeling that time, as we perceive it, doesn't exist. How pleasant it would have been to have finished the war and the rest of life in a metaphysical state of simply "being," where dying didn't matter because there was no such thing—really. But this is not the case.

You'd think that someone who experienced what I did in that idling helicopter would be somehow different. I am not. I am as reluctant to die as the next guy. There is simply too much more to do. There's a business to run and a fortune yet to be made. There are seven irons to be hit and dogs to be walked. There's family and friends to love and cherish and people who need help. There are more laughs to be had, more books to write and, at the end of the day, there's Scotch and soda, tall, with a twist.

Using mathematical calculations, spawned by quantum physics, Einstein reasoned it out in his mind. In that helicopter in the rice paddy, I saw it with my own eyes, and felt it in my heart—time is merely an illusion. So how come I still want all I can get?

Better make it a double.

CHAPTER 19

Infusion and Disneyland

BY THE END OF JANUARY 1967 the Christmas Truce was long forgotten and my stomach was back to normal after the rabies shots. The Cav was engaged in numerous battles throughout the Highlands, with casualties of both infantry and helicopter crews higher than usual. Although real numbers were impossible to come by, you could feel it. It was at this time that I learned a new word: "infusion." We were informed by battalion headquarters that the Army's brain trust in Saigon had developed a plan to balance out the combat experience level of its helicopter pilots in the various units throughout South Vietnam. Those of us with six months or more of time in country were considered experienced combat veterans. So we experienced pilots were now being offered the opportunity to volunteer to be reassigned from our unit to another unit. In other words I could, if I wanted to, get out of the Cav. After reading the infusion form it took me about 20 seconds to make my decision. I was out of there.

My decision was based on two factors that I was certain were accurate. One, no matter where they sent me the danger level would have to be less than in the First Cav. Two, no matter where they sent me, the living conditions could hardly be worse than in the First Cav. We were now spending almost all of our time in the field. On the bottom of the form, and this was a big plus, you could list units to which you did or did not want to be assigned. I did not know where I wanted to go, but I knew where I didn't want to go, and that was to the Ninth Infantry Division. I wrote this down. Then I signed the form and turned it in.

The reason I did not want to go to the Ninth was because it had come

First Lieutenant Joe Mulheran (Minnesota) with a gunship. He landed one, without a tail rotor, going 60 m.p.h. Joe was the best.

to Vietnam en masse just a few weeks before, from Fort Riley, Kansas. That meant there would be a preponderance of inexperienced combat pilots. Also, the Ninth was stationed at Bearcat, halfway between Saigon and Vung Tao in the Delta region of the country. I had heard that the weather in the Delta was beastly hot. Also, the Delta was as flat as Kansas. I believed it was safer to have mountains to fly around, and lots of palm groves to fly over at treetop level, rather than across totally featureless terrain. Naturally there were no mountains in the Delta, and I'd heard there were very few trees. In my mind the Delta was one huge rice paddy offering no natural protection. On all missions the helicopters would be wide-open targets.

Another reason I didn't want to join the Ninth was because I had been in contact with my flight school buddy, Joe Mulheran. He had been flying in the Delta for six months and had already been shot down five times! One of those times he had his tail rotor shot off but was still able to land safely. He kept flying fast enough so that his forward motion kept the helicopter's fuselage pointed straight. This counteracted the principle "For every action..." generated by the force of his spinning main rotors. He flew back to his base, which had a dirt runway for fixed wing aircraft. He came in fast, 60 miles per hour, and put the skids gently on the surface, cut the power, and slid to a stop. An incredible piece of flying. Even before this happened I had said often that Joe was the best pilot I knew. (He went with Northwest Airlines after the war.)

So I thought I made it very clear on the infusion form that my volunteering to infuse was contingent upon *not* being assigned to the Ninth. A captain in headquarters assured me my wishes would be honored. I felt very good about my decision. Yes, I would miss a few of the guys in the unit, but none of us had become fast friends or lifelong-buddies-to-be. So the missing would be short lived. What I would not miss was the constant action, the interminable stays in the field and the isolation of An Khe. South Vietnam was a real country with real cities. An Khe was nothing but a hamlet in the middle of the mountains.

It only took three days for my new orders to be cut and returned to me. I was in the tent at An Khe when the orders were delivered by the company clerk. I excitedly opened the envelope, and a few of the guys gathered around. The orders: Lieutenant James T. Joyce is hereby reassigned from the First Air Cavalry Division at An Khe to the Ninth Infantry Division at Bearcat. Report in three days. Transportation arrangements will follow.

"The bastards!" I said.

"What?" the guy next to me said and looked over my shoulder to see what I had just read. "Joyce has been assigned to the Ninth!" he called out and everybody laughed. "Joyce," said Hal Trout from Missouri, "Didn't your momma tell you never to volunteer in this man's Army?"

"Fuck you, Hal," I said, and now everyone was positively gleeful. I had been the only one in the tent to volunteer to infuse and I suppose this caused resentment. We were hardly family, but we were a team, sort of. But too late now, the deal was done and when I complained to the HQ captain who told me my wishes would be honored he just shrugged his shoulders, said he was sorry but there was nothing he could do about it. He then mumbled something about it being stupid to volunteer, anyway. I was off to the Delta, like it or not.

Writing about the First Cav wouldn't be complete without telling you about Disneyland. Disneyland was the nickname for the United States Army–sponsored compound for prostitution, which was located outside the camp's main entrance. It must have had a real name if the Army created it, but I never heard it. Disneyland consisted of approximately 20 buildings built side by side out of concrete block. The walls touched each other. The compound was rectangular and all of the doors to the buildings faced an open courtyard. There were no back doors to these buildings and only one way in and out of the courtyard. Army MPs guarded the entryway. Although Disneyland was outside of the Cav base camp, it was considered secure during the day. It was closed at night. All of the 20 buildings were the same type establishment, a combination bar and whorehouse. Only the signs over the entrances distinguished one from another: "Nooky Heaven," "Pussy Cat Inn," "Playboy East," "Honey Moons," etc. You get the picture.

Up to this point my only association with Disneyland was from the cockpit of a helicopter. There were many different approach paths for landing at the Golf Course, and one of them was directly over Disneyland. It was the shortest route in when approaching from the southwest. We would contact the tower and tell them our call sign and location and say, "Request Disneyland approach."

"Roger, Disneyland," the tower would say. "Clear to land."

We'd then come in low and slow over the compound, and the soldiers and the girls in the courtyard would scatter and run for cover, because they knew that one of the helicopter door gunners would probably drop a smoke canister. It became a tradition, and it was fun. It was fun for us to watch the people scatter and fun for them to be scattered, and it gave the soldiers a chance to give pilots the finger. A harmless diversion. But wouldn't you know that one day one of the young women—she must have been new—ran out of a building instead of into one and the canister hit her on the head. Although the canisters were light, she must have been hit by an edge, because stitches were required. It didn't take 24 hours for the order to come down from Division Command that there would be no more approaches to the Golf Course over Disneyland. This was a typical Army response—safety first.

On the day after my orders for the Ninth came through, I decided my education would be sorely lacking if I didn't go to Disneyland. The concept of a whorehouse established, sponsored, protected and ministered to by the United States Army really did boggle the mind. Our own 227th Battalion flight surgeons gave weekly, mandatory physicals (blood tests) to the young women. I had to see it.

One of the guys in the tent, Arnie Slade* from Texas, was a regular visitor to Disneyland whenever we were back at An Khe. He was always inviting me to go with him, and until now I had declined. But this day was different. I asked Arnie if he was going to Disneyland after lunch. He said he was and would buy me "a piece of tail" for a going away present. I told Arnie that was not what I had in mind, I just wanted to see it. "Sure, Joyce, sure. But wait 'til you see them VC women. You'll change your mind real fast."

So after lunch Arnie and I walked across the Cav base camp, out the main gate, and into the Disneyland compound. Arnie explained that all the bars were the same so I could take my pick. I chose Playboy East and we walked into it. I must admit I was nervous and never would have gone there alone, U.S. Army sanctioned or not.

The room was dark and it took awhile to focus after coming in from the bright sunlight. Arnie led me to a back booth along the side wall and we sat down. I gazed around the place and as my eyes adjusted it took on a familiar feel. Along the far wall was the bar with liquor bottles lined up behind the bartender. Laminated on the mirrors were the familiar logos of Budweiser, Miller and Schlitz. A fake Tiffany lamp hung over the Vietnamese bartender's head. There were booths along both walls and tables and chairs in the middle of the room, and in the far corner was a pool table. It looked no different from thousands of neighborhood taverns all across the U.S., with two exceptions.

First exception: Sitting all around this neighborhood tavern were young Vietnamese women wearing high heels, fish net stockings and mini-dresses with plunging necklines.

Second exception: There was a door between the bar and the pool table. Arnie said that was where you took the women. There were rooms with beds in them behind the door.

Before coming to Vietnam I had heard it said often that the Vietnamese women were the most beautiful women in Asia. So far, after being in country six months, I would have questioned that. The only Vietnamese women I had seen, up close, were the mama-sans who did our laundry. They were not beautiful to me. They sported few teeth and betel juice stained chins. The peasants working in the rice paddies couldn't really be seen looking down at their conical hats from a helicopter. So I was stunned when I looked around the place to see these cameo-faced young women with their small, perfectly proportioned bodies and their long, straight, silky, jet-black hair. "I could be in trouble," was my first thought.

Arnie asked me what I wanted to drink and I told him a bottle of Bud. He went up to the bar to get it and when he returned to our booth he had four bottles of Bud in his hands—one for me, one for himself, and one for each of the two young women he brought with him. They were beautiful. They were also giggling. Arnie took charge. "Lia, you sit there next to Lieutenant Jim. Li Li you sit by me." He placed the four beer bottles around the table.

Arnie sat down and explained to me that for $20 I could take Lia in the back room. Or if I wanted Li Li instead, I could have her. He'd treat either way. He asked me which one I wanted. I told Arnie that I appreciated the offer but I really wasn't interested. All I wanted to do was drink. "Suit yourself," said Arnie. " Li Li, baby, let's go!" And Arnie and Li Li headed for the door between the bar and the pool table.

I was now alone with Lia. I took a long swig of the Bud and Lia took a sip of hers. She was looking at me and I noted her hand was resting on my leg. High up on my leg. "GI think I'm pretty?" she asked as her hand moved. "Yes," I said, "You are pretty." Then she asked me if I'd like to "boom-boom" her.

"Excuse me?" I said.

"Boom-boom me. Fuck-fuck me. GI want fuck-fuck me?" she said, giggling.

I don't know why I was shocked to hear this blunt question but I was. I guess it was because no one had ever asked me that before. I took a long drink of the Bud. "No, thank you," I said. "Maybe later."

Her fingers moved higher.

"Lia, I just want to drink beer for awhile and talk to you. Wouldn't that be OK?"

"No, OK. Bye, bye, GI Jim, I no make money when I talk."

She stood up, took her bottle of beer and walked over to a sergeant who'd just sat down at the bar. He was glad to see her. He cupped her buttocks with his hands and pulled her toward him. She put her arms around his neck and kissed him.

In my ear I felt hot breath as sweet perfume engulfed me. "GI like boom-boom me?"

I looked up to see an Asian goddess. "No, thank you," I said, "I'm just drinking." She left in an exaggerated huff.

I went up to the bar, ordered two beers and took them back to the booth. I was barely seated when another young woman slid in across from me. She was coming out of the top of her dress. She leaned toward me and said, "You want fuck-fuck me?"

"No thank you," I said.

"I give you number one blow job, GI. You like?"

"No thanks," I said. "I just want to drink." She left, acting like she was hurt. I don't think she was.

I downed the two beers and got two more and was not approached again by any of the dozen or so women in the club. I guess the word got around that the guy in the back booth was a drink-drinker and not a fuck-fucker.

Then Arnie came through the door with Li Li right behind him. He came to the booth, and she went to sit with other young women at a table near the bar. He asked me what I was doing sitting there with all the beautiful women around. Again I told him I was not interested in getting laid. I was just simply going to sit there and get drunk. "It's my last day with the Cav. That deserves a drunk, doesn't it, Arnie?" Again he told me to suit myself and said he needed to go see a buddy of his over at Honey Moons. He'd come back and check on me later.

In the booth, by myself, I began, as solitary drinkers do, to think about my life and to try to get some perspective on it—some game plan, something to look forward to. I was making little progress. There was a war going on and I was in the middle of it, in the middle of my time in it. Tomorrow I'd be leaving for the goddamned Delta, which would probably be more dangerous than flying with the Cav. I thought of the guys I'd met, other pilots, who were now dead. I saw in my mind the dead soldiers and the wounded soldiers, and I heard the screams on the radios, "We need help now!" The Delta would produce more of the same. Six months of the same. Six months is an eternity. There was nothing to look forward to.

Usually, with a few beers things began to look brighter. It wasn't happening today. I switched from beer to vodka and ordered two doubles. My life was not real. I downed the drinks and ordered two more.

It was sometime into the sixth vodka when Arnie came back from Honey Moons. He ordered up another Li Li and took her through the door, promising he'd not be long. I got two more doubles.

That afternoon in Disneyland set my lifetime record for alcohol consumption. I do not remember leaving the place or getting back to the base.

It was the middle of the night when I woke up. I was on my cot in the tent, fully dressed and still in my boots, but the mosquito netting was tucked in all around me. My buddy Arnie Slade must have taken care of me. A few of the guys were gently snoring and one was quietly jacking off. I went back to sleep. In the morning I would board a Caribou for my trip to the Delta, never to see An Khe again.

Within one month after I left the Cav, two of the guys I shared the tent with were killed. One of them got word on his radio, just after take-off from the Golf Course, that he was the father of a baby girl, his first child. That was also the night he died.

I felt then, and I feel today, that had I stayed in the Cav I, too, would have been killed. Getting killed in the Cav had become too commonplace, too expected, too "normal." When we learned that a helicopter crewmember had been killed, our attitude was not quite "So what else is new?" but it wasn't far enough from it. The news no longer had shock value.

So I was going to the Ninth, and as much as I bitched about it, I was secretly glad it was happening. Change, any kind of change, was called for if I was to survive Vietnam. This I believed to my bones.

Whenever I have been asked over the years what I did in Vietnam, I simply say that I flew helicopters with the First Cav. To those who know about the Vietnam War, that statement says it all.

CHAPTER 20

Saigon

ON THE WAY TO THE NINTH Infantry Division we had a one-night layover in Saigon, 260 miles south of An Khe. There were four of us helicopter pilots traveling together who infused from the Cav and were bound for the Ninth. Lieutenant Bill Allen from Delta Company 227, who was a gunship pilot; Captain Ed Chastain* from the 229th, a slick pilot; and Lieutenant Zack Hatfield*, also a slick pilot from the 229th, rounded out the foursome.

For the trip we had been issued TDY (Temporary Duty) pay and unanimously decided to blow it, and then some, by staying at a fancy hotel. We took a cab from the US Air Base at Ton San Nhut to an old French hotel on Le Loi Street in downtown Saigon. Captain Chastain had stayed there before and declared it first class. Chastain was raised in Bloomfield Hills, Michigan. He should know first class—and he did.

On the way to the hotel we passed the beautiful Catholic cathedral on Phan Din Phurg Street. I had the 1960s Catholic thought of going to the church after we checked into the hotel to see if I could find a priest to hear my confession, but I dismissed it. Getting blind drunk was a serious sin, but at this time it did not seem so to me. Surely there was a dispensation written somewhere that said it was OK to get shitfaced in a war zone. Also, a confession is probably not valid if the priest and the penitent don't speak the same language.

The hotel lobby was elegantly appointed with a huge crystal chandelier hanging over its center. The Vietnamese working the front desk were warm and polite and spoke perfect English. When we were shown to our rooms we found them to be large and spotless. Each room had a sitting area by the window with a sofa, coffee table, and two wingback chairs. The bed was big and comfortable. In the bathroom was a bathtub and a separate shower. There was also a bidet. There are no bidets on the south side of Chicago, in the dorm rooms at John Carroll, or in Army barracks, so I'd never seen one. Chastain laughed at me when I asked him what it was, and then he explained it. "Oh," I said. We had all the hot water we wanted, and there was a thermostat that individually controlled each room's air conditioning. It was the best hundred bucks I ever spent.

On the roof of the hotel was an open-air restaurant appointed like a garden. It had a 360-degree view of the city. This hotel was where senior journalists, high-ranking military personnel and civilian bureaucrats stayed. They spent their nights in the garden restaurant drinking gin and tonics and watching the war. Bombs and rockets exploding and tracer bullets honing in on targets could clearly be seen in the darkness, just a few miles beyond the city lights.

We four ex–Cav pilots dined on the rooftop that night and enjoyed watching these real fireworks. When I had awakened that morning I had vowed never to drink again, but that was that morning. The recuperative powers of a 24-year-old are amazing. As we sucked down Scotch and sodas served with ice cubes in glasses made of glass, we all agreed this was the way to go to Vietnam. We ate medium rare steaks covered in a fabulous French sauce. The sauce had mushrooms in it. Life in Vietnam could be very good indeed.

After finishing supper we lingered at our table drinking coffee and snifters of Grand Marnier. We poured our own Grand Marnier, Chastain telling the waiter to leave the bottle on the table. A battle was going on that could not have been more than three miles from the city limits. Puff the Magic Dragon had been called in, and we were intrigued watching him work. We'd never seen him before. I will tell you about Puff later; we had a joint mission one night in the Delta.

When the bottle of Grand Marnier was empty Captain Chastain said he'd be pleased to show us Saigon's nightlife. We had been watching the battle and toasting our dead friends. Chastain wisely added that if we sat there much longer we'd all be crying drunk. He said we'd have the rest of our lives to do that if we survived the war. Now we should have some fun.

It turned out the captain had been temporarily assigned to Saigon for three weeks when he first got to Vietnam. He knew every bar and nightclub in town. With Ed as tour guide the four of us leisurely strolled down the streets of the city. The only irritant was that every couple hundred feet we would be approached by young men pedaling pedi-cabs, a form of bicycle taxi. "GI want ride? Take you to nooky bar," they'd say. We declined the ride and the nooky, and before long we all had the same thought: "How come these guys aren't in the Army?" They were the right age and obviously in good

The Vietnamese people were innovative.

shape. It upset us to think of all of the American soldiers getting killed defending Vietnam, while these Vietnamese men were riding their bicycles around Saigon working as pimps.

One of the things that impressed me most about Saigon was how safe we felt. Yes, some entrances to some buildings were sandbagged and guarded by ARVN soldiers, and concertina wire was strung along the tops of some walls. But the streets were full of civilians—Vietnamese, Americans and many other nationalities. In the space of a few blocks I heard Italian, German, and French. And commerce seemed to be in full bloom. The streets were brightly lit; hawkers stood on the sidewalks inviting people into their shops; mopeds, bicycles and cars zipped along the boulevards; fresh fruits and vegetables were in abundance. People chatted away, laughed often and seemed not one bit concerned.

Where was the war? It was someplace else. It was out there—we saw it from the rooftop. It was not in Saigon. I thought of Bob Hope and had to smile. I'd have given anything to have taken Bob on a combat assault into a hot LZ.

We walked and barhopped for hours. The only thing that was slightly unnerving, to me, was that every hundred yards or so I would see a rat dart in and out of the shadows. The sons of bitches were everywhere in Vietnam—but I could get used to every hundred yards or so. "I wonder how you get assigned to Saigon?" I asked as we walked along. "You got to know somebody important," Ed Chastain said. Of course.

When we'd finally had enough walking and drinking we were a long way from our hotel, so we hailed a cab. The driver, about 20 years old, spoke very good English. Bill Allen asked him why he wasn't in the Army. He laughed and said—honest to God—"Oh no, not me. Army too dangerous. Might get shot. I like Saigon."

Our curiosity was now piqued and Bill asked him how it was possible to stay out of the army if someone was young and healthy. Bill asked if Vietnam didn't have a draft for all young men like in the United States. The guy laughed again and said Vietnam did have a draft but it was not for everybody. When we got to the hotel he charged us about five times what he should have and then asked if we would like some nooky. "Girl fuck you in your room," he said. Ed Chastain told him that he should go fuck himself, and we got out of the cab.

We had been told back in the States that the Vietnamese soldiers were poorly trained, lacked discipline and would go out of their way to avoid a fight. This had not been my experience with them. Many times I'd flown combat assault missions for the ARVN and they acted just as aggressive and determined as our soldiers. Granted, my experiences were limited, but those Vietnamese troops that I carried eagerly jumped off the helicopter and charged into the battle.

But this night in Saigon showed me another face of young Vietnamese men. You could make a case for the American draft dodger back in Omaha, but how did someone justify dodging the draft when his own country was under siege? For the first time since learning I was going to Vietnam I could not stop a doubt from creeping up about the validity of our involvement in the war. In the Cav we were thoroughly isolated. Up in the Central Highlands we and the ARVN were the good guys, the VC and the NVA were the bad guys. We fought each other whenever we found each other. It was black and white. But I just heard gray when the driver told us not everybody had to join the Army. Here in civilization, I could feel bribes being paid and deals being cut. The smell of politics and favoritism fouled the air. "You got to know somebody important." I didn't like these thoughts. I'd been comfortable with the black and white of the war. Of course I knew that it wasn't black and white—nothing is—but it made it easier to be there.

Just before I went to sleep in my swanky hotel room I decided to start taking a more active role in looking out for myself. This night in civilization strengthened my resolve to avoid getting killed in Vietnam, thanks in part to the draft-dodging, cab-driving pimps who helped wise me up. If they weren't willing to die for their country, why should I be?

So I made a survival plan. I'd briefly thought of it before and discarded it, but now it was back and I would put it into action when I got to the Ninth Infantry Division the next day. I was going to increase my chances of going home alive. I was going to tell a lie to the Ninth. When I got to my new unit I was going to tell them that I was a gunship pilot. It was time to go on offense.

CHAPTER 21

Welcome to the Ninth

UNLIKE THE FIRST CAV'S BASE CAMP, which was located next to the little town of An Khe, the Ninth Infantry's base camp was located next to nothing. The Army plopped this massive division headquarters about midway between Saigon and the coastal resort town of Vung Tao and gave it the name Bearcat. The closest hamlet was miles away.

My orders were to Delta Troop of the Fifth Cavalry. This was a helicopter outfit whose overall mission was conveniently vague: Do whatever you can to support the infantry troops. Whereas the Cav, in theory, had enough Huey slicks to transport all of the soldiers from an entire brigade at the same time, this was not the case with the Ninth or any other unit in the Army. Helicopters had a large role to play here, but they weren't an integral part of almost every single mission as they were in the Cav. The Cav was helicopters, thus its official name, First "Air" Cavalry Division. In the Cav the helicopters were analogous to the horses of bygone days; now the horses flew.

I presented my orders to my new company commander, Major William Burleson*. Burleson was a big man, over 6' 3", I judged, being 6' myself. He was obviously a weight lifter. There was no body fat. I'd learned earlier that day he was a much-decorated Korean War veteran. He'd been an infantry lieutenant in that war and attended flight school afterwards. His physical size and no-nonsense demeanor were intimidating. He also had the brightest, most piercing eyes I'd ever seen.

"Welcome to Alpha Company, Joyce," he said as he shook (make that crushed) my hand. He told me to have a seat while he looked over my file. He walked behind his desk and picked up a folder. I ventured into the chair across from him. "So you came to us from the Cav, huh?" he said, looking me right in the eyes. "I heard it was rough up there."

"Yes, sir, it was pretty rough," I replied, trying not to look away.

"It's rough here, too," he said. "I don't want you to get the idea that this is going to be an easy assignment."

He asked me why I volunteered to infuse. His eyes, I was glad to see, had gone back to my file. "Frankly, sir," I said as a small laugh escaped, "I didn't think it could get worse than the Cav. I was ready for a change." This, I was about to learn, was the wrong answer.

He looked back at me—make that *through* me—with those eyes. He told me there were just as many VC in the Delta as in the mountains, probably more. If I thought I'd be better off here, then I had made a big mistake when I volunteered to infuse. He hoped I didn't have the attitude that the Cav was somehow better than the Ninth. "Yes, sir," I said. "I mean no, sir."

He returned to flipping through my file. "What did you fly in the Cav, Joyce?"

Here was the question, and although Major Burleson had me intimidated—at least a little bit—I was not going to crumble. My Saigon resolve was holding. If he caught me in the lie I was about to tell, I had a backup lie that I felt would keep me out of Fort Leavenworth, the Army prison. All the while I was reminding myself that the Army, or at least a captain in it, lied to me about winding up with the Ninth Infantry. "I flew gunships, sir."

"Gunships?" he said, still looking at my papers. "It says here you were a D model pilot. D models are slicks, B models are guns."

I explained to him that was usually the case, but in the Cav we had used both D and B models as gunships. I stated that D models were bigger and could carry more ordnance.

He looked up from the papers. I could tell he was skeptical, so I thought my lie could use some rapid reinforcement. I told him the Cav was also using Chinooks as gunships and added that they were pretty independent up there in the Central Highlands.

He got angry. That was exactly what he meant, he said, by an attitude. Just because the Cav experimented with gunships didn't mean they were better than the Ninth or any other unit in Vietnam. If I thought the Ninth was inferior because it was new in country I had another thought coming. He didn't want to hear me mention the damned Cav again.

"Yes, sir," I said, having a hard time not smiling.

He fell for it.

He looked back at my file and said he was going to send me on a mission that night. Because the Ninth didn't have D model gunships, I would be flying as co-pilot with Captain Doug Carpenter*. That way I'd be officially B-model qualified, and I'd have my own fire team after that.

"Any questions?" he asked.

"No, sir," I said as I stood up. "I'm glad to be here." I saluted him, and he returned it without looking up at me. I walked out of his tent. Yes! I was no longer just a target. Now I had become a shooter.

I did not know the actual percentage of casualties—flying slicks versus flying gunships—but I didn't care. I was tired of being a target. I did think guns were probably safer, however, because they never slowed down to a hover and they never landed except to rearm and refuel, and those areas were mostly secure. Also, the VC and NVA were frightened by gunships and rarely picked a fight with them. Too much firepower. Gunships took the battle to the enemy. The enemy took the battle to the slicks—slow approaching, hovering slicks with their cargo of infantry. Knock down a slick and you've killed 12 people, eight of whom were coming to seek you out and destroy you once they got on the ground. (I didn't learn until years later you were exactly twice as likely to die flying in a gunship than a slick.)

I was pretty sure there was something more about me that Burleson didn't like besides the Cav business, and I was certain there was something about him that I didn't like beyond the military tough guy affect. But it didn't matter. I would be one of dozens of pilots under his command, and I would simply avoid him and do my job. But my self-preservation scam still called for more deception. For instance, I had never been in a gunship, so I had no idea how to fire the weapons. The main weapons in gunships were fired by the pilots. The two door gunners only fired their M60 machine guns, which were in the same configuration as on the slicks.

The gunships I would be flying carried fourteen 2.75-inch self-propelled rockets—seven on each side. The Ninth's gunships also had mini-guns, one on each side. The mini-gun fired 7.62mm caliber rounds. The mini-gun resembled the old Gatling gun. It had six barrels which rotated as the rounds went through. But unlike the Gatling gun, which was fired by turning a hand crank, the mini-guns were automated and could fire, at the pilot's discretion, anywhere from 2000 to 6000 rounds per minute. The destructive force was unbelievable. The site for the mini-gun was a rectangular piece of clear plastic with a white dot of light in the middle of it. This site was pulled down from the cockpit ceiling in front of the pilot's face. Wherever the little light appeared to be on the ground is where the bullets landed. Literally pinpoint accuracy.

So I would not only have to learn how to arm the weapons systems and fire them, but also who—the AC or the co-pilot—would shoot what weapon and when. And what targets called for what weapons? Problems, yes, but not anything I couldn't overcome.

After my meeting with the major, I went to my new tent home to unpack and get settled. This tent was the same size as my tent in the Cav (a g.p. medium), but this one was raised about four feet above the ground, sitting on a wooden foundation. It had steps going up to a nice front porch, and it had a back porch, too. The wood was new and clean and smelled good. Only six guys were assigned to the tent, instead of eight, so my personal area was much larger. At the back of the tent there was a small bar painted red with four bar stools in front of it. Behind the bar hung a sign: "The Red Bar Inn." Under the sign was a working refrigerator full of cold pop and beer. Now we're talking living conditions.

I got settled in, met the other guys, and was careful not to talk about the Cav except in vaguaries. I sensed they didn't want to hear about it anyway, which made it easier. Any stories I told about flying in the Cav would have had to be switched around from slicks to guns, and no doubt I'd have slipped up. By the time I met Captain Carpenter and the other six guys I'd be flying with that night, I had figured out how to tell him that I did not know how to arm and fire the weapons of a gunship—me, a First Cav gunship fire team leader, with more than six months' experience in country.

On the flight line, as night approached, I met Captain Carpenter, and he introduced me to his team members, the other two pilots, and the four door gunners. A gunship fire team is almost always two helicopters. We climbed into our seats and strapped in. "Captain," I said, "I am not familiar with the operation of this gun system."

"Really?" he said, turning to look at me. "Major Burleson said you flew guns with the Cav."

I told him I had flown guns in the Cav but they were outfitted with grenade launchers (called hogs) instead of rockets and we had machine guns instead of the new mini-guns. (I think I'm correct in saying that the Ninth was the first unit in Vietnam to have mini-guns on its helicopters.)

"Oh yeah, OK, no problem," he said. He then told me the mini-guns were used just like machine guns and the rockets were much more accurate than the grenade launchers. He'd show me the difference during the mission. He said if we didn't find any Charlie to shoot at we'd find something else. He began flicking switches to start the helicopter, and I smiled to myself. So far my deception was going without a hitch.

Our mission that night was a routine patrol of the Mekong River. The Mekong was the main body of water in the Delta (the Mekong Delta), and it meandered back and forth and up and down, eventually emptying into the South China Sea. The river was used extensively by the Vietnamese people as a thoroughfare to transport people, produce, animals, trade goods, etc. They had wooden boats of every size and description.

The Mekong Delta at twilight as seen from the back of a Huey.

The Mekong was also used extensively by the Viet Cong to move troops, weapons, ammunition, and supplies, especially at night. The river had a dusk to dawn curfew imposed on it for all traffic. Any boat seen on the river at night was assumed to be Viet Cong and was to be destroyed without warning. No exceptions.

When the moon was full, or mostly so, it was no problem to spot river traffic at night while flying at "altitude"—about 1000 feet. When there was not enough light from the moon or the sky was cloudy the gunships flew low—about 100 feet, using their searchlights to scan the water's surface. The Mekong River was hundreds of miles long, so completely patrolling it to keep it clear of traffic was impossible, but any boats sunk were a plus for our side.

This night it was cloudy, so we used the search light method. We didn't shine the lights constantly, of course, because the VC would see us coming a mile away, enabling them plenty of time to get to shore and hide under the overhanging trees. So we shone the lights sporadically: on, off, on, off.

We had been flying for about an hour when our wingman, who was a few hundred yards behind us, radioed that he had just caught sight of a long, narrow, covered boat. He had flown over the top of it, so he hadn't had time to shoot. We, obviously, had flown over it a few seconds before.

"Rattlesnake Six,"—that was Carpenter's call sign—"it is heading north. There were people on deck. The door gunner saw rifles in their hands," said the wingman, Rattlesnake Five.

"Roger that. Attack formation," said Rattlesnake Six.

I'd like to tell you I remained calm hearing all of this, but I didn't. My heartbeat picked up and the adrenalin rush kicked in. My first time in a gunship and I was about to get into a fight. I had been flying the helicopter, but the captain now took the controls and began a steep, climbing turn to the right. He leveled off at 1000 feet and told me to take the controls back. He armed the weapons and pulled down the mini-gun site. The rockets were aimed by pointing the nose of the helicopter directly at the targets. They were encased in pods that didn't move. The mini-guns were on swivels and had a good range of motion.

Carpenter said that in the Delta, "gun runs" start at 1,000 feet. He asked what altitude we used in the mountains. "The same," I said, knowing a rhetorical question when I heard one. I noticed his voice was calm. He asked if I saw the outline of the river, and I told him I did. He said the target should be somewhere in front of us. He told me to point the nose down to begin the attack.

I pointed the helicopter's nose at the middle of the river, and our gun run now began. Carpenter opened up with the mini-guns. We were gaining speed rapidly in our dive but we had yet to see the boat. He punched off two rockets but then quit shooting. We pulled out of our dive about 50 feet over the water. "I see him!" said the left door gunner over the intercom and opened up with his machine gun, but too late. We were past the river and climbing back up. Carpenter asked the door gunner how far away the boat was. "About 200 yards," the door gunner replied.

"Rattlesnake Five, the target is 200 yards left of where we crossed the river," radioed Six to the wingman, who had just started his gun run from 1000 feet. "Roger, 200 yards, left."

We two helicopters in the fire team were now abreast of each other. We were climbing back up to 1,000 feet, and Five was diving toward the target. We could see his tracers and rockets going into the river. If this gun run was perfectly timed we would be starting down moments after he had pulled up. And it was. As we reached 1000 feet and turned around to face the river, Rattlesnake Five was beginning his climbing turn.

"Fuck, we missed him!" he radioed. He told us the boat was heading for the far bank. It had been directly below him. "Roger Five, we'll get him," said Carpenter.

I again pointed our nose at the river and our next gun run began. Carpenter told me not to pull up until he shot the rockets, as he fired short bursts from the mini-guns. He said at 300 feet I was to turn the search light on. "Roger," I said, the adrenalin still pumping. I was indeed on offense!

At 300 feet I flicked on the light. The boat was directly in front of and below us. As Rattlesnake Five had said, it was moving rapidly toward the bank. I could see no one on the deck, but the outboard motor was churning the muddy water behind it. I felt a bump on the cyclic as Carpenter popped it forward to lower our nose even more. And then, FWHOOSH-FWHOOSH, two rockets left our ship, and a half-second later they slammed into the boat.

"Pull up!" Carpenter yelled but he didn't have to because I had already started to pull up. As we passed over the boat, which was now in a million pieces, our skids could not have been more than ten feet above it, and we flew through a solid sheet of water that had come up in the air when the rockets exploded. "Turn on the windshield wipers, Joyce," said Carpenter, laughing, "I told you we wouldn't miss him this time." He called back to Five and told him the target was destroyed. "Fall in behind me," he said. We would go back to base to refuel.

At Bearcat we refueled and rearmed; then we continued patrolling the Mekong until dawn. We did not see any other boats. I had hoped during this time I'd learn more about operating the guns, but the night remained cloudy and the on-off, on-off business with the lights kept us too busy. But, again, I had a backup plan, so I was not too concerned. If the Army taught me one thing it was CYA (cover your ass).

When the mission ended we refueled a final time and then hovered over to our parking spots. I had done almost all of the flying and felt perfectly comfortable with the shorter and lower-to-the-ground Huey "B" model. I set it down gently on the skids and turned off the engine. Just like on the slicks, we pilots were protected on our sides by an armored plate that slid back and forth. And just like with the slicks, it was the door gunners' jobs to slide the plate back so the pilots could get out.

The door gunner on the captain's side opened his door and slid back the plate, but Carpenter remained in his seat, perhaps to debrief me on the mission and to explain more about the weapons. The door gunner on my side now appeared at my window. He opened my door and slid my plate back. His face was perhaps 12 inches from my face when, BANG! He was now about 12 feet from me writhing on the ground. The other door gunner had shot him.

Not on purpose, of course. It was an accident. The other door gunner had been "clearing" the mini-gun on my side and somehow a round was discharged. Obviously more safety procedures needed to be worked out with these new weapons. Door gunner one had shot door gunner two in the groin.

Carpenter leapt from the ship and ran to the wounded soldier. Blood was squirting all over the ground and he was screaming, "Shit, shit, I've been shot!" The captain knelt next to him and applied pressure to the wounded area, slowing up the flow of blood. The other door gunner was jumping up and down, half crying and at the same time yelling, "Medic! Medic!" In moments the medics arrived. They cut off the gunner's pants, applied a tourniquet and bandages, gave him a shot of morphine, and put the soldier on a stretcher and into the back of an ambulance, which raced off to the base hospital. We learned later that no vital parts had been hit.

Captain Carpenter was terribly shaken up by this accident. As the A/C he was ultimately responsible. There was no way I'd be getting any debriefing or training. I didn't even think to ask for it. I was pretty shook up myself, and to this day I cannot forget the look of shock and terror on the door gunner's face as he spun backwards through the air.

After getting some sleep I went to the OPS (operations) tent to get my next assignment. Sure enough, Lt. Joyce would be commanding a fire team that night. The mission was "River Patrol."

It was now very important that I find Bill Allen. He was the Cav gunship pilot who also was infused to the Ninth. I felt I could level with him with my ongoing deception, and I was right. He too had been screwed by winding up here.

He suggested we go to the flight line, where he would give me the short course on how to fly gunships. He said that after all the time I'd had in slicks I'd have no trouble flying guns. I agreed with him, of course, but it was nice to hear this from a real gunship pilot. I owed Bill, big time, for this confidence boost.

We found a parked gunship, and Bill got into the right seat while I took the left. There on the ground at Bearcat he walked me through the arming of the weapons and explained how to shoot them. He also gave me a tactics course on when to use which weapons on a variety of targets— hooches, tree lines, boats, men in the open, fortified bunkers, and so on. He said when I ran into ".50s," or hand held rockets, to concentrate on them first. He also outlined the basic fire team formations, depending on target, and told me the best way to protect slicks on combat assault. In less than an hour he said that I knew as much as he did. "Mainly just use common sense," was his parting advice. (I am pleased to write that Bill Allen survived Vietnam and wound up flying for Northwest Airlines. He also became a major general in the U.S. Army Reserves.)

It did not take long to get the hang of flying gunships instead of slicks, and no one ever learned that I'd lied to Major Burleson about my past. After a few missions I felt completely at home in the cockpit of a gunship, and I liked flying them. The difference between guns and slicks was indeed the difference between offense and defense. You definitely had more control over what would happen next.

There was one down side, however, unique to the gunships outfitted with mini-guns: the noise. The guns were mounted toward the rear of the ship—the ends of their barrels perhaps four feet behind the pilots. When we fired the guns a solid line of flame came out of the barrels ending just off of our ears. The noise was so loud it caused severe pain in the ear closest to the flame.

When we began a gun run at 1000 feet we usually used the mini-guns rather than the rockets. The mini-guns were more accurate, and we would save the rockets for the bigger targets or intersperse them with the mini-guns to further intimidate. There were only 14 rockets and with each punch two went off, one from each side. So our main weapon was the mini-gun, and by the time we ended a gun run, about 50 feet above the ground, the ear pain was extreme. I am mostly deaf in my left ear because of the mini-guns. We complained about this problem, and eventually we were issued earplugs. They helped a lot, but by then much damage had been done.

A mini-gun is like a machine gun in that bullets are constantly coming out of the barrel. But a mini-gun has six barrels spinning at high speed. Whereas a machine gun goes "ratta, tatta, tatta" a mini-gun roars "WHAAAAAA!" See that tree? WHAAAAAAA! Sawdust. See that hooch? WHAAAAAAAA! You mean that pile of rubble? Mini-guns are incredible.

After being in the Ninth for a month or so I was given another opportunity to increase my chances of living through my time in Vietnam by escaping for a full seven days. It was seven days out of the country through the program of R&R. One day Major Burleson announced he had a number of R&R passes to give out. Most of the guys in the Ninth were too new in country to take one, however, and didn't need a vacation yet. If they took one now they'd have ten more months without a break.

So Burleson asked those of us who had infused if we had yet had our R&Rs. Without waiting for an answer he smiled, winked at us, and began passing them out. This was most out of character for Major Ramrod but I accepted the pass, and before I knew it I was on a commercial airliner headed back to Honolulu with Mary on her way from Atlanta. We'd met there before during my R&R from the Cav.

CHAPTER 22

The Major's Story

I RETURNED TO THE NINTH FROM Hawaii more determined than ever to get home alive, because now I had more reason than ever. On the beach at Waikiki I'd gotten engaged to Mary. But while I was gone the Ninth had also become engaged in a very serious way to the Viet Cong. The action was now the heaviest the Ninth had seen since it got to Vietnam. It was especially heavy at night, and we fire teams were kept busy patrolling the Mekong, supporting troops on the ground, who were in contact with the enemy, and escorting slicks full of GIs into battle.

And there was a new development on the river. Our U.S. Navy had begun to patrol it with gunboats. These boats were heavily armed with both M-60 and .50 caliber machine guns. They were also heavily armored but were easy targets for hit and run ambushes from the shoreline, especially if Charlie was equipped with .50s and hand held rockets. So when flying around looking for trouble we would sometimes be called to support a gunboat that was under attack, flying to his location to strafe shorelines. For many weeks it seemed like an almost constant WHAAAAAA from our miniguns and FHWOOOSH-FHWOOOSH from our rockets.

Then one night I was told my team could take a break. We were really dragging and apparently it showed. So I took this opportunity to go to the Officer's Club tent after supper to do some serious winding down. I sat at a table with three other guys, two captains and a lieutenant. I was the only single one in the group and I kept asking the others about what it was like to be married. I was full of questions and they, of course, were full of answers—they were experts on the topic of marriage even though they frequently disagreed with each other on the answers to many of my questions. Good-natured arguments ensued, and we were having a wonderful time.

155

As the evening progressed I noticed that Major Burleson was at the table next to us and that he appeared to be listening to our conversation—more so than to the one at his. I didn't know how long he'd been there. He and I truly did not like each other and neither of us made any pretenses that we did. Whenever we had conversations, which were infrequent, it was all business. The chemistry between Major Bill Burleson and Lieutenant Jim Joyce sucked.

The drinking and talking at our table was going strong when I noticed out of the corner of my eye that the major stood up. "Good, he's leaving," I thought, but this wasn't so. He excused himself from his table and walked over to ours. This commander did indeed have a commanding presence: the height, the muscles, and the camouflaged bronze leaf on his collar. "Good evening, gentlemen," he said.

"Good evening, sir," we chorused.

"Joyce, I want to see you outside," he said. That was one of the things I hated about him. His bluntness.

Damn, I said to myself. He's learned about the gunship lie or perhaps I misunderstood his signals about the extra R&R. I followed him through the tent flap and into the darkness.

"Let's go over there, Joyce, so we can have some privacy," he said and started walking toward some parked helicopters with sandbags stacked around them. "He's going to beat the shit out of me," was all I could figure.

"Sit down, Joyce," he said when we reached the choppers. I sat on a sandbag wall.

He began by saying he had been listening to the conversation at our table, and heard my questions about marriage, and the answers the others had given me. He said he didn't know why he felt compelled to tell me about his marriage, but he did. "You're not exactly my favorite officer," he said, but then he smiled. He told me he was going to tell me things he had never told anyone before—all because I sounded sincere about wanting to be a good husband. He added that what he would tell me was personal and confidential. "Can I trust you?"

"Yes sir, you can."

Major Burleson then told me his story. It was a story of confusion, hurt, misunderstanding, deceit, and frustration. It was also a story of love, contentment, forgiveness, commitment, and joy. I listened in silence and in awe as he talked, sometimes stopping to wipe tears from his eyes. I did not fully understand it then, but I do now. The major was telling me about real marriage, not the wishful thinking kind that doesn't exist—like the ones I'd been hearing about in the club. He ended by telling me of his undying love for his wife and their children.

"So that's my story, Jim. I'm glad I told you," he said at last, adding that maybe someday it would help me in my marriage. I thanked him and said I felt privileged to have heard his story.

"You're welcome, Jim. Now let's talk business." The major wasn't good at segues.

He said he realized that I had been working hard lately and that I was doing a great job. As a result, he was going to give me tomorrow night off. He would take my place as the fire team leader because he needed some flight time, and it would be a relief for him to get back in the air. He said command duties were often boring and tedious—sometimes he wished he were just a pilot again. Then he asked how my wingman, Phil Harkness*, was doing. Phil was a captain from Iowa who had just arrived from the States and needed combat experience before he could take his own fire team. On the ground he outranked me but in the air, as the fire team leader, I was the boss. Phil did not have to be in Vietnam. His brother was killed there, which gave Phil an automatic ticket out. He elected not to take it. "I am a career officer. My duty is here," he once told me.

I told the major that Captain Harkness was doing fine and would be qualified to take a team very soon. He nodded and said he would evaluate Harkness when he flew with him the next night.

But I had one other thing to tell him, because Phil and I had one serious disagreement. Back in the States the flight school tactics instructors told students to turn all of the lights off when their helicopter was engaged in battle at night. The reasoning seemed sound—it was hard for the enemy to shoot something they couldn't see. However, experience taught me and many others that turning all our lights off could be a disastrous mistake. We felt like the greater danger, even while being shot at, was not the enemy but the possibility of running into another aircraft. When flying a helicopter in battle the pilots and door gunners were very busy and the sky above the battle area could get very crowded, very fast. Watching out for the other choppers was most important, and to do this we had to be able to see them.

I told Major Burleson that I insisted that the team leave its running lights on but that Phil still thought it was a bad idea. "Sir, I really feel strongly about this," I said, adding with a smile that I knew he didn't want to hear about my previous unit, but that was how the Cav flew at night. We had changed the no-lights policy after a mid-air collision.

Major Burleson smiled back. "I hear you," he said. He suggested we go get a drink and toast my engagement. As we walked back to the O'Club tent he asked what my fiancée's name was, where she was from, and how we met. Major Bill Burleson was my new best friend. I was already looking forward to more nights talking and drinking with him.

The next night, as planned, the major sat in my seat and took out the fire team. The mission was routine: patrol the Mekong and be ready to be diverted to wherever needed. A lieutenant colonel also climbed into the back of my ship and sat atop the ammo trays. The door gunners fabricated a seat belt for him. He had arrived in country that day and would be leading a battalion of infantry. He was not a pilot and wanted to learn all he could about the gunships who'd be supporting his troops. What better way to learn than to fly in one?

The two helicopters cranked up and I watched them take off. I was grateful for another free night. Two in a row was a recent record. I went back to the tent and sat at the Red Bar Inn sipping a beer and writing letters. By 10:00 I was asleep.

At 0100 hours I was awakened by an enlisted man from the operations tent. He said they had just gotten word that one of the helicopters in my fire team was down. He didn't have any more information, but Captain Miller* wanted me in the ops tent.

I pulled on my boots and ran to the tent. When I got there Miller was listening to the battalion wide frequency. A battle was in progress. There was yelling and swearing and confusion as usual, but between all this we began to learn, from what the infantry radio operator was saying, that two helicopters were down. Both were gunships. They had to be mine.

Miller scrambled a team of medevac rescue helicopters, our slicks, to get to the area. Lieutenant Roger Fraser from New Jersey led them. As a courtesy Captain Miller asked me if I wanted to ride out with the slicks.

"Ask the infantry if there's any survivors from the downed helicopters," I said.

He called the infantry radio operator. "Negative, base" came the reply.

"No thank you, Captain," I said.

I walked back to my tent and sat on the edge of my cot, my head in hands. I do not recall crying; I recall only the feeling of disbelief and loss. Major Bill Burleson, Captain Phil Harkness, the new lieutenant colonel, and my other six crewmembers were dead. Dead, dead, dead, dead, dead, dead, dead, dead, dead.

In the investigation that followed it was determined that the crash of the helicopters was not directly attributable to the enemy. The two gunships were engaged in a battle and had run into each other—head on.

Flying a helicopter has been compared to playing on a Ouija Board. If you think right, you'll start to go right; think left, you go left. Think up, you start up, and down, you go down. All I can imagine is that one of the team was low to the ground and the other one was above it to provide cover. Then they started to receive fire. The one who was low would unconsciously have wanted to get higher to get away from it. The high one would have wanted to get closer to the target to start shooting at it. Obviously the normal procedure for gun-run was not followed, since this procedure separates the helicopters. But then I wasn't there, goddammit, so maybe some circumstances overrode procedure. How the hell they came together, head on, I will never understand, unless all of their lights were off—which meant I was not forceful enough in selling my beliefs about keeping the lights on. I will always live with that regret.

I wrote condolence letters to the families of my team members. I also wrote to Mrs. Burleson. In the letter I told her that shortly before his last mission Bill and I had a long, private talk about marriage. I told her that his love for her and their children could not have been more pure, intense or, now, everlasting.

On the night before he died Major Bill Burleson made me the messenger of his eternal love for his family. I will always live with that honor.

When an officer was killed in Vietnam, the family could request that the body be accompanied back to the States by a fellow officer. Mrs. Burleson made that request, and another major from our unit performed that duty. When he returned he sought me out with a message from her: "Please tell Lieutenant Joyce that his letter meant everything. It will be cherished. He'll know what I mean."

The major then told me that Burleson had been keeping a journal. The journal was open on his desk when he'd gathered up Bill's personal effects, and he had read the last entry. It said, "I believe that I will not survive Vietnam. I cannot shake this feeling."

CHAPTER 23

The Ox Cart

I WAS WITH THE NINTH INFANTRY about three months when there was a change of command at the highest level. Our general had been promoted to a MACV (Military Assistance Command Vietnam) position in Saigon, so another general was coming to take his place. This called for a large ceremony. No organization likes a ceremony more than the Army. Many other generals from around Vietnam, including Westmoreland, would be attending the ceremony at Bearcat. This august gathering of stars would, of course, make a wonderful target opportunity for the Viet Cong. We put precautions into place.

For two weeks prior to the ceremony the word was put out to the local Vietnamese that on that date between the hours of 0800 and 1800 no one, and we meant no one, was to be within three kilometers of the perimeter of the Bearcat base. If found there they would be destroyed. Because the area was sparsely populated there was little doubt the local people got this word. My fire team was given the mission of patrolling the perimeter during the time of the ceremony, 1400–1600 hours. This mission was simple. We were to fly around the outskirts of the camp to insure no one was in the restricted area. If we found anyone in this area we were to kill them.

It took perhaps 15 minutes to fly the first complete circle around the camp. We needed to fly slowly over the wooded areas and peer down into the trees. The trees in this area of the Delta were unlike the jungle canopies in the mountains of the Central Highlands. These trees were more grove-like, and if we flew low and slow over them we could see between the leaves and branches all the way to the ground.

The first circle we flew was near the edge of the established perimeter, which was delineated by barbed wire and raised sentry shacks placed a few hundred meters apart. Then we flew in gradually wider and wider circles above the restricted area. With each completed pass we called the duty officer at base HQ and reported the area clear.

During the first hour we saw no one and returned to base to refuel. Refueling was accomplished in minutes, and we went back to patrol the next circle.

We were almost to the three kilometers point when we saw them. It was a group of about 20 people of all ages—men, women, and children. They were accompanying a long, wide, flatbed cart being pulled by two oxen. Piled on top of the cart was a stack of twisted firewood rising, precariously, ten feet above it. This would have made an excellent mobile hiding place for soldiers and weapons.

The oxen were moving as rapidly as oxen can move. Two of the men were striking them repeatedly on their rumps with long bamboo poles. The group was moving through a grove of trees which provided little cover for them. I came to a hover about thirty feet above them. My wingman, Gary Driggers, a chief warrant officer from Cincinnati, Ohio, hovered above and to the right of me. We armed our weapons and pointed them at the side of the pile of wood.

The men continued whipping the oxen, now even harder—the big animals were practically galloping. We followed at a hover and all of the people, including the children, put their hands in the air but continued to run alongside of the cart, as though it somehow provided protection. The word "terror" is not strong enough to describe the looks on their faces. Neither is panic. They thought they were looking up at death, their own, about to be carried out by screaming, air-slapping Huey gunships.

"Dammit," I said to no one and called the base. I told the duty officer, a major, that we'd come up on about 20 civilians and an ox cart full of firewood and gave him the coordinates.

"Roger, Gunslinger Niner, destroy. Over," said the major without hesitation.

I looked down at our targets and couldn't fathom doing what I was just told to do. These were civilians, at least the women and children were, and most of the men were beyond military age. I knew that everyone in Vietnam was a potential enemy—*but*.

"Base, this is Gunslinger Niner, these are civilians. Over."

"I rogered that, Niner, destroy. Do you read me? Over."

"Negative, Base, I do not read you," I said. I did not say, "Over." He called me again and repeated the order to destroy the target, emphasizing they were in the restricted area. He asked again if I read him.

"Base, Niner, you're garbled," I said. "I can't read you. Out." I did not

POWs were usually blindfolded for security reasons.

ask him to "say again," which would have been the proper radio procedure. The major now knew he was being ignored.

I told Gary, who heard my conversation with base, that we would stay with these people until they were out of the restricted area. I told him to hover over to the other side of the ox cart and not to fire his weapons unless he saw people hiding in the wood or weapons sticking out of it. I asked him to confirm what I'd just said. "I read you, Niner" he replied, "loud and clear." I could hear the relief in his voice.

The oxen were now going even faster as the men increased their whipping. Large sections of the wood started falling off of the cart. No one stopped to pick them up. As we continued to follow them their hands, tentatively, began to come down. Their petrified expressions changed to fear laced with hope. They were taking the shortest possible route to get out of the restricted area. Obviously they had gotten the word but decided to gamble on not being detected. We continued following them at a low hover, Gary Driggers on one side and me on the other. Our mini-guns and the door gunners' machine guns were trained on the woodpile. In a few more minutes the group crossed the line of the restricted area.

By now most of the wood had fallen off of the cart. There were no mortars or other weapons concealed in it, nor were there soldiers. We stopped

Sometimes POWs were women.

our forward hover, and as the group continued onward one of the women turned around and, running backwards, put her hands in the air and bowed to us, bowed to us, bowed to us.

We continued our mission and found no other people in the restricted area. I called Gary and told him to follow me home. "Roger," he replied, and then asked if I thought we would get into trouble for not shooting the people. I told him that he wouldn't get in any trouble but I would.

"I'm glad we didn't do it, Jim. Over," said Gary.

"Me, too, Gary. Out."

We landed back at base after confirming that the next fire team was on patrol. I expected to be met by my new C.O., Captain Jim Miller, Bill Burleson's replacement. I assumed he'd be accompanied by a couple of MPs. But this didn't happen. I left the parked helicopter and walked to the company operations tent, knowing for sure there'd be a message for Lieutenant Joyce to report immediately to some higher authority. Nope. Nothing.

I have often thought of this mission, and each time I think of it I thank God we didn't shoot. "Legally" I could have, and "legally" I should have—having been given a direct order, three times, to do so. But the major at HQ wasn't staring at those faces. Although the My Lai Incident had not yet occurred, perhaps the word "civilian" eventually meant something to him, and he decided not to pursue going after me. I'll never know.

At the time I was immediately thankful that we did not destroy the ox cart people, and as the years have gone by I've become even more thankful. Had I followed the orders to shoot, my soul would have a hole in it that all the rationalizations and a thousand confessions couldn't begin to fill. Now I can say with a touch of pride that there are people alive in Vietnam today who would not be if I hadn't disobeyed an order. And no doubt those people have had children, who have also had children. I also say this with enormous relief.

Although I can't begin to count the number of times I have thanked God that we didn't kill those people, paradoxically (and this is going to sound strange) I am also most thankful that we were given the opportunity to refuse to kill them. You know what I mean?

(I am pleased to report that Gary Driggers survived Vietnam and became the Vice Chairman of Mid Coast Aviation, Inc., in St. Louis, Missouri.)

CHAPTER 24

The Screaming

A FEW DAYS AFTER THE CHANGE of command ceremony at Bearcat our unit was sent to the field for an extended stay. Prior to this time our field stays with the Ninth Infantry had been brief and sporadic, a welcome change from life with the Cav. But now we were told we'd be gone at least three weeks. One of the division brigades was in almost constant contact with the enemy and was sustaining "unacceptable casualties." The brigade requested more air support from gunship fire teams, and our unit got this mission.

The field camp location was 30 miles directly south of Saigon. As we flew into it I saw, to my delight, that it was a well-established camp, which had obviously been there for many months. There was a PCP runway for STOL (short take-off and landing) fixed wing aircraft. The perimeter was heavily barb-wired and fields of fire were cleared. When we unloaded our gear we were taken to a tent that we did not have to erect ourselves. Nor did we have to fill sandbags; they were already in place. There were enclosed latrines so we would not be using piss tubes and honey buckets. A mess tent was in place. "This is not really going to the field," I said to myself—and kept it to myself.

This field camp had an amenity that not even our base camp at Bearcat had. In our tent there was a television set! I could hardly believe it. Someone had purchased, swiped or traded for a small black and white TV and concocted an ingenious antenna for it. We could pick up the armed forces network from Saigon. At first it felt weird, and somehow wrong, to come in from a combat mission and then sit down to watch *I Love Lucy*, but I quickly got used to this anomaly and it became a welcome diversion.

On the fifth night at the camp some of us were sitting in our lawn chairs, drinking beer and watching *The Ed Sullivan Show*. We had flown missions most of that day and were winding down. At about 10:30 the tent flap burst open and a Spec 4 from operations ran in. "Lieutenant Joyce, scramble your team! One of our units is about to be overrun!" He said he'd alerted our door gunners and they were on the way to the ships.

Three of us four pilots in the team were watching the TV. The fourth was asleep in his cot but heard the word "scramble." He jumped into his boots and we all ran to the helicopters, parked only 25 yards away. The door gunners had already untied the rotor blades and hustled us into our seats. In less than two minutes we were up in the air again.

The operations officer on duty gave me my destination coordinates over the radio as we were on climb out. He told me the unit under attack was company sized and added that it sounded like they were in deep shit. I estimated our flight time at about seven minutes, at a heading of 130° (SE). When we were three minutes out from its location I contacted the company. "Alpha Company, this is Gunslinger Niner. We are a fire team en route to your location." I told him we were about three minutes away approaching him from the northwest. "What is your status? Over."

Back to me came a young man's voice. He was screaming, "We're getting the shit kicked out of us! Three minutes is too late! You gotta get here sooner!" His voice went up even higher: "We're gonna be overrun!"

I assured him we'd get there as fast as possible and asked where he was, in relation to the enemy. In his terrified voice he said that when we got to him Alpha Company would be on our left and that Charlie was coming across the field to our right. He said we'd see the tracers. Then he screamed, "Oh God! The captain's been hit! I've got to move back! They're coming! Fly faster!"

My wingman was again the warrant officeer Gary Driggers. Gary also heard the screaming on his radio, and we were both pulling all the speed we could from the Hueys. It was possible to put a Huey onto a high-speed stall, from which there was no recovery, but that was not now an issue. If we didn't get to Alpha Company before it was overrun, Alpha Company and the Viet Cong would be intermingled. Where would we shoot?

In a few minutes we saw the tracers streaking back and forth on the dark ground in front of us. The two opposing forces were very close together— Alpha really was about to be overrun. I called Alpha and told him we were within sight of the battle. "Can you see us?" I asked.

"Yes, yes. I see you! Start shooting! Start shooting!"

Behind his screams we could hear the racket of the battle. I told him I was going to punch off a short burst of the mini-guns and asked him to tell me if that was where he wanted the fire. In a firefight people naturally get very confused. Left becomes right and north becomes south. I did not want to kill any Alpha with "friendly fire." This happened too often. I squeezed off a two-second burst.

"Yes! Yes!" yelled the radioman. "That's it! Keep shooting! Keep shooting!"

Alpha radio had been correct. The VC were on our right, in the open field; Alpha was in a grove of trees on the left. We could now go to work. We did not take time to go into the traditional gun run formation. Gary came alongside of me and we opened up with both mini-guns and rockets. We were 300 feet above the ground and now slowed down, to be able to lay down as much ordnance as possible before over-flying the target. "Yes! Yes! That's great! Keep shooting! They're pulling back!" screamed Alpha radio.

We over-flew the field where the VC were and could tell by their tracers that they were retreating toward a dense tree line about 500 yards long. I turned 180° hard left, and Driggers turned 180° hard right. We wanted to get as many of them as possible while they were still in the open. We formed up and started another gun run. By now, of course, we had become the prime targets of the VC; tracers were streaking past us as we flew toward them. Then we saw—goddammit! They had a .50 at the edge of the tree line. Tracers from a .50 caliber machine gun at night looked like fiery bowling balls. They were huge. The flame from a .50 caliber machine gun's tracers wrapped around the shells so you could see them coming from any angle. Fifty caliber machine guns got everyone's attention. They were devastating. Our armor plating was useless against them.

As we pilots carpeted the area with rockets and mini-gun fire I told the door gunners to try to locate the .50 and knock it out. They did. It was silent before we finished this second pass. Our door gunners were magnificent.

When we turned back to make another pass, somebody turned the lights on. I do not mean the lights of the helicopter; I mean the lights of the world! The entire battlefield was now as bright as if the sun had mysteriously risen. "Puff the Magic Dragon" had arrived on the scene.

Puff the Magic Dragon was a C-47 (the civilian name is DC-3). It was a twin-engine propeller-driven airplane with reciprocating (not jet) engines. It first gained fame in World War II. (The "C" means it carried cargo, or it could transport about 30 troops in its fuselage.) One of its unique features was that it was the first multi-engine airplane that could maintain straight and level flight, and then safely land, with only one of its engines functioning. It had retractable landing gear and variable pitch props. It was a tail-dragger.

In Vietnam the military got the bright idea—and it *was* a bright idea—to make a gun platform out of the C-47. Because it could fly very slow and carry tons of ordnance, it made a great fixed wing "gunship." Puff was outfitted with three 7.62 side mounted mini-guns, giving it awesome destructive force. There were about five "Puffs" (also called "Spookies") in the Vietnam theatre at this time, and one of them was now circling above us, dropping flares.

Puff showing up was like the good news and the bad news for us. The good news was that we now could clearly see the enemy's positions and also see the last of the enemy soldiers running to the tree line. We noted that these soldiers wore uniforms, indicating they were NVA regulars, not Viet Cong. It could be a long night. On the down side, the NVA could now clearly see us. Prior to the light coming on we had been all but invisible. The only lights on our helicopters were the small red and green running lights. These were almost impossible to see from the ground through all the smoke.

Another problem Puff posed for us, and probably a more serious one, was that the flares he was dropping were attached to parachutes. We had to take extreme caution to avoid them, and there were many of them at different altitudes. The flares burned out well above ground level, creating a treacherous obstacle course for us. If our rotors struck the parachute ropes or canopies we would certainly crash. But as long as the burning flares above us kept the daylight coming, we could see the spent flares' chutes and avoid them.

We made another run across the area. I concentrated on the edge of the tree line and Driggers started shooting about 50 yards behind that. This being an NVA unit, there were probably many of them and they'd be deep into the trees. The open area was now cleared of enemy soldiers. The distance from Alpha Company's tree line to the NVA's tree line was only about 100 yards. When we arrived the NVA had been more than halfway across it. If we had been about 60 seconds later ... but then we weren't, so there's no sense thinking about that.

As soon as we realized Puff was on the scene I called him to be sure he knew we were there, too. Dodging his parachutes was one thing; dodging his mini-gun fire would be something else. "Puff Six" assured me he would hold his fire until we returned to base to re-arm. After one more run—this time coming at them from directly over the top of Alpha—the Gunslinger fire team was out of ammunition. I radioed this information to Alpha radio and Puff, telling them we would return in about 20 minutes. Puff's door gunners could now go to work.

They were waiting for us at base with a fresh supply of rockets and ammo for the mini-guns. We were refueled and re-armed in less than three minutes. During those procedures the engine was not shut off, it was only slowed down, which slowed the spinning rotor blades. The door gunners jumped back on board and we brought the engine up to full rpm and took off. As soon as we got a few hundred feet in the air we clearly saw our destination. It was that bright round spot on the horizon, surrounded by black sky.

When we arrived at the battle scene we set up our next gun runs and started down, but now the light was getting dimmer and dimmer, and suddenly the sky went black. I called Puff Six and asked him what was going on. He told me he had just run out of flares. This meant there were a dozen spent flare canisters hanging from parachutes and we were flying among them. Turning right, left or back around would have made no difference. We were surrounded. I called Gary and told him to stay with the gun run. "Roger, Niner," he replied. I was sure I heard him gulp.

The next ten seconds were perhaps the longest ten seconds of our lives. If we struck the canisters, the harness ropes, or the canopies, we would almost certainly die. But there was nothing we could do about it, so we said a quick prayer, fired our weapons, and eventually flew out the other side. The pucker factor was 10^2.

I then got a call from base. Six slicks full of infantry were en route to the area to reinforce Alpha Company. We were told to accompany them into the LZ. So Gary and I went high and circled to wait for them. The fire on the ground was now sporadic. Alpha radio said the company was regrouping and were assessing casualties. He said there were many and they had gotten the shit kicked out of them. "The captain is dead!" he cried. He was very relieved to hear that reinforcements were minutes away.

I contacted the slick team leader and told him to follow me into the LZ. I would not be landing, of course, but would tell him when to "flare" and set down. There was a long LZ behind Alpha's position which would accommodate all six helicopters at one time. I had noticed it when the lights were on. The slicks would have a grove of trees and Alpha Company, at least what was left of it, between them and the enemy position.

I got word from base that another fire team would be joining us and the six slicks, which by now were coming out of the LZ, would be returning two more times with more troops. The other fire team and ours were to coordinate getting them in and out of the LZ, at the same time continuing to place ordnance on the NVA position. I called the team leader and we worked out the details. After the last of the reinforcements were dropped off, the slicks remained in the LZ to take on wounded. They would pick up the dead later. The other fire team stayed behind to accompany them out, and we returned to base to re-arm and refuel. Alpha company was now reinforced and apparently secure. There was no more firing coming from the NVA positions.

I thought the evening would be over for us, but I was wrong. After we refueled and re-armed we were sent ten miles due south of the base. This new mission was to destroy a hooch where VC were suspected of hiding. This was easy—hooches don't move—and we received minimal fire during the attack. We were then told to fly west to the Mekong River where a navy gunboat was taking fire. The Mekong meanders like a serpent. Depending on its location it could be heading in any direction on the compass. When we came upon it, it was heading due west. We approached from the east. We contacted the navy gunboat commander, who told us he had taken sporadic rifle fire from the shore; the rifle fire had been no problem for him, but now he'd encountered a .50, which was a problem. I had to wonder where all these fucking fifties were coming from. He informed us it would be on the right bank on our approach, and we would see the tracers.

In moments we did see them. We were at 1,000 feet and I told Gary to come up next to me. We would again attack together. I told him we'd use the mini-guns, down to 500 feet, and then punch off rockets until we pulled out. This was not a normal gun run formation, but we were already lined up perfectly to begin an attack. The surprise of it should make up for the lack of traditional tactics. And it did. Their own weapons were making so much noise they didn't hear us coming.

"You got him, Gunslinger, you got them all!" said gunboat, as he shone his spotlight back and forth along the bank.

We again returned to base to refuel and re-arm, but the night was still not over. The NVA unit had regrouped, and Alpha Company was again under attack. It was daybreak before we were relieved and told we could go home, and stay home. We were dead tired, having spent 20 of the last 24 hours in the air.

After re-arming and refueling one last time we hovered over to our parking spot, between rows of sandbags, and finally shut down the engines. I unhooked my harness as the door gunner slid back my armored plate. I stepped out of the helicopter, and though I was exhausted, I was still wired from all the excitement. I decided to take a short walk before going to the tent. I wanted an uninterrupted cigarette. I wanted to try to get some perspective. This evening had begun while I was watching *The Ed Sullivan Show*. Less than ten minutes later I was listening to the screams of the Alpha radio operator as his unit was about to be annihilated. I'd heard many screams before but none so desperate—and none that came from someone who sounded so young.

I started walking down the side of the PCP runway which ended at the camp's perimeter. My thoughts were a jumble, mainly having to do with my own survival, and my chances of getting home alive. During the night we'd heard that three choppers in the Delta had gone down, two slicks and a gun. I had less than two months left in country, but if I had many more days and nights like this one my chances of surviving were not good.

When I first got to Vietnam I knew, for certain, that I would get through it alive. I knew this because I was young and stupid. I was still young, but after ten months of living with death, I was no longer stupid. Helicopter pilots and their crews were dying at an unnerving rate. All the guys I knew who were now dead got that way doing the exact same things that I was doing. So if I kept doing what I was doing, I was going to die too. It was just a matter of time. Would my time in Vietnam run out before my time on earth ran out? That was the question. I lit another cigarette.

My mind then wandered back to our tent at Bearcat. Somehow, a *Chicago Tribune* newspaper had wound up there. On the front page there was a picture of a prominent businessman who had done something newsworthy. From the picture the man looked to be in his seventies. When I saw this picture my first thought was "Wow. Look at that. People actually get old."

I had been walking with my head down, paying no attention to my surroundings. But then I heard voices, and a "thump" sound, and I looked up. At the end of the runway, about 50 yards in front of me, I saw a two-and-a-half ton truck. Its back was facing toward me and its tailgate was down. On the ground behind it were large piles, which looked like a jumble of cordwood or perhaps railroad ties. I couldn't see them clearly because of the heavy fog.

Two soldiers were working with the pile directly behind the truck. One got on one end of a piece of the heavy wood and one got on the other. They picked it up off the pile and swung it back and forth to get momentum, then tossed it into the truck. *Thump.* I now saw there were two other soldiers in the back of the truck, arranging the wood to make room for more. I continued walking toward them wondering why soldiers were loading wood into a truck ... and then I was stopped, cold. I now saw that these heavy objects were not large pieces of wood, they were bodies—the bodies of our soldiers killed during the night.

A Huey slick now approached. I stood frozen as I watched it hover up next to the truck and set down. One of the door gunners jumped out and yelled something to the soldiers who were loading the bodies. They stopped their work only long enough to point to an area just off the runway. That's where they wanted the next pile to be.

CHAPTER 25

A Medal
and a Promotion

AWARDING MEDALS FOR HEROIC DEEDS performed during battle has always been a military tradition. During my six months with the Cav I don't recall hearing much about medals other than Air Medals. These were given automatically when 25 hours of combat assault time were logged. For slick pilots, flying troops in and out of battle or flying medevac under fire constituted combat assault. Routine resupply missions or flying VIPs or POWs didn't qualify. For gunships, all time spent flying was considered combat assault. These Air Medals were not passed out or pinned on in any kind of formal ceremony. They were simply, and I suspect haphazardly, noted in our official files.

Each unit had an officer who was designated the awards and decorations officer. This was a minor, extra assignment. The A&D job consisted of reviewing a write-up that someone submitted, suggesting that Soldier So and So deserved a medal for what he did on such and such a date. The A&D officer would then check out the story as best he could and recommend to the CO that the medal be awarded as suggested, or perhaps he might suggest upgrading or downgrading it. The big medals like the DFC (Distinguished Flying Cross), the Silver Star, and the CMH (Congressional Medal of Honor) would have a committee of officers verify it was merited. No one simply "got a medal for heroism." Someone had to suggest, in writing, that it be awarded.

In the Ninth Infantry medals were taken a lot more seriously than in the Cav. Our awards and decorations officer, Captain Harold Fitch*, actively pursued these write-ups. Fitch was a career officer. He would come around

The author (left), unidentified door gunner, and CWII Gary Driggers of Ohio. This photograph was taken for macho purposes only. Pilots didn't really load ammo.

after particularly difficult missions and start asking questions with note pad in hand. It was like he had a quota to fill with a bonus attached. It was rumored within the company that he had suggested to more than one person that they write him up for a medal. But that was just a rumor.

I couldn't stand Captain Fitch for many reasons, including the fact that he was a slacker. He flew less hours than anyone in the company, using the silly A&D job as an excuse. Once I commented about this to someone while Fitch was in earshot. He hated me for that.

One of the warrant officers in my fire team wrote me up for a medal. I was unaware he'd done it. He had suggested that I receive the Distinguished Flying Cross and that the other members of my team receive the Bronze Star. Fitch sent word that he wanted to see me, and I went to his tent. He showed me the write-up and asked what I thought about it. I was caught completely by surprise.

I told him that I did not believe I should get a medal higher in prestige than my team members. Obviously they were there, too. He then asked if I thought we deserved the DFC. This was a loaded, unfair question. Was I going to argue that I was heroic? Hardly. First of all, I did not feel heroic, and secondly, I wouldn't give this dickhead the satisfaction of asking him for anything. I told him I had no idea what we deserved—that it was someone else's call—and left his tent.

One time I landed my gunship at an unfamiliar field camp, setting it down at what I thought was a safe distance from a .155 Howitzer. The barrel was pointed way above us, but when the gun fired the concussion shattered my door window. Some Plexiglas cut my face. The cut was minimal, requiring only a Band-aid, but Fitch seriously wanted to put me in for a Purple Heart. He had to be on commission from somebody.

Some weeks later our battalion had a medals ceremony at Bearcat. We stood at attention as the CO came along pinning medals to our chests. My team members and I got Air Medals with "V" device, two levels down from the DFC. Captain Fitch got his revenge. He also, somehow, got a Bronze Star.

I was offended by the politicking associated with the medal awarding process. I felt then, and still do, that with very few exceptions medals should be awarded to the spouses or parents of those who died in combat or to those who were permanently disabled. Getting out of Vietnam in one piece should be all the award, and reward, necessary for those who fought in the war. But that's not the way it was. Medals were important to accumulate if you planned to make the military your career. It was also nice to be a Bronze Star recipient if you planned to run for public office. So people sometimes hustled for medals. The medal business could also cause problems for those in administrative posts in Saigon, Vung Tau, Cam Rhon, or other cushy places. How did you get a medal for bravery with those assignments? Some, of course, found ways.

With about seven weeks to go in country I was promoted to the rank of captain. This promotion was automatic. The deal at the time was second lieutenant for 18 months; first lieutenant for 12 months; and then, unless you really screwed up, captain. I was glad to become a captain for two reasons: There was a nice pay raise associated with it, and it showed the rest of the military world that under no circumstances could I be considered a rookie. I had paid my dues and I was proud of the two white stripes on my collar instead of one. An ego thing.

There was one small downside to getting promoted. The military had a tradition that when an officer got promoted he had to throw a "promotion party" to which all fellow officers in the company got invited. All drinks, all night, were paid for by the promotee. The NCO bartender expected a large tip. A promotion party could be very expensive.

When I got my promotion from second lieutenant to first lieutenant I had been in the last week of the Huey school at Benning. Hardly anyone had noticed when I'd showed up for class wearing silver bars in place of gold. And there had been no time for a party. In a few days we'd be scattered all over the world.

When I got promoted to captain, things were different. Unfortunately for me, on the night of my promotion party the entire company was back at Bearcat. Although the food was free, catered by the mess hall, I'd be buying beer and booze for about 30 officers and warrant officers. And these guys could drink. But there was nothing I could do about it except enjoy myself. I dressed for the occasion, being one of the few guys in possession of civilian clothes. While I was in Honolulu on my second R&R Mary had bought me two coordinated outfits—Hawaiian shirts with matching Bermuda shorts. Although wrinkled from being in the bottom of my duffel bag, they were festive and, I thought, appropriate for this big night. I put one of the outfits on.

One of my tent mates, slick team leader Lieutenant Roger Fraser, complimented me on how nice I looked and asked if I had another civilian outfit. "As a matter of fact, Roger, I do," I said and reached into the duffel bag for the second one. It, too, was a beauty.

"Would you let me wear it?" he asked.

"Be my guest," I said and tossed it to him.

So Roger and I went off to my party looking great. We wore tennis shoes—no socks of course—the outfits from Hawaii, and on my head was my brand new captain's hat with the two white bars sewn on.

There was nothing remarkable about the party. It was the same as others we'd had—30 guys got drunk. However, when the party was almost over and just a handful of us were left standing, it took a different twist.

I was at the bar going over the bill with the sergeant. He was explaining how he had given me a discount here and a discount there, and I was nodding my head like I was listening. Meanwhile, I was staring at the bottom figure which was now due and payable and didn't include the tip. It would take two months of extra captain's pay to recoup the party's cost.

Then the sergeant commented on my outfit. He said it was beautiful and wondered if there was any chance I'd sell it to him. He was going on R&R next week and needed civilian clothes. It took me less than a second to reply. "How about this, Sarge? I'll give you the outfit and we'll call that your tip."

"Yes, sir, that's a deal!" he said.

First Lieutenant Roger Fraser (New Jersey) evolved from the cockpit of a Huey slick in the Vietnam Delta (*top*) to the cockpit of a U.S. Airways 330 Airbus en route to Rome (*bottom*).

So I took off the shirt and the Bermuda shorts and put them on the bar. Naturally I was not wearing underwear. Everybody went into hysterics, especially Roger. He was pointing at me, laughing and saying I was crazy.

I asked the sergeant what he thought of the outfit Lieutenant Fraser was wearing. He said it was a beauty also and asked if I thought the lieutenant would sell it to him. I told him it did not belong to Lieutenant Fraser—it was mine, and it was definitely for sale.

"I'll give you twenty bucks for it, Sir."

"It's yours, Sergeant," I said. I turned around and looked at the still guffawing Roger. "Take off my outfit, Lieutenant Fraser, and that's an order," I told him, pointing at the captain's bars on my hat.

Roger quit laughing and the rest of the guys starting chanting: "Take it off, Roger, Take it off, take it off." Roger hesitated but then stood up. As the guys continued to chant, he did an imitation of a stripper, and then placed his outfit on the bar. Roger, of course, wasn't wearing underwear, either.

The very end of the evening is somewhat hazy. I do recall nonchalantly standing at the bar with Roger having one last drink, compliments of the sergeant who had already changed into one of the outfits. I recall flash bulbs popping, and I remember thinking that if I ever ran for public office and these pictures surfaced, I'd have some explaining to do to the voters. And I remember walking with Roger back across the compound to our tent. We passed two soldiers who were walking guard duty, and even though they could clearly see by the two white bars on my hat that I was a captain, they did not salute me. They were laughing too hard. Roger pretended to be pissed off. "You privates," he yelled. "Have you forgotten your manners? You're supposed to salute an officer!" They stopped, looked us up and down, and as they saluted one of them said something about our privates. And they broke up laughing again. When the Army coined the phrase "out of uniform," I bet it had no idea just how far out of uniform two of its officers would get.

Roger Fraser was the second best pilot, after Joe Mulheran, that I ever knew. He had been nicknamed "Super Slick" for his deftness in getting a Huey D model in and out of impossibly tight LZs on medevac missions. He saved many lives. He survived the war and became a pilot for Piedmont Airlines and, later, US Airways.

Being a captain made no difference in my day-to-day life. I was still a fire team leader flying the same type missions as before—river patrol, combat assault escort for slicks, etc. One morning, however, we were on patrol and got called to come to the aid of an infantry company under intense artillery fire. The initial word on the unit's status did not make sense because the Viet Cong did not have artillery and as far as we knew the NVA's had not yet made it this far south.

When we got to the scene we were able to determine that the incoming artillery rounds landing on the infantry were actually coming from their own battalion's artillery battery, three miles away. We made some frantic radio calls and got the shelling stopped, but lives had been lost to this "friendly fire." When we landed to refuel at a field camp a captain came running up to my ship and started yelling at me that my gunships had just fired on U.S. troops and there would be severe repercussions. He demanded to know my name and what unit I was from, and he told me to get out of the helicopter.

Now, being a captain myself, I was able to look at his name tag and address him by his last name. I told him he didn't know what the fuck he was talking about; it had been his own artillery killing his own infantry, and we were the ones who got it stopped. I told him to look at our magazines and rockets. He would see we hadn't fired one round. I stepped out of the helicopter and took off my flak jacket so he could clearly see he wasn't talking to a lieutenant or a warrant officer. I told him I agreed with him that there'd be repercussions and that I hoped, for his sake, he wasn't in the artillery. I could tell by his collar insignia that he was. He got a panicky look on his face, turned around, and ran away.

CHAPTER 26

Our Allies and
the Last Mission

TWO OTHER COUNTRIES SENT ground troops to help the United States during the Vietnam War: South Korea and Australia. The South Korean Army was appropriately nicknamed the "ROK Army." This name made sense because (1) ROK stands for Republic of Korea and (2) a rock expresses no feelings and is tougher than nails. The ROKS did not interact much with the U. S. forces. They were given certain areas to control and to keep cleared of the Viet Cong, and they performed their duty to perfection. It was said during the war—and debated for years after—that if the ROKS encountered any armed resistance when they entered an area, they killed every man, woman, child, pig, goat, water buffalo and chicken. They were vicious fighters and the Viet Cong (and everyone else), were terrified of them. Their area remained clear of the enemy throughout the time that I was in Vietnam.

Years after the war I had a Korean business associate, Mr. B. C. Kim from Seoul. Our business relationship evolved into a friendship, and one day I asked him if he had ever heard how tough that ROK Army unit was. (I used the word "tough" to give him an out.) His cheeks flushed just a tad, and then he chuckled and said, "Oh yes, Mr. Jim, ROK Army unit go to Vietnam they tough. Those soldiers were orphans. Very angry people."

The Australians, on the other hand, worked frequently with the U. S. forces. They were open, friendly, and always jovial, and no Army guys, or any guys, could drink more beer. Once our unit had a joint mission with the Aussies and we bivouacked at their base camp at a rubber plantation near Nui Dat, southeast of Saigon. We lived with them for two weeks, and it was the most enjoyable two weeks I spent in country. There was very little enemy activity in their area. Some days we only had one mission and some days none at all. Army intelligence had it that the Aussie camp was going to be hit big by an NVA unit to teach our allies "a lesson." It didn't happen while we were there.

Every night we pilots were invited to their officer's club to drink beer and play darts. Their O'Club was like the officer's latrine at An Khe. Much thought had gone into its construction. It was a real building, not a tent. We had our priorities and the Aussies had theirs. Next to beer drinking, playing darts was their passion and they were very good at it. Gambling was involved, of course.

I am one to brag. After the third night I was beating every Aussie in the place. The game of darts came to me like no game ever had, before or since. The Aussies called me "Champ" and genuinely thought it funny that a Yank was beating them night after night at their own game. I can't remember ever being so proud of myself.

The Aussies liked teasing us Americans about the way we dressed: long pants, long sleeved shirts, flak jackets and steel pots. Their uniforms were Bermuda shorts, short-sleeved shirts, soft floppy hats, and no chest protection. They called us sissies and it wasn't long before us sissies started wearing their uniforms. We liked the comfort and, of course, the rakish look. But this pissed off our new C.O., Major Regan*, who chastised us for being out of the uniform of the United States Army. "Where is your pride?" he yelled and told us to give the uniforms back. ("How tight is your sphincter?" we wanted to ask.)

With 43 days to my DEROS, my left hand began bothering me again from the imbedded glass. The pain had been on again, off again, ever since the accident. Usually a few days after the pain came, I could feel a tiny piece of glass just below the skin, and then a day or two later it would break through and I could pull it out with tweezers. The pain in the past had been sharp like pin pricks. It was not unbearable and had not affected my flying. Very little pressure was needed to lift up or push down the helicopter's collective or to twist the throttle. This could be done with fingertips.

But now my hand was throbbing with pain even though I couldn't feel any glass near the surface. I was having a hard time sleeping, so I decided to go to our flight surgeon. He was a laid-back southerner from South Carolina. "Show me where it hurts," he said. I pointed to the area, and he placed his thumb on it and gently pushed down. I flew out of my seat and practically to the top of his tent. "Ouch!" he said. "Gawddam, I'm sorry, Captain!" When I caught my breath I told him, "No problem, Major. It has never hurt like this before. I need some painkillers."

He looked over my medical records and said that a piece of glass must have dislodged and was now moving to another area. It must have broken through scar tissue, he said. I needed to get it surgically removed. I told him that my DEROS was July 15th. I asked if he could somehow set up surgery in the States for me when I got home. He picked up my chart and noted that I had been in country almost 11 months and had been carrying that glass around for two years. Enough, he said, was enough; he was sending me home for surgery. "When?" I asked.

"Tomorrow," he said and I nearly went into shock.

The doctor phoned Major Regan and told him his decision. He listened a moment, and then I heard, "That will be up to Captain Joyce. I'll ask him and call you back." Flight surgeons were god-like when it came to a pilot's well being.

He said the major asked if I could fly one more mission, tomorrow. He'd have an experienced fire team leader infusing from the 101st the next day but there was a C/A scheduled in the morning and he needed me. The doctor said he could give me some painkillers that wouldn't affect my motor skills or judgment, but the decision was mine. I immediately said that I would fly the mission. I told him I was feeling guilty as hell. My time in Vietnam wasn't up yet. I had never expected he'd send me home. I was stammering. The major laughed and shook his head. He asked how I could possibly be feeling guilty after flying for 11 months in combat. "I've always said you helicopter pilots were crazy," he said.

He told me he'd write orders to send me to the MASH at Ton San Nhut the day after tomorrow, and from there they'd make arrangements to get me home for surgery. I walked out of his tent shocked, euphoric, and riddled with guilt. And then I thought, "That's five times in the last four years I've been called crazy. Maybe I am."

My last mission as a helicopter pilot was, like the CO said, a combat assault. We would be accompanying six slicks carrying a platoon of infantry. Only light resistance was expected, if any. One last time I climbed into a Huey in Vietnam and cranked it up.

It was a 20-minute flight to the LZ. The LZ was large, so with a tight formation all six aircraft could land at the same time. I contacted the slick leader and learned that was his plan. I was on his left; Lieutenant Jim Thomas*, my newest wingman, was on his right. Ten seconds before the slicks touched down we both punched off two rockets and then raked the tree lines on either side of the LZ with our mini-guns. We did not get return fire, and the slicks were in and out of there in 20 seconds. Time to go home.

Well, not quite. I got a call from base telling me to contact Hell Fire Six, an infantry company commander. I contacted Hell Fire and learned

The author with the cutest kids on earth. They would say, "G.I. number one! VC number 10." They probably didn't mean it, but we gave them c-rations anyway.

he was only a five-minute flight away. We found him after he popped smoke. One hundred yards northwest of the smoke there were two hooches. He was drawing fire from them and they were slowing him up. He asked me to take them out. We were already at 1000 feet so I told Jim to circle at that altitude and wait for me to finish the first run, then to make his run. A standard gunship attack.

We located the targets and started down. The familiar puffs of white smoke could be seen coming from the hooches' windows. At 800 feet I punched off two rockets and the hooch on the right was disintegrated. Slight pressure on the left anti-torque pedal and I was lined up on the left hooch. At 500 feet I punched off two more rockets. Direct hits. I had become very good at this. (It was sort of like playing darts.) We turned the helicopters back toward Bearcat.

The "Rules of Engagement" in Vietnam were clear-cut when flying from place to place. You could not shoot at anybody unless they shot at you first. Then they were fair game. About ten minutes out from Bearcat my right door gunner said that he thought we were taking fire from a tree line ahead. At the same time, Jim Thomas called and said that someone was shooting at us from three o'clock.

Ever since learning I was going on my last mission, I had been thinking about the "getting killed right before you leave," syndrome. Also, there was something wrong with gunships at altitude being fired upon as they were flying past. It smelled like an ambush. Jim called to ask if we were going to engage. I thought about it for less than two seconds and said, "Negative. Fuck him. I'm going home. Out."

I heard "click-click" in my headset and it made me smile. To talk over the radio, to another aircraft or to the ground, you pushed a button on the front of the cyclic. You held it down to transmit and released it to receive. If you pushed it and immediately released it the other person heard a "click." Thomas had "click-clicked" his microphone button. This "click-click" meant, "Roger, I understand, I agree. Out."

At the MASH hospital, which bordered the airport at Ton San Nhut, I was given a bunk in the tent where the surgeons lived. They needed all available hospital beds for the wounded who arrived around the clock by helicopters and trucks. The doctors treated me as an equal, and I guess I was, since most of them were captains, also. The ranking officer of the MASH was a big, gentle lieutenant colonel, a neurosurgeon from Louisiana. He told me I was free to go anywhere I wished, but he advised me not to go into Quonset Hut number 3. He said that's where the head wounds were treated and that they were horrible to see. I took his advice.

After supper three of the surgeons and I sat around the tent drinking beer. They were full of questions on what it was like to fly a helicopter in Vietnam, and I was full of questions about what it was like to be a doctor there. One of them, a general surgeon from Oklahoma, said that the worst part of his job was when the soldiers knew they were dying. "They cry for their mamas," he said. "They do it every time. That really breaks me up."

The next day I boarded a giant C-141 "Starlifter." It was a flying hospital. Instead of seats, the fuselage had rows and rows of stretchers stacked almost to the ceiling. IV bottles hung everywhere, and Army nurses scurried up and down the aisle tending to their patients. There were only four window seats on the aircraft and I was assigned to one of them. I was one of the few passengers on the plane who could walk.

As the C-141 began its take-off roll, I stared at the ground below us. Slowly, at first, and then faster and faster the ground sped by until there could be no stopping. When I was sure we were going fast enough, I leaned forward in my seat and tightened my stomach muscles—to lift the plane off the ground. As we slowly gained altitude I continued looking out the window and marked it off: 300 feet ... 700 feet ... 1200 feet ... 1500 feet! I let the Starlifter pilots take it from there. I relaxed, sat back in the seat, closed my eyes, and said three words. Thank you God.

CHAPTER 27

Welcome Home

THE FINAL DESTINATION OF THE C-141 was Andrews Air Force Base near Washington, D.C. En route from Saigon we stopped twice to refuel, in Tokyo and again in Fairbanks, Alaska. Our route of flight over the Pacific took us directly above the Aleutian Islands. It was awesome to gaze down and see the islands get bigger and bigger as we headed east. Small rock formations barely above the water level evolved into enormous rock islands that seemed to come halfway up to the belly of the plane. They must have been looking at the Aleutians when they coined the phrase "stark beauty."

At Andrews I was taken by an Army bus to Dulles Airport. The bus bypassed the terminal and drove directly to a United Airlines 707, chartered by the Army to take troops to Vietnam. The plane made a stop in Chicago, however, and that's where I got off. The military had a thoughtful policy for those needing medical attention when returning from Vietnam. If this included a hospital stay then it would be at the military hospital closest to your home. In my case this was the Great Lakes Naval Base north of Chicago.

At O'Hare a Navy enlisted man was waiting for me and drove me in a van to the hospital. I was met by a nurse who escorted me directly to my room. No check-in, no paperwork, nothing. My room was, in fact, two rooms, one with the bed and chairs in it and the other like a parlor. Both had a beautiful view of Lake Michigan. There was a walk-in closet and a large bathroom. The bathtub had a whirlpool in it. Now we're talking welcome home. This was first class.

A Navy nurse, an ensign, came into the parlor where I was sitting enjoying the view of sailboats on the lake. She introduced herself and welcomed me to the fourth floor. She said they'd be taking good care of me. The doctor would be in to see me shortly; he was, she said, a wonderful surgeon.

He'd make my left hand as good as new. As she was talking I noticed she had a puzzled look on her face.

Finally, she said, "If you'll pardon me for saying so, Sir, you are the youngest looking captain I have ever seen." Now I was puzzled. I told her I was 24 years old, which was the age when most guys make captain. She looked at my chart again and started to laugh. "You're not a Navy captain, you're an Army captain! That's why you look so young. We've made a mistake!" And that's why the room was so plush and that's why the royal check-in treatment. A Navy captain is just one step below the rank of admiral. She quickly added that it was the Navy's pleasure to have me and that I would be staying in this room. She thanked me for going to Vietnam and welcomed me home. And then she gave me a hug.

The next day the Navy surgeon removed a piece of glass from my left palm. It was spike shaped, three eighths of an inch in length. He also removed three smaller shards and was very pleased with himself. In those days glass did not show up on an x-ray and he had to guess where to cut from the way I described the pain. He told me he was sure he got it all, but said that the scar itself would be tender to the touch for the rest of my life. He was correct.

I was released from the hospital and now had a two-week leave of absence before returning to duty. My parents drove me home, and during the two-hour ride we got caught up on family news and generally reconnected. By the time we got to the house I was out of stories, at least for the time being, and so were they. I was itching to get to Chris Quinn's Tavern to link back up with the guys in the gang—my other family.

When I walked into Chris's, about 7:00 at night, none of my gang was there but another friend from the neighborhood was. I took the stool next to him as Chris, the 87-year-old proprietor, bought me a beer. My friend started telling me about a wild party he'd recently attended. He went on and on and on about who was there, who got drunk, who threw up, who got laid, and who said what to whom. His rambling monologue could not possibly have been more uninteresting to me. A week ago I was being shot at in Southeast Asia and he thinks I'm interested in a party he attended? Not once did he ask me anything about the last year of my life. Finally, and fortunately, some of the guys in the gang started coming in, and they bought me beers and properly welcomed me home.

Some veterans got genuinely screwed up from their Vietnam experiences. A person cannot live with constant fear, constant death, constant killing, constant hate, and constant guilt and not have these constants leave emotional scars. These veterans, mostly the grunts, saw too much, too soon, to assimilate.

It is difficult for me to say how much negative emotional baggage I am carrying because of the war. I have had some Vietnam nightmares over the years and my (final) wife, Barbara, wakes me up before I start throwing punches. Also, I could not go into an Oriental restaurant for many years after the war without a mild to medium onset of agoraphobia. Get me out of here! And once—this is embarrassing—in the town (hamlet) of Hana on the jungle-covered island of Maui, I saw the Japanese tourists with cameras turn into Viet Cong soldiers with AK-47s. This was many years after I left Vietnam. I was on vacation with Barbara. "Honey, I can't explain it but we've got to get the fuck out of here. Now!" I told her there were VC behind the trees. She took me to our room and calmed me down and then drove us back to Lahaina. Once we got out of Hana I was fine.

I have to smile as I think about one residual effect of the war that I was totally unaware of until I wrote this book. I have been, for the past 15 years, with a corporation that does business around the world. Often foreign customers have come to our company headquarters to visit. We have had people from Australia, Brazil, Canada, Denmark, England, Egypt, France, Germany, Greece, Scotland, South Korea, and Switzerland. When they visit they stay at a local hotel. Barbara and I live in a house with a separate apartment in the lower level, but only twice did we offer this apartment to our foreign guests—those from South Korea and those from Australia. That's probably not a coincidence.

Because of the nature of our business I can live anywhere I wish, and I have chosen the mountains of North Carolina. From the air they look very similar to the Central Highlands of South Vietnam ... and there's a golf course directly behind my house. But that's probably stretching it.

In 1986, eleven years after the war was officially over, there was a Welcome Home Vietnam Veterans Parade held in Chicago. It was to be a long overdue "Thank You" to those who served. The "returning vets," many now in their 40s, marched through downtown led by none other than General William Westmoreland. This parade was the brainchild of an ex-sergeant, Thomas Stack, who had served with valor and distinction in the Ninth Infantry Division two years after me. When Stack first proposed his idea for the parade it was met with less than mild enthusiasm at City Hall and among assorted veterans' organizations. "Who would march? Who would watch?" were objections Stack had to overcome.

But Stack, one of the most tenacious people on earth, persisted and finally got permission from the mayor's office to have the parade. He then set about the difficult and tedious tasks of advertising and organizing the parade to make it a success.

And it was a huge success. More than two hundred thousand Vietnam veterans came from all across America to march in the parade. Over 100 Aussies showed up and even a handful of ROKs. A half million spectators lined the parade route waving flags, cheering and crying for, and with, the veterans. Hundreds of Chicago policemen lined the parade route and as the veterans walked by the cops saluted them. It was a cathartic experience for many, and after Chicago's success other cities did the same. One of the guys in the gang was Cyril Watson, who also flew helicopters in Vietnam a couple of years after me. When Cy (who became a judge) and I heard of the plans for the parade we briefly discussed marching in it. But in a few moments we decided against it. Too late, we agreed, at least for us.

Tom Stack was the youngest of 11 children. When he was two years old and I was three, the Stack family moved into the two-flat next to our bungalow. Only the ten foot wide gangway separated our houses. We were first friends, and good friends, until we left our homes for the Army. Tommy was a decorated war hero, and his battlefield exploits are legend, but his great contribution to his country was in healing wounds. He died, prematurely, of cancer—quite possibly caused by his high exposure to Agent Orange.

CHAPTER 28

I Get a Job

ALTHOUGH SAFELY OUT OF VIETNAM I was not out of the Army. I still had five months of active duty to serve to complete my three-year obligation. My final assignment was back to Fort Rucker where I was an administrative assistant. My duties were so nebulous I do not recall what they were, but I did accomplish two things during this time. I became an expert with a .45 caliber pistol, for the hell of it; and I got certified in the fixed wing Beaver, for ulterior motives.

My plan for my future civilian life was to go with the airlines as soon as I got out of the Army. I contacted American, United, and TWA, and all expressed interest in hiring me, but all three encouraged me to get more fixed wing flight time, if possible. They verified what I had heard before, that helicopter time did not count for much with them. So I spent many hours in the Beaver, boring holes in the skies over Southern Alabama, simply logging time.

With about four months to go before my termination date I heard about a man in Daleville who owned a DC-3. He used the plane in his real estate development business flying customers to Florida and the Bahamas. His name was Lou Herring, and I made an appointment to see him. He was a big man with an affable, almost jolly demeanor. I liked him right away. I told him I had heard he had a DC-3 and that I wished to fly it for him. I explained that this would be good for me, because DC-3 time would count for a lot with the airlines, but it would be good for him, too. I would not charge him any money to be his pilot. "What do you think?" I asked.

To Mr. Herring's credit he did not laugh in my face. He politely explained that there were hundreds of pilots at Fort Rucker who would pay him to fly his DC-3 for the same reason I wanted to fly it. He said I was correct about the airlines, the DC-3 time would be helpful, but he didn't need a pilot. What he needed was a pilot who was also a salesman. He asked if I thought I could be a salesman. I thought about this and said, "Yes, I think I could sell, but only if I really believed in what I was selling." He said that the following Saturday morning he was taking a group to Melbourne, Florida, and invited me to join them.

After the weekend in Florida I was sold on becoming a salesman, and every weekend from then on I flew as the co-pilot of the DC-3. The A/C was a retired Air Force lieutenant colonel named Jack Cornell*. We called him "Colonel Jack."

Taking off and flying the DC-3 is like every other airplane: nothing to it. Landing it, however, could be difficult. Remember that the DC-3 (C-47, "Puff the Magic Dragon") was a tail dragger. There are two ways to land tail draggers: the "three point landing," as with the J3 Cub and Birddog, or a "wheel landing" where the large wheels under the wings touch the runway first, and then the small wheel under the tail touches, some seconds later, as the plane slows down. The wheel landing was the proper procedure for the DC-3.

Wheel landings are easy if there is no wind or if the wind is coming straight down the runway into the airplane's nose. But often the wind is coming from the side, called a "cross wind," and then the DC-3 is a bear to land. In those few seconds when the main wheels are on the runway and the tail wheel is still in the air, the crosswind is exerting force against the plane's large, vertical tail section. If the pilot does not have the expertise to counter this force the plane will tend to run off the runway. In extreme cases it can actually spin around, which is called a "ground loop." This is a very ugly and very expensive landing. Damage will be done.

Flying can be very exciting, even when people are not shooting at you. For instance, although Jack was an excellent pilot he sometimes took chances. Once on a flight from Melbourne to Dothan we were climbing through 10,000 feet directly over Mac Dill Air Force Base in Orlando. We were surrounded by thunderheads and the air was extremely turbulent. The cloud tops were at 12,000 feet and Jack decided to fly over them. We knew from PIREPS (pilots reports) that conditions would improve when we got farther north, near Tallahassee, and we could descend back below 10,000 feet. Technically you are supposed to have a pressurized cabin or wear oxygen masks if you fly over 10,000 feet. This was a technicality Jack ignored. We didn't have any oxygen.

As we were weaving our way in between thunderheads and continuing to climb, all of a sudden both engines quit. Faster than the speed of light Jack's hand shot up to the ceiling over my head and hit a toggle switch. The engines came back to life. "What the fuck!" I yelled as my heart went into my throat.

"Mechanical fuel pump!" he yelled back. "They're known to be bad on these planes!"

"Don't you think we should put down? Mac Dill's right below us!" I yelled.

"Nah," he yelled as the plane bumped, jumped, dropped, rose, skittered, and vibrated through the air. "We'll be fine!"

I took him at his word because I had no choice. He was the A/C. I kept reminding myself he'd flown many missions in DC-3s "over the hump" in India during World War II. But I was not comfortable. If the auxiliary fuel pump failed we'd be in serious trouble. DC-3s are way too big for most farmers' fields.

Two hours later, however, we landed safely in Dothan. We had 28 customer passengers on board and many were pilots from Fort Rucker. Only one of them realized we'd briefly lost our engines over Orlando. Such was the severity of the turbulence and the swiftness of Jack's reflexes.

It was now mid–December and I would be discharged January 5, 1968. TWA and United invited me for interviews. But Lou Herring had other ideas and threw me a slow, hanging, curve ball—one he knew I couldn't let pass. He offered to make me the sales manager of his company, with a share in all profits. I now had a difficult decision to make, but really not that difficult when you factor in my personality. Lou had further sunk the hook by saying that after one year, if all was going well, I would become his partner.

In the three months I had worked for Lou Herring I had made more money than the airlines would pay me in the next two years. I now had to frankly admit that becoming a pilot with the airlines fell into the category of "What else can I do?" As an English literature major in college I was qualified only to be a teacher—an occupation I would not consider. I was now forced to admit that I was not, and never really had been, in love with flying. Take-offs were always fun and landings were always challenging, but the time spent flying from place to place was, for me, excruciatingly boring. The airlines flew very high, and always on instruments, which would make cross-country flying even more boring, if that were possible. I decided to go for the business challenge (the fast buck) and put the airlines on hold for a year. I figured I had nothing to lose.

Note: Fifteen years later, after passing up the airline opportunity, I returned to Chicago—stone-broke. I took a job with Prairie Materials Sales, Inc., selling concrete. I was given a company car, a Volkswagen. Sometimes I'd be driving past O'Hare and look up at the commercial airliners and think, *I could be driving one of those, instead.* That was painful.

CHAPTER 29

The Last Flight

WITH ME ON BOARD FULL TIME in the Florida Tradewinds Corporation, Lou was able to move with his family from Alabama to Florida. Mary and I moved to Columbus, Georgia. I was no longer flying the DC-3; we'd recruited other flying salesmen who needed multi-engine time. I no longer needed it or wanted it. My focus was now all business.

Sometimes we would fly down to Melbourne on the DC-3 with the customers. We did this one weekend in June of 1968. We had planned to return on the plane Sunday night, but Lou asked me to stay over for a meeting with the developers on Monday. This would leave us in Florida without a way back to Georgia. But that problem was quickly solved. In our company we also had a Cessna 172. Lou suggested I fly the Cessna to Columbus. It was coming up on an overhaul, which was done by mechanics at the Columbus Airport. I agreed, but Mary was very apprehensive. She did not like the idea of flying in such a small plane. But after much persuasion from Lou and me she reluctantly agreed.

A Cessna 172 has two fuel tanks located in the wings. Proper procedure when flying cross-country is to run all of the fuel out of one tank and then flip a lever to begin drawing from the other tank. After doing this you should note the time, deduct the departure time, and then you'll know approximately how much flying time you have left. This procedure is a double-check against the fuel gauges, an extra safety measure.

In the case of our 172 the fuel gauges weren't working, so it was important that I check my time. The only drawback to this procedure is that when you run out of gas from the first tank the engine coughs, sputters and sometimes quits before the fuel from the second tank begins feeding into it. When an engine quits it gets very quiet, and this can be unnerving. So to do Mary a favor—she was really nervous and the air was very bumpy—I decided to skip this procedure. When I knew we were over halfway to Columbus I switched fuel tanks and noted the time.

Shortly after this the air smoothed out and the vast South Georgia pine forests were now below us. I noticed from our ground speed that we had picked up quite a head wind, but I'd made this trip many times and knew we had plenty of fuel. Soon the air was like glass and there were no clouds. We had blue sky above and the green carpet of forest below. It was serenely beautiful. Mary was able to start reading a book. Her toy poodle, Michelle, went to sleep on the cockpit floor. All was well, life was good, we'd be in Columbus in half an hour ... and then the engine quit.

Before taking off in any aircraft the pilot is supposed to "pre-flight it." The pre-flight consists of making sure the tires aren't flat, checking for foreign objects, checking for loose nuts, checking the oil level and the fuel level, and so on. To check the fuel level in a 172 you're supposed to remove the gas caps on top of the wings and stick your finger into the holes to be sure the level of gas is to the top. That's what you're supposed to do. But when you're a Huey helicopter pilot veteran of the Vietnam War you can't be bothered with a thorough pre-flight of a little Cessna 172, which you will be flying on a simple route from Florida to Georgia. The Viet Cong were 13,000 miles away. Besides, I was sure the guy at the airport in Melbourne told me he had topped off the tanks.

There is a truism in flying that goes: "There are old pilots and there are bold pilots but there are no old, bold pilots." I had become a bold pilot and now I was in trouble.

"What happened?" Mary yelled as I switched back to the first fuel tank and the engine sputtered back to life. I checked the time and it was obvious that if both tanks had the same amount of fuel we would be dry within minutes.

"We're almost out of gas," I told her in the calmest voice I could muster. "I'm going to have to land somewhere." Mary, appropriately, became catatonic.

I began a slow climbing turn to get more altitude to better find a place to land and to head the plane directly into the wind. I began searching for a field or road. I knew I could land safely if only I could find enough room. But in all directions it was solid trees. "Mary," I said, "pick up the dog, we're going to crash." I added she shouldn't worry because I knew how to land in trees. They told us in flight school. I said we might get banged up a little bit, but we wouldn't die. She picked up the dog.

In flight school they really did tell us the proper way to land in trees. I'll never forget it. "Drop full flaps and when the wheels start hitting leaves bring the plane to a stall and wallow it in. On the way down start saying the words, "Our Father who art in heaven...." So I'll admit I was scared, but not terrified like the night in flight school when I had the electrical fire. I really believed I could pull off a tree landing. (There's your proof. I was nuts.)

As the nose came around pointing directly into the surface wind, there, like a miracle, was a field. It wasn't very long and it was almost directly below us, but it looked like it would work. I began a 360-degree turn to start losing altitude and to set up a final approach. The engine was still running, but I was afraid to get too far out, knowing it could quit at any time. I had to stay close enough to the end of the field to do a "dead stick" landing if necessary. When I came around I was still too high, but I didn't feel like I could afford another 360 degrees.

There is a procedure known as "slipping" an airplane. This entails full left rudder and full right stick or vice versa. It's called "cross controlling." A plane will lose altitude very rapidly, like a rock falling, but it will not be in a stall. Slips can be very tricky at low altitudes, but I had no choice.

It took me three extreme slips with full flaps to get low enough to land. We came over the tree line and I dropped the Cessna into the field, but we were going too fast. We were gliding over the grass and the plane wouldn't quit flying, so I violently twisted the yoke back and forth. This was a maneuver I had only heard about—it was not taught in flight school—but it worked. We lost our lift, stalled, and touched down on the grass. I stood on the brakes. We came to a stop about three feet from a wooden fence with giant trees behind it. The engine quit.

"That was close," I said to Mary, who was rapidly coming out of her catatonic state and grabbing at the door handle. She wanted out of that plane, now. "Wait!" I said. "Don't open the door yet. We have to watch out for the bull."

She gave me an incredulous look. "What are you talking about? A bull?"

I explained to her that the Army taught us that when you land in a farmer's field you've got to be sure there's no bull in it. If there was, he'd attack you. I told her we had to stay in the plane a few minutes.

From the cockpit, facing into the forest, we looked back toward the field, as best we could, over our shoulders. No bull showed up and no cows either. I got out to have a good look and the field was clear. Mary got out of the plane carrying the poodle, and we walked to a dirt road. We couldn't see any houses because of all the trees. We walked about a hundred yards down the road, and as it curved a mailbox on a post appeared in front of us. We continued walking toward it, and then a small yard came into view with a weather beaten, unpainted house at the back, nestled into the trees. There was an elderly lady on the front porch sitting in a rocking chair. We approached the porch and the lady stood up. She looked at us more with curiosity than apprehension. She could tell we were not from this area because we were dressed like city folk and we were white. "Good afternoon, ma'am," I greeted her. "I'm wondering if you have a telephone we can use?" I explained how we'd landed our airplane in the field down the road. I told her I ran out of gas and needed to call Columbus to get somebody to pick us up.

"Good Lordy," she said, "I thought I heard an airplane." She then told us how lucky we were because that was the only field for miles around. She said she had a telephone and we were welcome to use it. Later she told us that last year four helicopters had landed in that field during a thunderstorm. "How'd you get an airplane in there?" she asked. "Ain't that field too small?"

I called a buddy in Columbus who said he would drive out to get us. While waiting for him we sipped iced tea on the nice lady's porch.

The next day I went to the Columbus airport to find Charlie Phipps, who owned the flight service station. He was also an instructor pilot in Cessna 172s. I asked him to go with me back to the plane to check it over. The landing had been hard and his eyes would be better than mine to see if any damage had been done. He agreed to do this.

We got a five-gallon can, filled it with AV-gas, and drove to the field. The trip took about 45 minutes, and all the way there I was debating whether to ask Charlie to fly the 172 to Columbus. But by the time we got to the plane I decided that I must fly it out. It was my carelessness and cavalier attitude that put the plane in the field, so it was my responsibility to get it out of there.

Charlie thoroughly checked over the plane as I gassed it up. He declared it sound and we turned it around, with its tail just an inch from the fence, to give me as much "runway" as possible. I climbed into the cockpit, strapped myself in tight and turned on the engine. At first it didn't want to start, but fiddling with the choke eventually brought it to life.

"See you in Columbus," yelled Charlie as he backed away from the plane and gave me a thumbs up. I dropped the flaps 20 degrees. When the engine needles were in the green I stood on the brakes and pushed the throttle all the way forward. The little plane shook and rattled and then started to move a little. I got off the brakes and it leapt forward.

There was no discernable wind, the ground was fairly smooth and I was picking up speed rapidly. By myself, and with only five gallons of gas, I was light. But the big trees in front of me were getting real close, so I rotated a few miles per hour slower than I would have liked. If the engine didn't sputter I knew I'd be fine. I gingerly added a little more flap, and cleared the trees with about three feet to spare. No problem.

I flew to the Columbus airport, landed, and taxied to the apron in front of Charlie's flight service station. I found a place to park, cut off the engine, unhooked my seat belt, got out of the plane, put chocks against its tires and tied down the wings. I didn't know it then, but that would be the last time I ever piloted an aircraft.

Epilogue 1: Flying

As THE DAYS AFTER MY FORCED landing went by I got more and more freaked out by how careless I had been, and I came to the conclusion that guys like me should probably not be pilots. Although I had the physical skills proven in flight schools, Vietnam, and most recently in the farmer's field (that was one great landing), I did not have the temperament. Running out of gas, politely referred to as "experiencing fuel starvation," was inexcusable.

To be a good pilot you must be a safe pilot, and that means you must pay close attention to details. I don't like details. I like big pictures, concepts, theories. To be a good pilot you need to know and respect the machinery you are flying. I do not like machinery. I have owned many cars and in most cases never bothered to raise their hoods. Not interested. To be a good pilot you must value and enjoy rules, regulations, and meticulous procedures, especially when flying IFR. I like short cuts. To be a good pilot you've got to like to talk about it, brag about it, and revel in your exploits. This one fits me perfectly—but one out of four is not enough.

To this day, I have my FAA pilot's license in my wallet, Certificate Number 1694742. It states that I am a commercial pilot, single and multi-engine, land, instrument airplane, rotorcraft-helicopter. I'll bet less than 5 percent of all pilots have those ratings, and I am proud of myself. I like to show off the license, especially to other pilots who most appreciate it. But I also realize that had I continued to fly it would merely be a matter of time before my carelessness, or lack of single-mindedness, caused disaster. My last take-off was out of the farmer's field, and the last landing was at the Columbus, Georgia, airport. You should have seen it. It was a beauty. I painted that baby right on the numbers and the tires went, "erk-erk."

Epilogue 2: War

GOING TO WAR IS A GRUESOME and unfortunate way to begin adult life. The experience stains the participants, and in some cases, the memories of the horrors may overwhelm them. War becomes their preoccupation and they can't stop talking about it. We all know them. They seek out the VFW Halls and the American Legion posts where they are most apt to find similarly wounded companions. They will share their experiences over and over in an attempt to purge the unbelievable from their minds. This eases their pain for a time, but it will be back—relentlessly haunting. They deserve our sympathy and support.

The majority of combat veterans are able to put their experiences behind them, for the most part. They don't talk much about war, and they get on with their lives, armed with a diminished capacity to be shocked. They have learned to expect the unexpected. Perhaps they cannot sustain joy as they once could, but their ability to accept human folly—their own and that of others—has been enhanced. They make decisions more by instinct than by reason, having learned the gut is often smarter than the brain.

The instinctual decision I made in Vietnam, switching from slicks to guns, was the correct one, even though it probably defied reason. That was when I made the transition from experiencing war up close (to further my education) to becoming a fighting participant. In a bizarre way that made being in combat healthier, emotionally speaking.

In the slicks the door gunners had the weapons. We pilots could order them to shoot but that's not the same as shooting them ourselves—it is vicarious shooting and that doesn't count. When we approached the LZs we became the prime target of the Viet Cong and NVA and there was nothing we could do about it except hope, pray, pucker up and go on in.

Being specifically targeted by the enemy (who is aiming to kill you) is terrifying, and when it happens day after day and night after night you can't help beginning to think of yourself as merely a target. That's a lousy way to go through war—and through life. Time in the gunships balanced this out. It was a "Shoot at me, you son-of-a-bitch, and I'm going to shoot right back" sort of a posture. Believe me, that made it better.

But no matter how one experiences it, war is horrific. On the physical plane it is blood, guts, dead bodies and body parts scattered all over the place. On the emotional plane it is rage, terror and anguish run rampant. So to call the overall experience positive is impossible.

Positives are there, however, on a smaller scale, and can be cherry-picked. Visiting foreign countries and seeing different cultures is broadening. Living with others in close quarters is character building. Witnessing acts of courage is heartening. Facing up to danger is ego fortifying. Observing sacrifice is humbling. Sharing hardships is unifying, and surviving deadly situations is exhilarating. These are positives that all combatants experienced, and we find solace in them. They lessen the overall impact of the horrible— but lessen it is all they can do. The stone in the heart will never go away.

After returning home from Vietnam I wrestled with the question, "Am I glad I went?" The answer was "No." The experience took my soul, my spirit, or whatever you want to call it and ... torqued it. The answer was also "Yes." I heard my country's call and did my duty. Ambivalence was mine. It still is. It always will be.

Military History
of James Joyce

James Joyce received his commission as a second lieutenant in the United States Army in June 1964 upon graduation from John Carroll University in Cleveland, Ohio, where he participated in the school's four-year ROTC program. His Army branch of service was the Transportation Corps.

Joyce began active duty January 5, 1965, reporting to Fort Eustis, Virginia, the Transportation Corps headquarters. After attending the eight-week Officer Basic Course he remained at Fort Eustis awaiting orders for Army flight school. While at Eustis he served with Charlie Company of the 714th Transportation Battalion, where he was designated a Trainmaster. The 714th was a railroad battalion operating electric, diesel and steam powered locomotives on narrow-gauge tracks which spanned the fort. The unit's unofficial motto was "Main gate and back."

In June of 1965, Joyce began U.S. Army flight school at Fort Rucker, Alabama. He was a member of Officer Fixed Wing Aviation Class 66-2. The class nickname was "The Green Dragons." Joyce completed the nine-month course and received his Army aviator wings in February of 1966. He then answered the Army's request for volunteers to cross-train from fixed wing aircraft (airplanes) into rotary wing aircraft (helicopters).

Joyce remained at Fort Rucker, becoming a member of Rotary Wing Qualification Course 66-5, where he learned the basics of helicopter aviation in the H-13, a small two-place aircraft with a reciprocating engine. Joyce graduated from this basic helicopter transition school in May 1966 and was then assigned to Fort Benning, Georgia, where he attended the UH-1 Transition School. Here he learned to fly the large, jet-powered helicopter now known as the "Huey," which was becoming the symbol of the Vietnam War. While at Fort Benning, Joyce was promoted to first lieutenant.

In July of 1966, Joyce arrived in Vietnam, where he was assigned to Bravo Company, of the 227th Assault Helicopter Battalion, in the First Air Cavalry Division based at An Khe in the Central Highlands. He became an aircraft commander and team leader flying Huey "slicks." The helicopters were used in combat assaults carrying ground troops in and out of battle. They were also used for medevac, resupply, POW transfer, psychological warfare and various other missions.

In February of 1967, Joyce volunteered for the Army's "Infusion Program" designed to balance out the combat experience level of helicopter pilots throughout the war zone. He was assigned to Delta Troop, Third Squad of the Fifth Cavalry, Ninth Infantry Division based at Bearcat in Vietnam's Delta region. Here he was a fire team leader, in command of a team of Huey gunships. These attack helicopters, which carried 2.75 inch rockets, .30 caliber machine guns and 7.62mm mini-guns, provided air support for the Huey slicks during combat assaults, and for ground troops engaged in battle. The gunships also provided cover for patrol boats that plied the Mekong River and were employed as initial strike aircraft in advance of infantry ground attacks. While Joyce was serving with the Ninth Infantry he was promoted to the rank of captain.

In June of 1967, Joyce ended his Vietnam tour of duty and was assigned to the U.S. Army Aviation Center at Fort Rucker. He was honorably discharged on January 5, 1968.